Theorizing Fandom: Fans, Subculture and Identity

Theorizing Fandom: Fans, Subculture and Identity

edited by
Cheryl Harris
New School for Social Research
Alison Alexander
University of Georgia

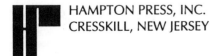
HAMPTON PRESS, INC.
CRESSKILL, NEW JERSEY

Printed in the United States of America

Library of Congress Cataloging-in-Publication Data

Theorizing fandom : fans, subculture, and identity / edited by Cheryl
  Harris, Alison Alexander
     p. cm. -- (The Hampton Press communication series)
     Includes bibliographic references and indexes.
     ISBN 1-57273-114-1. -- ISBN 1-57273-115-X
     1. Literature--Societies, etc. 2. Fans (Persons) 3. Science
fiction--Societies, etc. 4. Comic books, strips, etc.--Societies,
etc. 5. Mass media--Audiences. 6. Popular culture. I. Harris,
Cheryl, 1961- . II. Alexander, Alison, 1949- . III. Series.
PN21.T44 1998
306.4--dc21   97-43498
                                           CIP

Hampton Press, Inc.
23 Broadway
Cresskill, NJ 07626

Contents

PART IV: THE RHETORIC OF FANDOM

▶

About the Contributors

Cheryl Harris is Graduate Faculty in Digital Design and Technology at Parsons School of Design, The New School for Social Research, New York City, and President of Northstar Interactive, Inc., which studies the sociology of online audiences and virtual environments.

Alison Alexander is chair of the Telecommunications Department at the University of Georgia.

*   *   *

Nancy Baym is an associate professor in the Department of Communication at Wayne State University.

Harry Benshoff recently received his doctorate from the University of Southern California's School of Cinema-Television and is currently teaching at the University of California, Santa Cruz. His Dissertation, Monsters in the Closet: Homosexuality and the Horror Film, will be published by Manchester University Press.

Mirna Cicioni is a Senior Lecturer in Italian Studies in the School of European Studies at La Trobe University, Melbourne, Australia. Besides slash fiction, her research interests include Italian sociolinguistics, women in post-war Italy, and Italian Jewish writers. Her book *Primo Levi: Bridges of Knowledge* was published by Berg Press in late 1995.

Steven Classen is assistant professor in the Department of Communication at California State University, San Bernardino.

Chad Dell is assistant professor in the Department of Communication at Monmouth University. His current work concerns the study of historical broadcast audiences.

Cinda Gillilan is completing her doctoral degree in Media Studies at the School of Journalism and Mass Communications at the University of Colorado at Boulder. Her interest include television zine fans, fandom, representations of Native Americans and Vietnam veterans on primetime, and interdisciplinary cultural and feminist theory.

Shoshanna Green has studied, taught, and worked in the fields of history, mathematics, computer science, linguistics, editing, and film and television studies. She has been a fan for almost 15 years, during which time she has written and published a fair amount of fan fiction and helped run a lot of conventions.

Cynthia Jenkins has a J.D. from the University of Wisconsin-Madison. She is currently happily not utilizing her legal training as housemaster of an MIT dormitory and is reveling in the luxury of the time to read broadly in a variety of humanities disciplines. She has been participating in fandom for the last 25 years.

Henry Jenkins is the Director of the Film and Media Studies program at the Massachusetts Institute of Technology (MIT) and the author of *Textual Poachers: Television Fans and Participatory Culture.*

Andrea MacDonald is a doctoral student at the Annenberg School for Communication, University of Pennsylvania.

Jonathan Tankel is an associate professor in the Department of Communication at Indiana-Purdue University.

Thomas R. Lindlof is an associate professor in the College of Communications and Information Studies at the University of Kentucky. His research interests are in mediated communication processes, audience theory,k and qualitative research methodology. His books include *Natural Audiences, Qualitative Communication Research Methods,* and *Constructing the Self in a Mediated World.* His current work focuses on the social action and interpretive strategies of the "culture war" in the United States.

▶I

INTRODUCTION

▶1

Introduction Theorizing Fandom: Fans, Subculture and Identity

Cheryl Harris
New School for Social Research

Mass media, popular culture, and its artifacts (such as recordings, books, magazines, merchandise, TV shows, movies, and stars) increasingly define western postindustrial society. Arguably, individuals and social groupings form relationships with mediated content that present a continued problematic for both scholars and the culture industries: How do we constitute an "audience?" Audiences in and of themselves cannot be said to "exist" anywhere, and they do not hold still. They are mutable, fluid, dynamic, and interactive, with endless overlaps and resistant to ideological closure. Further, within the notion of audience, how do we explain and understand the surprisingly intensified relationships created by a special category of audience—"fans?"

To be "a fan" is an accepted colloquialism in our culture—one can be a fan of a restaurant chef, a television star, a political candidate, or even a good sunset. Although we use the term with abandon, fans and their

3

social and cultural environment ("fandom") are profoundly untheorized in the social sciences. We know virtually nothing about what produces fandom, what specific practices are associated with it, what role fans may play in social and cultural processes, or who is likely to become and remain a fan. Clearly, the topic is still in its infancy for all its pervasiveness.

Only in the past few years have fans become a focus for academic researchers, and as with all new areas of inquiry, the first work on fandom was primarily descriptive in nature, falling prey to what author Steve Classen sympathetically calls "functionalist pitfalls." In other words, describing what fans do provides some necessary insight, but in doing so we tend to lose sight of how fans fit into the larger picture. More specifically, although we have many descriptions of fans of various people or things, in the past much of the literature has tended to examine fan practices closely but has not successfully integrated existing or new theoretical models into explanations of why fans do what they do.

Part of the reason for this is that fans, like "audiences," are constantly in flux. Worse, they are prolific. There are as many fans and fan movements as there are meanings to contest and negotiate, and it is almost impossible for a single researcher to carefully follow several fan groups over an extended period of time, keep up with newly formed groups, and keep tabs on the boundaries of fandom as a whole. Still, in pulling together multiple perspectives on fan phenomena we can begin to see patterns that may help explain fan culture.

Once audiences were thought of as unified in their thoughts, desires, and needs—a "mass" who would generally respond similarly to the same content and whose behavior could consequently be predicted along certain lines. If this were ever true, it certainly is no longer. Yet, as discussed earlier, we are still in the earliest days of theoretical development in thinking about and applying models of how audiences might be different from one another. This is true in academe as well as in the popular culture industries where millions are spent on trying to determine audience composition and response to content. Many questions remain for those who attempt to pay serious critical attention to the problem of specialized audiences with very intensified relationships to content—those who do not have to be pursued because they are already captive in their "fanatic" devotion to a star, text, or icon. In this volume, several different yet related arguments are made in an attempt to build explanatory models for these special audiences—"fans."

Looking at the surprisingly scanty literature on fandom readily illustrates that there are numerous and inconsistent perspectives, perhaps as many as there are interested players. To the media industries, fans have traditionally represented an important constituency to be measured, controlled, co-opted, institutionalized, and appropriated for their value as a ready market for products and as a public relations tool. The press, on the other hand, seems well-invested in the idea of fandom as highly stigmatized, marked by "danger, abnormality, and silliness" (Jensen, 1992, p. 1), in which fans engage in "secret lives" without much purpose. The functionalist pitfall of academics is of a different kind. Academic researchers fall prey to the tendency to focus on "objectifying, exterior perspectives . . . which slight the insider's dimensions of . . . audiencehood" (Ang, 1991, p. 11). In other words, much of the discussion around fandom has essentially pathologized it without leading us much closer to understanding this important phenomenon.

In the discussion around fandom, the authentic voices of fans themselves are rarely heard. Fans who exist within an organized web of interpretive communities define themselves and their roles very differently from any of these groups, as Henry Jenkins's chapter ("Normal Female Interest in Men Bonking") which lets fans speak for themselves demonstrates.

The following chapters develop distinct theoretical perspectives on the phenomenon of fandom, going beyond description of what fans do toward an understanding of why fandom is a fundamental and widespread social role in contemporary western society.

The authors represented here employ different strategies of analyses, but common to many of them is the work of Bourdieu and de Certeau, whose examinations of the relationship between heirarchies of power and alternative uses of cultural resources provides an interesting foundation for a discussion of fandom. In postindustrial societies becoming more, not less, class divided, one's subordination may be a source of anomie and despair. Looked at this way, some individuals may seek to express their otherwise silenced identities through a common interest in a symbol, icon or text, and, then, redress their alienation through the social nature of fan practice.

This is the position taken by Harris, Classen, and Dell in their separate chapters. Steve Classen aptly describes how "couponers" resist institutionalized marketplace norms by exploiting "gaps" in patriarchial strategy. Similarly, Chad Dell shows how traditional roles may be challenged and even inverted through fan practice. Using postwar female fans of professional wrestling as an example, Dell convincingly argues that the development of fan movements can be specific responses to significant historical social and cultural shifts that threaten or displace social identities.

Virtually all researchers find the social or shared aspect of fandom a critical consideration. In "A Sociology of Television Fandom," Cheryl Harris summarizes the history of one national fan organization, "Viewers for Quality Television," over a 5-year period and its attempts to contest the distribution of cultural space on television by influencing programming decisions. Using a sociology of culture perspective, fandom is reconceptualized as a spectrum of practices engaged in to develop a sense of personal control or influence over the object of fandom (such as a star or text), in which the outcome of one's involvement is not as important as the involvement itself—recognized membership and interaction centering around a common object. As in Nancy Baym's observation of fans interacting in a computerized environment, fan discourse works to create a specific kind of community that becomes more important than the object of fandom itself.

Fans are also motivated by self-invention, in which fandom provides an opportunity to live in and through a set of symbols that are expressive of ones aspirations rather than "reality." As Henry Jenkins notes, "What many . . . fans enjoy is the sense of creating their own cultures . . . which more perfectly expresses their own social visions and fantasies."

In his chapter, "Normal Female Interest in Men Bonking" Henry Jenkins points out how academic accounts of fan phenomena differ from fan accounts of themselves because academics and other outsiders, not privy to the fine gradations of meaning embedded in every aspect of fan practice, will miss much. Jenkins shows how fan culture and the production of literature are frequently inseparable and discusses a special instance known as "slash" fiction. He does so by allowing fans themselves to speak about why they do what they do and provides an unusual example of grounded theory, in which his observations are taken back to his subjects and developed interactively. Fans show an uncanny awareness of academic and mainstream points of view and how they are positioned within and outside of these perspectives. Jenkins develops an analysis of science fiction "slash" fans and reveals how fans seek multiple theories of themselves. Further, he shows how their writings mediate the relationship between fans and media culture.

Fan writings seem to be central to the practice of fandom: newsletters, fanzines, "slash" fiction, and songs are some of the communications produced. Jenkins, Classen, Baym, Gillilan, Harris, and Cicioni all discuss specific examples of fan writing. Some of this writing involves explicit appropriation, with "slash" as a prime example (Jenkins). However, fan culture also has other means of appropriation: an active, acquisitive material culture in which the collection of objects central to the practice of fandom serves both as an admission to fandom and as a form of ritualized maintainence. Fan acquisition of paraphanalia, therefore, must be carefully considered in developing overall theories of fandom.

Tankel, Murphy, and Smead in "Collecting Comic Books: A Study of the Fan and Curatorial Consumption" view the process of collecting objects or artifacts related to one's fandom as placing the consumer in a social strategy in direct contradiction to the needs of consumer capitalism. Looking at comic book fans and their "curatorial consumption", the authors conclude that this fan practice tends to supercede the immediate use dictated by industrial production and produces unanticipated outcomes. Interestingly, whereas most research on fans foregrounds female participation (in fact, many claim that fandom is primarily female), the comic book audience is overwhelmingly male. The authors discuss how cultural forms, fandom, and gender membership might be related.

A growing frontier of fan interaction is cyberspace—computer bulletin boards, online services, the Internet, and other electronic forums. Examining fan culture in this environment presents special problems because we still know little about the nature and effects of computer-mediated communication (CMC). However, the immediacy and high interactivity of this means of communication insures that it will continue to be of interest to fans. The rhetorical nature of fandom is the focus of "The Talk of Fandom: The Importance of Social Practices of Soap Opera Fans in a Computer-Mediated Discussion Group" by Nancy Baym. In addition to reviewing and critiquing the existing literature on soap opera viewers, this chapter also analyzes hundreds of soap opera fan interactions on the "Usenet" computer network. The author describes fan discourse as highly interpretive and differentiated, going beyond previous typologies of viewing behavior.

Andrea MacDonald in the chapter "Virtual Fans" also ventures into cyberspace to.analyze fan interactions over the "Usenet" and "Netnews" computer networks via the global Internet system, focusing on the way that this new interface has changed the workings of fandom and fan expression. Because computer-mediated communication has profound implications for future social and cultural development, ways in which individuals and social groups make use of this resource in developing identities deserves our serious attention.

Several authors in this volume are concerned with the role of fan fiction and the maintainence of fan relationships. Mirna Cicioni continues this discussion in "Hatstands and Nurturance: Male Pair Bonds and Female Desire in Sci-Fi Fans 'Slash' Writing." Specifically, she looks at a number of character relationships in which two men share adventures and dangers in a bond that is nonsexual but takes precedence over other relationships, both in the British television series The Professionals and in so-called "slash" fiction (fan writings that use established characters but subvert textual conventions). The author argues that within the fan community this type of character relationship stimulates unusual fan interactions and discourse.

Harry Benshoff continues the discussion of fan relationship with content in his chapter on Dark Shadows fan culture and how fan texts are being used to negotiate issues of sexuality and gender by subverting the conventions of both gothic horror and science fiction.

The authors in this volume generally propose issues of social class and power as dominant themes in understanding and building theories of fandom. However, gender constructions and roles go hand in hand with considerations of power and agency. Although not all fans are female, the literature strongly suggests that many are. Interestingly, Cinda Gillilan argues that fandom is itself a "feminine" or "liberated" space, a protected location for oppositional or alternative constructions of dominant discourse.

Finally, Thomas Lindlof, Kelly Coyle, and Debra Grodin ask "Is There a Text in This Audience? Science Fiction and Interpretive Schism." The status of text in mediated communication has been a problematic from the standpoint of classical audience theory, particularly in developing theories of the "reader." Lindlof et al. share some conclusions that challenge accepted concepts of audience and "readership" based on primary research with science fiction fans.

DEFINITIONS: A LEXICON OF FAN SLANG

Part of becoming a "fan" is immersion in a special lexicon often less than intelligible to outsiders, a practice common to membership initiation rituals in many social groups. The authors in this volume use this specialized vocabulary frequently. To avoid excessive repetition, some of the terms to be encountered and their basic definitions are summarized below.

> *Cons*: Fan conventions, often hotel-weekend affairs involving parties, panels, guest speakers, and appearances by celebrities
> *Filking*: Writing, performing, and recording fandom-related songs (particularly in science fiction fandom). The products of filking are referred to as "Filk" or "filksong."
> *Slash*: Fiction written and read by fans themselves centering around the objects of their fandom, such as in Star Trek Slash fiction. Often sexually explicit, slash is also frequently politically conscious. In addition, slash is invariably a complex and constantly evolving genre.
> *'Zines or Fanzines*: Fan fiction circulated in self-published newsletters or magazines. These may be written or edited by a single person, or may be "APA" (Amateur Press Association) collaborative activities.

REFERENCES

Ang, I. (1991). *Desparately seeking the audience*. New York: Routledge.
Jensen, J (1992). Fandom as pathology. In L. Lewis (Ed.), *The adoring audience* (pp. 9-29). New York: Routledge.

▶2

Normal Female Interest in Men Bonking: Selections from *The Terra Nostra Underground* and *Strange Bedfellows*

Shoshanna Green
Cynthia Jenkins
Henry Jenkins

Yes, fans analyze because they're fans. Or are we fans because we analyze?—Barbara Tennison (1993, November)

[Is slash] anything other than normal female interest in men bonking?—M. Fae Glasgow (1993, August)

Slash is one of the most pervasive and distinctive genres of fan writing. Most fans would agree that slash posits a romantic and sexual relationship between same-sex characters drawn from film, television, comic books, or popular fiction. Most often, slash focuses on male characters, such as *Star Trek*'s Kirk and Spock or *The Professionals*' Bodie and Doyle. However, the parameters of slash are under constant debate and negotiation within media fandom. Many fans would point out that the relationships are not always romantic, the characters are not always drawn from other media, and the central characters are not always male. Slash stories circulate within the private realm of fandom, are published in zines, distributed through the mails, through email, or passed hand to hand among enthusiasts. The noncommercial nature of slash publishing is necessitated by the fact that these stories make unauthorized use of media characters.

Although a private, subcultural practice, slash has, over the past five years, increasingly become the focus of academic and journalistic scrutiny.[1] The slash fan's peculiar relationship with American mass culture has become almost emblematic of recent work in cultural studies, referenced on the cover of *The Village Voice Literary Supplement* or ridiculed in *Lingua Franca*, cited in law review articles, and discussed at the Modern Language Association conference. If the initial academic interest in slash came from people who were themselves tied to the fan community, attentive to its traditions and familiar with its own theoretical and critical categories, slash has quickly become a point of reference for writers who know of it only secondhand and who seem to have no clear grasp of the concept. (More than one writer refers to "slasher" fan fiction,[2] for example, while literary critic Mark Dery (1993) uses the term "slash" to refer to all forms of "textual poaching in which tales told for mass consumption are reworked to suit subcultural needs" (p. 853), as if it encompassed the full range of fan production.) The differences in the ways academics and fans talk about slash are striking:

1. Most academic accounts center almost exclusively on Kirk/Spock stories, primarily because academic writers and readers are most familiar with *Star Trek* references. In fact, slash is written about a broad range of fictional characters, and some slash fans speak of being fans of slash itself, rather than or in addition to being fans of a particular show or set of characters. Many fanzines, both slash and nonslash, publish

---

[1]No listing of the complete bibliography of slash criticism would be possible here. Basic works would include: Bacon-Smith (1992), Jenkins (1992), Lamb and Veith (1986), Penley (1991a, 1991b) and Russ (1985). A sample of secondary works that have built on this literature would cut across recent research in cultural studies, women's studies, critical legal studies, and cyberspace, and include a good deal of popular journalism and unpublished conference papers. All of these works to varying degrees and with varying explanations suffer from some, though rarely all, of the blind spots we list here. (This article was written in 1993.)

[2]See, for example, Viegener (1993) for a generally sympathetic, but totally inaccurate and obviously secondary account of slash as "slasher novels, such as those written by the fans of *Star Trek*, which involve sadomasochistic scenes between Captain Kirk and Dr. Spock" (p. 235). As Trek fans know, Spock was always referred to as "Mr. Spock," whereas "Dr. Spock" is the pediatrician Benjamin Spock. We have delighted in imagining such stories, but as far as we know, they do not exist.

stories based on a variety of sources; fans call such collections "multi-media" rather than "single-fandom" zines.

2. Academic accounts of slash tend to deal with it in isolation from the larger framework of genres within fan fiction. Fans, on the other hand, understand slash in relation to many other rereadings and rewritings of program material such as hurt/comfort (which focuses on nurturing but not necessarily sexual relations between characters) and heterosexual romance.

3. Academic accounts of slash seem preoccupied with the question of why straight women write stories about gay male characters, seeing slash as a heterosexual appropriation of queerness. In fact, lesbian and bisexual women have always participated alongside straight women in slash fandom and people of all sexual orientations have found slash a place for exploring their differences and commonalities.

4. Academic accounts tend to focus on slash's uniqueness, its difference from other forms of popular culture. Fan critics are interested in exploring slash's relationship to other forms of commercial fiction (ranging from gay erotica to popular romances, from Dorothy Sayers to Mary Renault) and to traditions of retelling and rewriting within folk culture.

5. Academic accounts often consider slash to be a static genre, making generalizations that assume a consistent subject matter and thematics over time and across all slash stories. Slash fans, on the other hand, see the genre as always in flux, and are interested in tracing shifts in its construction of sexuality, story structures, character relationships, and degrees of explicitness.

6. Academic accounts have tended to be univocal in their explanations of why fans read and write slash, looking for a theory that can account for the phenomenon as a whole. Slash fans, on the other hand, are interested in exploring the multiple and differing—sometimes even contradictory—motivations that led them to this genre.

Almost all of the theoretical explanations of slash that academics have proposed are refinements of theories that have long circulated within the fan community. This chapter presents some fannish discussion of slash in the early 1990s, selecting excerpts from two apas: the *Terra Nostra Underground* and *Strange Bedfellows*.

The term *apa* originated in science fiction fandom as an acronym for "amateur press association." It describes a sort of group letter, regularly circulated to its members. Each member writes a contribution, called an *apazine*, and makes a copy of it for each member. She or he then sends them to the apa's editor, who collates all the contributions and sends a complete set to each member. Apas can serve as forums for discussion, as a way of circulating fiction and other writing by their members, as regular business conferences, and the like.

Terra Nostra Underground (TNU) was founded in Fall 1989 as a quarterly apa for discussion among slash fans; it began with eight members, and its membership had reached 23 when it folded 3-1/2 years later. Shoshanna Green founded *Strange Bedfellows* (SBF) as a successor to the TNU, and its current membership is 39, including the three authors. Members are mostly female, but three men regularly participate at present and others have in the past. The group includes bisexual, gay, and straight people. About half of the members have written fan fiction and/or published fanzines and that proportion is not, we think, too far above that in media fandom as a whole; the fan community tends to assume that everyone can write and that some people simply have not done so (yet). There is no sharp distinction between readers and writers in most of the discussion that follows. Both are considered creative. Apa members come from various educational and class backgrounds, although most are middle class and tend to have at least a college degree; most are American, but there are eight European members (including one living in the United States) and one Western woman living in Japan. We believe that in the period covered by these excerpts there were no non-white members, but because the apa is conducted through the mail rather than in person, we are not certain.

Discussions vary widely. In addition to the kinds of analysis excerpted here, members talk about everything from the NAMES Project quilt to their summer vacations, from Tailhook to ice skating and the exigencies of apartment living. Apa writing can be personal and confessional or more abstract and speculative. Often, arguments are made through collaboration and brainstorming among group members and are understood in relation to previous discussions both within the apa and elsewhere in fandom.

In any one issue of the apa, then, there are up to 39 apazines written by as many members, ranging from 3 to 30 pages long, each adding to ongoing conversations and introducing potential new topics for discussion. It is rather like a party with many conversations going on at once and people moving from group to group, or like a printed version of an electronic bulletin board.

This chapter excerpts some of the discussions undertaken in these two apas in the early 1990s. We have chosen these particular apas as sources, rather than any of the many other apas, letterzines, and the like that we might have used, simply because we are members of them. This meant, first of all, that we had easy access to six years of history of these discussions; however, it also meant that we compiled this essay *as fans* as well as academics. We participated in many of the conversations we are reproducing. We are not claiming that the membership of these apas is statistically "typical" of slash fandom as a whole (although we do not think it is misrepresentative either), nor do we mean to imply that the topics we have selected for presentation here are the most important ones to fans.

As we circulated drafts of this chapter among the fans we are quoting, some argued strongly that certain themes we were pursuing were secondary and misrepresentative of overall fannish concerns; often these same themes were ones that other members felt were central. What is central often depends on where you are standing. We drew on discussions that seemed important and could be clearly and interestingly presented here. Some complex and important discussions could not be included exactly because they were so involved; they were too long to be summarized, too complex to be excerpted, and so embedded in media fan culture that nonfans would require long explanatory prefaces. These included fine grained analysis of particular slash stories, meditations on subgenres within slash and the attitudes of fans and academics toward them, arguments about the mechanics and ethics of fan publishing, and much more.

Academic respondents have also expressed discomfort with this project and its goals, discomforts that illuminate some of the contradictions within contemporary cultural studies. One critic of the manuscript dismissed it as a collection of "highly personal and nonrigorous analyses of texts and psyches, that assumes (and this is the biggest weakness) that the producers are centered and knowing, not caught up in confusing struggles that are further complicated by their insider biases." The writer treats "highly personal," "nonrigorous" and "insider biases" as negatively valued traits of fan criticism, contrasting it with an academic mode of criticism that is presumed to be valuable precisely because it is distanced, rigorous, and objective. Fan criticism does differ from academic criticism in significant ways: the subjective and empassioned engagement with the material, the rejection of specialized technical language and theoretical authority, and the tendency to focus on personal rather than institutional explanations. Yet a refusal to acknowledge that alternative modes of criticism might produce valuable insights seems the worst kind of academic elitism. Academic writing, after all, has increasingly been subjected to the opposite sets of criticism: academic writers often deny their own personal stakes in the objects under study, their rarified language does not engage closely with the particularity of popular culture and therefore lacks the rigor of most fan criticism, a false distance may be highly distortive to our understanding of the complexity of popular culture. Taking fans seriously means critiquing academic modes of thinking and writing and recognizing our own blind spots, silences, and failures to rise above "confusing struggles."

What is at stake here is who gets to speak about popular culture, in what kinds of languages, in what contexts, and with what authority. Traditional distinctions between art and craft, professional and amateur cultural production, mask hidden assumptions about class, race, and gender. Such implicit assumptions underlie academic anxieties about allowing fans to speak in print about their own cultural production. In the study of avant garde or canonical artworks, the publication of manifestos, documents, and personal reflections on artistic goals and aesthetic principles has a long tradition. No one questions that such statements, however subjective and "insider" their focus, make a contribution to our understanding of these artworks, even if we also recognize that artists may not fully understand the implications of their own work. In the area of fandom, craft, or other forms of amateur and folk cultural production, however, academic authority asserts itself at the expense of the voices of the cultural creators, choosing instead to treat such groups as ethnographic subjects.

We urge a reconsideration of the concept of popular expertise, a recognition and respect for the sites of amateur cultural production that accords them the same privileges to speak as are accorded to other spheres of the art world. In compiling this chapter, we have not operated on the assumption that fans know or can explain everything about their own activities; the fans continue to explore the whys and wherefores of slash precisely because they want better explanations for their tastes and actions. We have, however, taken as a given that the fan community has meaningful things to contribute to an understanding of slash and that cultural studies will be enriched by listening to them speak.

Academic work on popular culture pays a price for its insistence on isolating itself from other kinds of critical discourse: We sacrifice both the ability to understand experientially and the ability to more fully participate in public debates about popular culture. As the academy turns toward a reassessment of the role of the "public intellectual," we need to accept the fact that not all expertise resides within the academy. We, thus, urge a more open dialogue between academic writing and other modes of criticism. For that reason, we have chosen not to construct yet another academic theory of slash or to arbitrate between competing and often contradictory fan claims.

In refusing to offer our own summaries and conclusions, we do not deny that some form of selectivity shapes this presentation. In fact, this task of reconstructing a community dialogue has raised questions about the ways that all forms of ethnographic writing foreground certain voices and marginalize others and the need for greater self-consciousness about this process. In putting together this selection, we have tried to balance our desire to represent the texture of fan discussions with our desire to allow fans to more directly respond to issues or concerns raised in academic writing about slash. We want our readers to remember that we cannot do justice here to the full breadth, richness, and variety of fan discussion even in these two apas, let alone all of fandom. Rather than leave readers of this chapter with a sense of certainty about what slash is and why it is written, we want to pose new questions and spark new debates. We are simply offering a sampling of a complex and sophisticated conversation, allowing fans to speak in their own words to other fans and to non-fan readers of this book about what we do and how we think about it all.

WATCHING TELEVISION, CREATING SLASH

Where does slash come from? Does it originate in the series text or in the fan's reading of it? These questions have occupied fans much as they have interested academics. Cat, a French fan, has offered one explanation for why female viewers construct homoerotic fantasies. Her account focuses on narrative conventions and female identifications in television.

> Why are so many women interested in slash in the context of media related material? TV is a convenient source for fictional materi- al that can be shared with a great number of people and benefits from the structure of general fandom.[. . .] This explains why slash is media-related and why I have never heard of any mainstream Fag-Hag APA to this date. [. . .] To enjoy television that way, empathy with the fictional characters will have to be strong and rewarding. The woman (me, you, whoever) views the fictional piece from the character's point of view, and her emotions parallel his: anguish when he is hurt, tri- umph when he wins, etc. . . . (One identifies with more than one char- acter, usually, and can easily switch from one to the other according to need, but let us say that the "hero" is the main reference.) So in this society, someone enriching/feeding their fantasy life with TV fare will come across variations of the traditional pattern: the hero (dashing); the buddy (his confidant and accomplice); the screaming ninny (his romantic interest). [. . .]
>
> In this threesome, there are reasons to identify with the hero:
>
> (1) He is usually the main character (the heroine being seen less often, usually a supporting character).
>
> (2) He does all the exciting things and seems to enjoy them. He is the one to whom the adventure happens and the one who makes it happen. He must pit his wit and resources against danger and foes. (If the woman has spunk, it is not a value in itself but a source of excite- ment or annoyance for the hero. At worst, it is considered as cute.)
>
> There are reasons not to identify with the heroine:
>
> (1) A woman, having internalized the values of our culture, might feel that women are devalued per se, regardless of script, thus the woman-heroine becomes a worthless object of identification.
>
> (2) When female characters are shown to be effective and power- ful, it is often through their "feminine wiles" (unless they are ugly frus- trated lesbians. Who wants to identify with a loser, such as the Russian general played by Lotte Lenya in *From Russia with Love*?) As to women powerful through the use of their beauty and seduction (i.e.

their power to manipulate men to further their schemes), they could easily become alien, incomprehensible creatures for "average" women full of self-doubt or teenage angst, since they represent values that are not only difficult to achieve, but also considered obsolete. [. . .]

So you don't want to be her, you don't want to enjoy the emotions she feels. The male hero is easier to "feel" the adventure with: what he is made to feel you enjoy. And if you are of the daydreaming kind, you will "borrow" him, to make him feel some more interesting things.

If you do not want sex or romance to be absent from your day-dreamings and you are identifying with the male hero, seeing the adventure from his viewpoint, who the heck are you going to use as a romantic interest? Not him, because since you are living the adventure through him, the point is to make *him* feel the feelings of sex and romance, and *then* identify with it. So he has to have a relationship with someone other than himself, with someone who produces emotional reactions in him that you find interesting. And that person is unlikely to be the screaming ninny (because, if you liked her, you would have identified with her and "tinkered" with her to start with). Of course, you can daydream a female character you'd enjoy identifying with or fancying, but to create from scratch an original, interesting character is hard work, and she might not feel as real as the faces on the screen. Also, by that time, you could have internalized enough of our society's values to make the prospect unexciting. Or you can day-dream yourself into the script. (Hi there, Mary Sue.) [. . .]

This is where the male buddy comes in, since he is the only one (with the screaming ninny and the enemy) who shows a sustained interest in the hero. The woman who has empathy for the hero will enjoy the emotions produced in the hero by the Buddy. (She does not have to find the buddy breathtakingly attractive herself [some are willing to overlook Napoleon's chin for Illya's sake, for instance], but it helps.) And what type of relationship do buddy and hero have? One version could be that on the screen, there is a caring relationship. It is not tainted with sexism, with expectations of a given role, because the one is female and the other male. It is equality. Not in practical terms: the buddy can be less or more strong or skillful than the hero. But his weakness is not perceived as something that makes him in *essence* inferior or different. It has a different cultural meaning. They are attracted to each other's personalities, not because they're made blind by their gonads or "devalued" prettiness. [. . .]

That was one version. If that relationship is attractive because it is equal, why is there a non-negligible number of slashzines where one male partner dominates the other[. . .]? Why do they often seem to be motivated by raving lust rather than sheer delight in each other's intellect? [. . .] Seems that even if some fan fiction depicts one partner as dominant and the other as whimperingly submissive (Vila is a prime offender here) the lovers are not different in nature: a woman can safely indulge in S&M and rape fantasies, submissiveness, aggression and a whole load of other non-politically correct behaviors without guilt feelings, without it being gender identified.[. . .] Identification with the other gender means liberation from one's own gender related taboos. However, we have no personal, direct, experience of the cultural constraints the other gender has to submit to, so these constraints, although known to us, are not felt as being as binding as our own. This I would call the "Tourist approach." One feels freer to behave differently in a place that is not directly relevant to everyday life, and where the landmarks, although not very different, have shifted enough to create new perceptions: you are free of the rules of your country of origin, but not bound by the rules of the holiday country because you don't know them, or if you do, they don't mean the same things to you as to the natives. (Anestopoulo, 1990, August)

Barbara offered a different explanation for the slash potential of a program; she stresses that the ways women watch television shape their responses to the conventional representation of male sexuality.

One explanation I've heard about why slash seems so natural to fans has to do with how fans perceive TV characters. Instead of taking emotions and speech as directed at the audience, the fan game is to see everything in context of the show itself. If an actor, or a pair of them, are busy projecting rampant sexuality, the fan mindset is to look within the program for the object. In a cop-partner show (for instance), there are typically two men projecting subliminal sex appeal for all they're worth, and nobody else on screen with any regularity. Certainly, no female characters. Strictly within the show framework, there's nobody but the two men themselves to justify the sexual display, so the concept of slash (instead of the fan just thinking what a sexy, appealing show it is to her, herself) arises. (Tennison, 1991, May)

M. Fae Glasgow, among others, rejects the idea that her interest in slash involves identification with the characters, asserting a pleasure in exerting her own authorial control over sexy male bodies.

Oh, such delight! Someone else who doesn't think that the slash writer necessarily inserts herself into one of the personae! Isn't manipulation and watching so much fun? That's what I do; I never, ever, insert myself (perhaps because I lack the necessary plumbing? Sorry. Facetiousness is a hobby of mine . . .) into the character or the story. I may be present in the form of a narrative voice, but that's more because of my heritage of storytelling and the typical Scottish style of writing which almost invariably has a very strong "voice" or lyricism to it. To be honest, I don't even identify with any of the characters. I'm just fascinated by them. Plus, I'm prurient and salacious and simply *adore* to watch. (Glasgow, 1991, November)

Sandy and Agnes contributed observations about why slash's focus on male protagonists may facilitate identification more easily than would stories focusing on female characters.

> As an experiment last week, I gathered all of the female slash I had into one pile (largely Blake's 7, since it has more strong females than the rest of slash fandom's favorite shows put together . . .) and read it all one after another. I realized that my distance from the material is different in female slash. I *have* all of that equipment, I *have* sex with women—I wasn't able to go with the flow so much. There was an intermediate level doing the rather stupid job of checking each piece of action and thinking, "would I like this," "have I done this," "would I do this with (Jenna (Y), Beverly (Maybe), Gina (Y), Trudy (Y), Cally (Y), Dayna (YES, YES, YES), Servalan (not unless I had someone holding a gun on her at the same time)". I don't know what this means, but I'd love to hear from other women about it—queer and straight. (Hereld, 1992, November)

> Your comments to Barbara about female slash, about familiarity (with the equipment, the activities, etc.) making it more difficult to "go with the flow," reminded me of the discussion of "PC slash" on the email list, when a few folks complained about the tendency of some slash to be too "realistic" or concerned with accuracy to the real world as we know it, which they felt interfered with the fantasy. I've been trying to figure out ever since discovering slash just why it might be that two guys getting it on would be exciting to women, and especially to lesbians, and I think this may have something to do with it. Writing (and reading) about things we can't experience directly, we can fantasize that these relations can be far beyond the best sex WE may have ever had, not limited by or interpreted through our own direct experience. I'm reminded of a passage from Henry Miller (in one of the Tropics, I think—it's been a while) comparing the size of his childhood universe (a few blocks in reality, but limitless in imagination) with that of his adult world (far more extensive in reality, having traveled widely and seen many parts of the world, but as a consequence proportionately limited in imagination, because once he *knew* what some place was really like, he could no longer imagine it any way he wanted)—so that, in a curious way, the more he experienced in his life, the smaller were the possibilities of his imagination. (Tomorrow, 1993, May)

The question of the role that identification plays in reading and writing slash is frequently raised in the context of why straight women would be interested in the intimate relations between two members of the same sex or why lesbians would be interested in the sex lives of men.

By now it must be obvious that slash readers include women of all gender preferences. A more universal form of your question about why lesbians would want to read about men is, why should anyone want to read about characters who aren't anything they could ever be, and would actively dislike in life? Why do we read (with relish) about space pirates, neurotic rock stars, or melancholy Danish princes? Fiction isn't about reasonable wish-fulfillment or simple identity matches. Why should any of us watch *Professionals*, starring as it does two macho-prick studs? (Tennison, 1992, Winter/Spring)

REWRITING MASCULINITY

Slash also represents a way of rethinking and rewriting traditional masculinity. Sarah argued that slash's appeal lies in its placing "emotional responsibility" on men for sustaining relationships while men in reality frequently dodge such responsibility.

> In a letter I just wrote to Jane Carnall, I talked about it in terms of seeing men take on emotional responsibility for, and interest in, relationships. If the story is between two men, and if it depicts a somewhat satisfying relationship, you're guaranteed at least one man who's actively involved in the emotional realm. I know for me that's extremely sexy.[. . .] It explains why we already see, or read, sex into TV shows whose male characters have a supposedly platonic, yet intimate relationship on screen. We see that intimacy and experience sexuality.[. . .] [1] I think part of what slash is about is reading intimacy between peers as itself erotic. They don't just happen to have sex, their sexuality is a natural product of their mutual feelings of closeness.[. . .] We need our pornography to be about people we know and are interested in exploring as many different scenarios as we can imagine.[. . .] In a way, just as the characters' sexual relationship is an expression of their intimacy, we as slash readers also need that intimacy with the characters we write about. That's where the sexual excitement for us comes from; or at least that's one source of it." [2] (Katherine, 1992, November; 1993, February)

Henry suggested that slash addresses some of the social forces that block intimacy between men.

> When I try to explain slash to non-fans, I often reference that moment in *Star Trek: The Wrath of Khan* where Spock is dying and Kirk stands there, a wall of glass separating the two longtime buddies. Both of them are reaching out towards each other, their hands pressed hard against the glass, trying to establish physical contact. They both

have so much they want to say and so little time to say it. Spock calls Kirk his friend, the fullest expression of their feelings anywhere in the series. Almost everyone who watches that scene feels the passion the two men share, the hunger for something more than what they are allowed. And, I tell my nonfan listeners, slash is what happens when you take away the glass. The glass, for me, is often more social than physical; the glass represents those aspects of traditional masculinity which prevent emotional expressiveness or physical intimacy between men, which block the possibility of true male friendship. Slash is what happens when you take away those barriers and imagine what a new kind of male friendship might look like. One of the most exciting things about slash is that it teaches us how to recognize the signs of emotional caring beneath all the masks by which traditional male culture seeks to repress or hide those feelings. (Jenkins, H., 1993, May)

MISOGYNY

The female slash writers have struggled, however, with the genre's primary, if not exclusive, focus on male characters. Should they be writing stories about women? Should slash deal with lesbianism as well as male homosexuality? Is slash's frequent exclusion of female characters misogynist?

My only problem with slash is that I miss women. Sometimes reading about male bodies feels foreign, and I find myself wishing for the familiarity of a woman's body, or even just a significant, three-dimensional, female character. (Katherine, 1993, February)

A thought occurs to me about the unfortunate lack of female slash stories. The majority of slash is based on characters who have a preexisting, strongly emotional relationship in the show where they appear: a lot of slash is expansion on something to be seen in the show (as the slash fan sees it). Female characters, even if you can find more than one in a given show, are unlikely to have an intense, highlighted friendship with each other—if they have any strong relationship, it's likely to be with a male character.[. . .] [1] Male buddy-shows are attractive to us because they show something that's rare in men. One point is that it's not rare in women.[. . .] It's the cold-loner depiction of a woman that stands out in the media; and by their nature, cold loners don't run in pairs. In one sense, slash shows men as honorary women: doing what women-as-we-perceive-them do normally. It's extraordinary and sexy because the men don't (usually) lose the strengths of men-as-we-perceive-them; the slash character is a hermaphroditic combination of the best of both types.[2] (Tennison, 1990, August; 1992, August)

The writers of the series [*Blake's 7*] showed much more imagination when pitting the male characters against each other, in complex multi-layered interrelationships which continue to stimulate discussion, while the female characters were primarily pawns and patsies, taking little active part in the working out of their destinies.[. . .] I think it's commendable that there have been *so many* fan stories involving the female characters, given the material as presented in the series, and that this demonstrates the determination of writers to expand on potential barely hinted at. (Tomorrow, 1990, August)

I still think that misogyny plays a significant part in some segments of slash writing and reading. Some stories leave women characters completely out. For instance, even though *The Professionals* routinely depicts women as full members of CI5, many B/D slash stories posit CI5 as an all-male force. Other stories will "feminize" a male character (Doyle, Vila, Illya, sometimes Avon) and then pile explicit sexual humiliations on him with the overt or covert implication that he "really wants it"; this shows a certain amount of homophobia as well, i.e. bash the "pansy." Some stories portray strong women characters in a show as jealously shrewish, completely evil bitches; some of the depictions of Ann Holly or Dr. Kate Ross (both from *Pros*) or T'Pring (*Trek*) immediately come to mind. A few slash readers, writers and/or editors have expressed overt distaste or disgust at the idea of Lesbian sexuality, all while extolling the glories of male/male relationships.

But I'm now sure that misogyny is not the only reason for the vast overabundance of men.[. . .] As women, reading and writing about men in a mostly women's "space" may be a way for women to deal with their feelings about men in our male supremacist society. Even Lesbians have to learn about how to deal with men (most of us can't go off into a "womyn's paradise"). Lesbians don't usually engage in sexual relationships with men, but we see men in their positions of power. Straight and bisexual women usually have to deal with men in a more intimate way. (Boal, 1991, May)

I'm still bloody insulted by people in general insisting that I need "strong female role models." Some of us already have one. It's called a mirror. (Glasgow, 1993, May)

Nina, who has written slash stories involving female characters, commented on some of the difficulties she has encountered.

Actually, I've found it MUCH more of a challenge to write about female/female sexuality. First, I find I have to wean the women from the feeling that they MUST center their lives around men. Then I have to convince these characters that they DON'T have to then "retreat" to a lesbian separatist commune. It's not rejection of men, it's affirmation of women. Once that is done, men can become human rather than be gods whom women are supposed to worship. It definitely goes against the grain of societal conditioning to make the women the center of the story rather than adjuncts to the male characters. (Boal, 1990, November)

HOMOPHOBIA AND GAY IDENTITY

Making the characters in a slash story lovers leads to the question of whether they are gay. Some slash stories explicitly situate the characters as gay or bisexual people facing a homophobic society; others briefly raise the problem of homophobia only to dismiss it; and some deny that the lovers are "gay" at all. Some stories relocate the characters into science fiction or fantasy contexts, putting them in cultures that are not homophobic or in which "sexual orientation" itself may be a meaningless concept. For some fans, a queer awareness is a crucial part of slash; for others, it is irrelevant or intrusive. The question of whether slash is or should be about gay and bisexual men, the existence of homophobia both in slash writing and among slash fans, and the relationship between gay male and female sexualities have been topics of conversation and debate in the apas since the founding of the TNU. In the first few issues of the apa, several fans explicitly connected their own sexual and political orientations with their enjoyment of slash.

> I am a lesbian, so some of my approach to slash is political—I want to see how a gay couple (of any gender) reacts to and is reacted to by their society. The stories that assume society accepts such couples without question are a lovely relief and often fun to read, since they can concentrate on the individuals and their relationship. Stories which try to face a here-and-now reaction to homosexuality are more, well, contemporary and realistic (though I admit they're more fun to write than to read . . . usually).[. . .] I firmly agree that much attraction in slash is the concentration on what is common to all humans, since sexual differentiation has been bypassed. The characters have to relate as different individuals, not as members of different sexes. (Tennison, 1990, May)

Fans who see queer identity as part of slash are distressed by what they see as evidence of homophobia in the slash community. Nina's and Shoshanna's comments sparked continuing discussion.

> Most people who are involved in slash fandom are hetero women. Some of these women bring their own homophobic baggage into slash fandom. They thrill at the idea of two men doing it, and they see themselves as INCREDIBLY open-minded. But this sort of fan

would be repulsed by the idea of two women doing it.[. . .] Homophobic slash fans also tend to say things such as "(the partners) aren't Gay, they're heterosexual men who just HAPPEN to fall in love with each other." I've even read a letter in a Kirk/Spock letterzine where a fan said that K & S aren't "limp-wristed faggots; they're MEN!"

Fortunately, I've met many slash fans who aren't homophobic. They speak out for Gay rights, and sometimes do such things as volunteer for AIDS organizations. And they'll speak out for Lesbian as well as Gay male rights. When I show them my Uhura/Saavik story, they read it with interest and curiosity.[. . .] I have a feeling that Lesbian slash makes some women uncomfortable because they fear exploring the varied aspects of their own sexuality. (Boal, 1990, May)

Having recently read a huge stack of Bodie/Doyle and Napoleon/Illya slash, I'm on a slow burn about homophobia in the genre.[. . .] Many writers generally accept without thought, as something natural and inevitable, the marginalization of gay people, pairings and love which straight society tries to impose, and participate in it, continue it, in their stories. Sometimes it's the "they're not gay, they just love each other" excuse (which I paraphrase as "we're not gay, we just fuck each other.") Often the authors seem to think that it wouldn't bother the characters to have to hide (which N/I would have worse than B/D, since they're ten years earlier), that they wouldn't get frustrated and humiliated and angry. *Blake's 7* slash is generally not so bad at this, but often only because they haven't got a conveniently handy tawdry gay underculture to denigrate. ("Have you ever—done this with a man before, Napoleon?" "Y-yes . . . but they were only one night stands; it's never been like this before.") The "it's never been like this before" can be another form of marginalization by putting the love affair on a pedestal—it's so wonderful nothing else could ever compare, therefore it is entirely different from everything else and has no relation with anything else. (It can also easily slip into really dreadful misogyny—"no woman could ever understand/be so good a lover/make him feel so secure.") Without denying the existence of homophobia, both in their settings and quite possibly in the characters themselves [. . .] it is still possible to create a story in which the men are gay and human both. (Green, 1990, May)

"They're Not Really Gay, But . . ." usually goads me too! Often though, it's a matter of whether that opinion is that of the author or of the characters. Denial is part of coming out, and a couple of old closet cases like Illya and Napoleon really would have a hard time with that. I can believe they'd deny it to themselves even while they were doing it—but a good writer will make it clear that's a symptom of their times, their agency, their lifestyles and NOT something the reader is expected to agree with.[. . .] I'm not defending homophobic slash with these comments. They only touch on a couple of borderline cases to try to clearly see that line and fine-tune the definition. There is homophobic slash. It's ugly. Most of the time it's repulsively blatant. Liked your point about "It's So Wonderful Nothing Else Could Ever Compare." What I find ironic is that both excuses are things I've heard often from people in the process of coming out. At the point where they haven't come out to themselves and they're scared to death. These ideas can be gut-real and gritty if the writer knows what comes next in the process and makes some progress towards getting there—or points up the tragedy of it if the characters don't grow.[. . .] Is it possible that this type of homophobic story is the same process for the writer? That slash writers who aren't gay still have to go through a process of coming out to themselves about their own stories and accepting that they like them? (Morgan, A., 1990, August)

Nice to know I'm not the only one who gets annoyed with slash fiction where the characters never have to worry about being openly gay, and other unrealistic depictions of gay/lesbian/bi life. Another thing that croggles my mind no end is the type of slash story where A is desperately in love with B and the fan author decides to solve it by simply having character A blurt out his undying love to B without ever having given a thought to B's reaction to the news that A is gay in addition to his being in love with B. Super-unrealistic happy ending! I'm not against happy endings but such hastily written stories leave out the weeks or months of soul-searching it takes to work up the courage to approach that other person who is of your own gender because you don't know whether or not she is straight. Sometimes, I've had a crush on another woman and I've never told her my *true* feelings for her because I was so in love that I was afraid of losing a friendship . . . forever. (Frame-Gray, 1991, February)

I have heard the statement a lot that many female writers, particularly the early ones, are not interested in writing about gay men. I have heard and read the rationales behind this many times. I'm still baffled by the whole issue. For me, it is vitally important that slash *IS* about gay men (and/or lesbians). Slash doesn't work for me unless the characters are clearly gay (even if they are in various stages of denial about it). The vibrant fantasy here for me is that the flaming hets I see on TV come out of the closet and turn out actually to be GAY!!!! (Boal, 1991, August)

But, for other fans, slash is not a gay genre and should not be evaluated by political criteria.

Homosexuality has as much to do with Slash as Civil War history did with *Gone With The Wind*. Burning Atlanta gave Scarlet something to deal with and homosexuality has given Bodie and Doyle something to deal with—sodomy. But *GWTW* wasn't about the causes of the Civil War, the plantation economy, battle strategy and slavery, just as slash isn't about gay rights, creating positive gay identities for Bodie and Doyle, or exploring the gay male sex scene.

Two *heterosexual* males becoming involved in a sexual relationship is my standard definition of slash. Why specifically "heterosexual" males? Because I view slash as a product of female sexuality, and I'll be frank here [. . .] slash is an intricate part of MY sexuality and a sexual outlet. Bodie and Doyle are both men, so homosexual is technically accurate, but hardcore porn is technically heterosexual but I don't see my sexuality in that, either. What I want as a woman, how I view sex and intimacy is not reflected in male homosexuality.

My attraction to a fandom starts with the televised character. If I am attracted physically to at least one guy and the character lends itself to being slash (this isn't a given with me), then I'm hooked. I am not physically attracted to homosexual men. Portraying Bodie and Doyle in a "realistic" gay milieu is taking them from the realm of my sexuality.

Two heterosexual males *becoming involved* in a sexual relationship.[. . .] To me slash is the process of getting these characters into bed.[. . .] This process can be Pon Farr, a knock on the head, the gradual dawning of whatever lust/love, the point is that beginning with the aired characterizations gives us a common starting point. And like the Math test where the teacher wants to "see the work" seeing the author's process X lets us recognize the guys who end up snogging in bed together.

Two heterosexual males becoming involved in a *sexual relationship*. To say that there is no relationship between homosexuality and slash is absurd. To say that slash is just another name for homosexuality is equally absurd. We have appropriated men's bodies and sexual activities for our own gratification. Sounds a lot like complaints about male porn made by women, doesn't it? I'm waiting for a demonstration by gay men where they carry placards complaining that we are using them as "relationship objects." [. . .]

Three years ago I wouldn't have made a distinction between sexual and homosexual. Since the beginning, slash writers have appropriated what we want from the physical side, adapted it to fit female hot buttons, and pretty much kept the relationship female oriented in terms of "true love," virginity, h/c, monogamy, etc. Now the situation has changed.

Somewhere along the line, our appropriation of the physical act of homosexual sodomy [. . .] has been coupled with the obligation to portray these acts realistically and to also give the characters the emotional make-up of homosexual men. The failure to do this is taken as evidence of the writers' 1)naivete; 2)homophobia; 3)social irresponsibility; 4) all of the above.

My question, selfish and self-serving, is where do I fit into this? Something that was an extension of me is now being reality checked to fit the sexuality of a group of people who don't even READ slash because—like Wilford Brimley and oatmeal—it is the right thing to do. [. . .]

Why is it our duty to accurately reflect the gay male experience? Is it the duty of gay male writers to accurately portray the lives of spinster librarians? How they interpret my life will be done through the filter of their own sexuality.

What is the difference between the slash and gay characters? "Slash" characters excite by being extensions of female sexuality while the "gay" characters excite by being a window into an alien sexuality, that of homosexual men. It is internal vs. external in a way. The writers who prefer their characters gay can find more conformity because they are reworking a culture that actually exists—that of homosexual men. There is no island of slash men with sociological texts detailing their behavior. To find where slash comes from we must look inside ourselves.[. . .] My "sick" stories (the ones I'll never write) are the dark places in my sexuality. The issues I will write about, power and trust, concern me as a woman, not Bodie and Doyle as gay men. I am fulfilling my kink, not accurately portraying the kink of gay men.

That said, if YOUR kink is gay men, then state it as a kink, not as the realistic way to write slash or the morally responsible way or the two letter designation that also abbreviates Personal Computers. (Shell, 1994, May)

Barbara offers an alternative account of the relationship between women and gay men.

As long as you ask, I'll be happy to ramble on about how and why slash stories are written about gay men, yet are not "about" gay men. (This is normally so obscure a point that I see no reason to bore people with my fine gradations of meaning.) Slash stories are, typically, narratives featuring two male characters from a TV show who fall in love. And have sex, usually. This defines them as carrying on a homosexual affair, and characterizes them as gay or bi within the meaning our society understands.[. . .] At the same time, the writers are (with few exceptions) middle-class British and American women, expressing their concerns to an audience of peers through story-writing. Their reasons for writing are not gay-male reasons, but female-middle-class-sexual-orientation-unspecified reasons. The stories are written to address, not gay men, but the author's own feelings and sometimes those of her friends and fan audience. The male leads become metaphorical representations of the writer and, if she communicates well enough, the story's readers.

On the level of writing which creates plot, surface detail, and setting, a slash story about male TV characters is about gay men, and should plausibly include gay male styles of action. (Bodie should wear leather and not lace in public; government employees in Britain fear losing their jobs; Starsky finds that being fucked anally feels good (or bad).) The less immediately-obvious aspects of a story, such as theme and moral stance, are very much governed, in slash, by the female writers' perceptions of the world and their ideas of what is good and bad. Much slash is primarily about love or lust—which are shown as positive in general, and as the catalysts for a permanent relationship. This is an expectation trained into our culture's women. The emphasis on partnership and cooperation (even in stories that don't postulate the characters as lovers) is also something women are taught is impor- tant, while men more often focus on competition. The sexual descrip- tions often reflect what women know about their own erotic feelings, and omit what they don't know about men's; extensive foreplay, for instance, and extragenital erogenous zones are common in slash sex scenes, but not in men's descriptions of their own sexuality.

In good writing, these two sets of meanings work together to rein- force the overall message. Slash is so evocative and important to its fans because the position of gay men in society and the position of women correspond in many ways: excluded from the entrenched power structure, emblematic of sexuality, having an often-clandestine network (or a need for it) with other gays or women, able to communi- cate nonverbally with other gays or women to a degree, suspected of even greater communication and collaboration with other gays/women than is true, seen by straight men as "artistic" and "emo- tional," and so on and so on. A story about men in a tight relationship, as a metaphor for how women see love, can illustrate that both sexes need affection and support, that the need is simply human.[. . .] The cross-gender metaphor carries much of the bite of slash: men and male couples as symbols (not really stand-ins) for women suggest what we feel we are, as opposed to how we're seen, how women are forced to think of themselves, in our culture. (Tennison, 1992, Winter/Spring)

Members of the apa often debate what is and is not homophobic.

I *don't* think it is (always? primarily?) homophobia that leads to the I'm not gay, I just want to fuck you. Sometimes it *is* just a cheap device to up the stakes of their relationship. In romance, the more rivers they have to cross, more mountains they have to climb the bet- ter.[. . .] I don't want to belabor the point, but if neither of them has ever acted on a homosexual thought, it "shows" how special their love for each other must be. (Hereld, 1991, November)

I don't like stories in which the author, usually through Bodie and Doyle's mouths, maintains vehemently that they're "not gay." [. . .] I believe that this vehement protest often indicates an underlying belief on the part of the author as well as the characters that, first, there are two alternatives, gay and straight; second, that being gay is distasteful or unpleasant; third, that B & D's involvement is qualitatively different from that of any two given men, because "any two given men" would be gay and B & D aren't. Their sexual love is something else, something above, and hence not gay and distasteful.

A: Gays are icky.

B: Bodie and Doyle are not icky.

C: Therefore, Bodie and Doyle are not gay.

This is homophobia. It's also a form of biphobia, if only in the absolute invisibility of bisexuality.[. . .] Of course, it's possible for the characters to think being gay is icky, while the author does not. It's also possible for a story to be good—well written, well paced, good characterizations—while still displaying political views which I dislike. (Green, 1991, November)

Just as these intimate fantasies of ours (rape, anal sex, romance and happily-ever-afters) need no justification, neither do the stories that merrily ignore the threat of AIDS, syphilis or herpes.[. . .] Sandy, thank you for wording so clearly the "I'm not gay, I just want to fuck you" argument. You said, ". . . if neither of them has ever acted on a homosexual thought, it shows how special their love for each other must be." There is no malice on the part of the writer of such a scenario; in fact, those people who have come to enjoy slash fan fiction generally tend to become the greatest proponents of gay rights. It serves as a consciousness raising tool for many of us. (Willard, 1992, Winter/Spring)

I have never seen slash writing as being gay writing. Rather, it has always struck me as being what Joanna Russ called "the first truly female writing"—by women for women without any political agenda or being filtered through the censorship of commercial publishing. Sure, there are fannish conventions and taboos, but these have been broken since day one. There's always howls of outrage, but that's the point—if we aren't free to write what we like in fandom, where are we? This doubtless accounts for [another member's] perception of a lot of fannish writing as two heterosexuals transposed on same-sex couples. A lot of the early readers of slash seemed to me (sweeping generalization here!) straight middle class women from the Midwest/East. But there's always been a much higher gay component of slash writers and readers than what I'd observed in media fandom in general, which has brought in a genuinely gay perspective as well. (Resch, 1992, November)

FACING THE REALITY OF AIDS

How far reality should intrude on our romantic and erotic fantasies and, indeed, when reality becomes intrusive, remains a long-debated issue. The encroachment of AIDS upon us has given new impetus to this old question. If slash is about gay men, as some apa members argue, then do those characters need to be aware of safer sex practices or confront the risks of AIDS? Responding to concerns raised by another apa member, M. Fae, a prolific fan writer, wrote about her own treatment of AIDS.

> Nina, I've just done a pile of stories that deal with AIDS to some degree or other, simply because of the time in which they were set. I understand why a lot of people don't want to deal with it, and that's fine, but I can't thole sweeping it under the carpet in a setting where to ignore AIDS is both stupid and suicidal. I'm interested that you found my story "Silence=Death" depressing and had to write a somewhat more upbeat sequel: isn't it a bit of a contradiction to want stories to deal with AIDS yet not be depressing? How can it not be depressing that Bodie has just wasted away and died, leaving an infected Doyle behind to face his own death alone? AIDS is the bane of our existence and before we can get people activated to fight it, we have to show them the horror of what it is, in a way that will touch them personally, e.g. having their favorite characters suffer and die from it. I recognize that you want to show that AIDS is not necessarily a complete destruction of personality and living until death finally claims the patient, and that there is still a kind of hope, but "Silence=Death" wasn't about that. It was about what our society, in its blindness and its deafness and muteness, is condemning so many of our people to. (Glasgow, 1991, November)

Others responded:

> I think that as much as we like our slash fiction set in an ideal world where bigotry and homophobia do not exist or can at least be easily hidden from, we need realistic stories that deal with everyday horrors. From a purely educational point of view a slash story on AIDS may be the only place some readers can see the grim reality of the disease. Even today AIDS education is not exactly top of the list in health education, at least it is not in England—I don't know about the USA. Yes, we need fantasy and fantasized reality but we also need the true reality and it sounds like your [M. Fae's] AIDS stories provide that. (Hehir, 1992, Winter/Spring)

> I've been thinking about my reaction to AIDS stories. I guess basically it's this; all the *Professionals* AIDS stories I've seen have fallen without exception into two categories. In one, Bodie or Doyle have to go for an AIDS test, suffer a lot during the waiting period, but prove negative and presumably live happily ever after. In two, Bodie or Doyle have either just died or are dying of AIDS, and that is just another death story with AIDS as a minor twist, and for death stories "I have a

loathing of such depth that you could never measure it." The reality of AIDS for me is walking around for three or four days being hit, every five minutes, with "So this is it, he's going to die." The reality is having a friend who tested HIV positive, most of whose friends tested positive, some of his friends have died of AIDS, he is now in second-stage AIDS. The reality is for a week not even knowing if he would get AZT and the other treatments on the NHS (and if he hadn't, basically, he would be dead or dying now). It lasts a lot longer. It hurts a lot more. I'm not ready to write a story about it now. (Carnall, 1992, Winter/Spring)

"IT'S THE SEX!"

The push towards realism in slash writing has provoked some uncomfortable responses within the fan community. M. Fae, a writer of some of the more "adventurous" slash stories, discussed the relationship between her highly psychological, highly sexual stories and the larger slash tradition. As the discussion has continued, M. Fae has become increasingly vocal about her frustration with both fannish and academic accounts of slash that dismiss or fail to address its erotic and bodily pleasures.

Well, as a NEW fan, people would ask me what I liked most about slash, why I had got involved in it, etc. And then would appear shocked when I said, "Oh, that's easy. It's the sex!" The standard answer was still the "love, romance, caring," etc., and the majority were very taken aback when I said that I was open to any fandom, as long as it was slash and as long as we had at least two men buggering each other into next week. Now, no-one bats an eye at that. [. . .]

By the way, I think there is some room for the argument that I often don't write slash. I don't follow many of the rhythms of slash stories, I frequently approach the same topic from a diametrically opposite point of view from fan canon, I often discount such supposed cornerstones of slash as love, romance, friendship, equality, trust and of course, happily ever after. I rarely write my stories from the traditional skew of "how do we get them to love each other forever and/or commit to each other?": I almost invariably write them from the point of view of "what makes people tick? What would motivate a man like this, if we were to focus on *this* aspect of his personality?" Apart from that, it's usually for the sex itself, or to explore some interesting question that's come up either in the programme/book or in society in general or in slashdom.[. . .] I rarely feel the need to write the nicer stories, simply because there are so many good ones already being done. [. . .]

I'm very well aware of my own world view colouring certain things I do—but equally, the characters very frequently express things that are purely them, and opposite to me. I really don't write slash as any kind of allegory for women's issues: they are simply allegories for human issues, which I consider transcends the limits of gender. They are also, to get to the core of it for me, stories of sexual and/or emotional satisfaction, attractive fictional men manipulated as much as possible to give as much pleasure as possible. (Glasgow, 1992, May)

I am sick and tired of being told Why You Write Slash. I am sick and tired of being told what the deep, dark psychological reasons are. I'm sick of being told I'm a misogynist because I don't include women in my stories[. . .]. I am sick and tired of having other people tell me what I *really* think and feel—as opposed to what *I* think I think and feel. I am really tired of being told I'm writing "from my pain" or my guilt, or my inhibitions, or my lack of self-worth, or my repressed this that or the next thing. I am tired of being told I'm writing this or that because society has forced me into a box, a corner or subcultural ghetto. I'm tired of being told I'm doing this because I'm a feminist or a misogynist, a conservative or a liberal, a poor pathetic wee thing or a poor, misunderstood, down-trodden wee thing. I'm sick of being told I'm writing this because I'm revolutionary, overthrowing a patriarchal society, emasculating men, gelding men, or just screwing them into exhaustion. I am truly fed up with hearing that I identify with "him", or that he is me—I am he and he is me and I am the bloody Walrus. I'm tired of being told that everything I write is about *me*—why, thank you kindly for saying I'm too stupid to make up bloody sex stories! [. . .] I'm tired of being told I'm writing because I want a man, want to be a man or actually am a man and just didn't know it. I'm tired of being told it's because I idolize men, exalt men, kowtow to men, respect men, envy men, hate men, or just want to be a man. I'm tired of being told it's penis envy or vagina hate. And I'm really, really tired of people going on and on and on and on, reams upon reams upon reams, and not one of them ever mentioning one very salient fact. [. . .]

Some of us (gasp, horror, shock) read slash because it turns us on. Some of us read slash because it's sexy, arousing, fine, one-handed reading, as satisfying to the emotions and the intellect as it is to the libido.[. . .] Slash is often a masturbatory aid, or a marital aid, or just inspiration for a rollicking good time. Slash is not purely an intellectual exercise, nor is it exclusively a sociological experiment.

It's sexy stories. About sex, and men, and men having sex. It's about emotional orgasms, and physical orgasms, lust and/or love fulfilled. It's about libidinous excitement, descriptions that make us quiver—or to speak the unspeakable, descriptions that make us wet, and randy, and finally, happily basking in the afterglow.

Slash is about having fun, whether that fun is reading the equivalent of a classic romance structure featuring two men instead of one man and one woman, or whether that fun is reading a really good "weepy," where one lover dies in the arms of a man who loves him.

Slash is a romp in the grass, a roll in the hay, a wallow, a rollercoaster ride, a gallop through a dark and stormy night, a bucolic interlude of unsurpassed sweetness—or a dark delving into scream-filled dungeons, hurt and comfort, pain and surcease, domination, submission, sadism and masochism. [. . .]

I don't read slash as an academic, sociological, abstract exercise. And I'm not the only one. Let's not forget that there are some very basic, very straightforward reasons for slash, as well as more rarified ones.

After all, if all we wanted were good character developments, further explorations of an aired universe, more adventures of beloved ship's crews, then we could and would read gen. If all we wanted was the emotional intensity, then we could read and write male bonding stories till the cows come home. If all we wanted was the breaking down of barriers, and then the emotional intensity, then we could read h/c [hurt/comfort]. But some of us don't, at least not exclusively. We read, and write, slash.

Never underestimate the appeal of sex. (Glasgow, 1995, May)

"INAPPROPRIATE" FANTASIES

Have fans increasingly broken from the conventions of the traditional romance in more recent stories? What relationship exists between slash and mainstream pornography? Fans have debated what to make of a growing number of stories that incorporate less overtly "romantic" sexual content. Cynthia uses slash to reassess the feminist critique of pornography.

YOUR PORN IS OK, MY PORN IS OK

I agree with you that romantic slash is more tolerated because the fantasies are "acceptably feminine" whereas rape, hurt/comfort etc. are not. Looking at larger societal debates over pornography, the anti-porn movement, when they admit to positive sexuality at all, seems to want to distinguish between good sex (feminine sex that is relationship oriented, caring, tender, and based in mutual love) and bad sex (typified by the bulk of mainstream pornography, which is alienated, emotionless, sometimes not sweet and frequently does not occur within a secure relationship).[. . .] The dominant streams of thought within this movement do not allow much room for fantasy. Somehow all fantasy and representation are seen as leading towards actualization of the ideas or images.[. . .] The assumption seems to be that our fantasies control us, not that we control our fantasies. [. . .]

In many ways slash can be seen as the ideal "feminine erotica." It is relationship oriented as hell, oh so caring and tender, and all about love. The hiccup comes in with some of the harder edged slash that has started to surface more recently. There is a temptation to see romantic slash as good porn, which is to say as reflecting a feminine sensibility, as erotica v. harder edged slash as bad porn, which is to say reflecting a more masculine sensibility, to see it *as* pornography in the negative-value-laden sense of the word. [. . .]

The types of fiction that provoke virulent response are precisely those that draw on the tropes of male erotica. Those slash stories mess up all those nice neat categories people are used to thinking in. Rape? Tying up your partner and flogging him? Esoteric practices like pissing into his bladder? Long tender descriptions of mutilated bodies? These are tender scenes of love?

The damnedest part of it is, that for the most part, they are.

When slash develops s&m or b&d it usually does so in the context of the same relationship that structures more vanilla stories about sex and love. The relationship is consensual and the sex is the expression of a very mutual, caring and usually permanent bond. Part of what is curious is that the anti-porn argument suggesting that inherent power inequalities make it impossible for women to give real consent to participate in sexual games involving power (like s&m scenes) falls to pieces if both characters are acknowledged as masculine.[. . .] But slash stories assume that games can be just that: games. Or they assume that roleplaying can serve some therapeutic purpose. But they virtually always see the people as controlling the games, not the other way around. They actively construct an argument against anti-porn fears that power differential is fixed, that it is invariably harmful, and that pain- or power-centered imagination and bedroom practice will corrupt the way we interact outside the bedroom. The point of the stories is to situate these practices in the context of a relationship and examine how they function as a part of that relationship. [. . .]

Rape stories, though they may start out with male porn cliches about desire overwhelming control, or some such, usually go on to deal with the ramifications of the act. The point of the story isn't the rape; it's how the characters deal with the rape. Can they salvage anything from the wreckage created by the violence? Do they want to? Alternatively, if the rape is rewritten (either within the course of the narrative, or within sequels) so that it isn't really a rape (he really liked it) the narratives still focus on the dynamics of the relationship.

Hurt/comfort stories often contain enough gore to send shivers down the back of activists concerned with the conflation of sex and violence. [. . .] How can anyone get off on seeing a character suffer from gunshot wounds or auto accidents? Why does this so often lead to sex, and so often to highly improbable sex, at that, while the wounded partner is still suffering to a degree that renders erotic response improbable? It is as if the vulnerability of the physical body is being used symbolically to illustrate the vulnerability of the emotional makeup of men. The breakdown of the physical body leads to a breakdown of personal barriers, of emotional defenses. And this (in slash) leads to a breakdown of physical barriers and to sex. Yes, there is lots

of pain and suffering, sometimes very precise descriptions of which
bones are broken or which internal organs are bruised, or how bloody
the wound is, or how labored the breathing patterns are. But once
again, unlike the material I suspect h/c is implicitly being analogized
to, the hurt is not so much directly erotic as it is the means by which a
sufficient degree of vulnerability and openness is achieved that an intimate relationship can develop.

So the sub-genres of slash that all too often provoke wondering
looks, or less polite queries as to how the fan could like *that*, strike me
as curious hybrids of romantic feminine-style sex and elements of
masculine porn that are central to debates concerning the availability
and impact of sexually explicit material. Those elements of the pornographic imagination that are least accessible to many women are co-
opted and explored within the context of the familiar romantic relationship. True, romantic stories are seen as acceptably feminine, but I
would argue that slash stories about beating your partner until his
backside glows in the dark are also "feminine" by the same criteria.

Thoughts? Does this make any sense? (Jenkins, C., 1993,
November)

A UNIVERSE OF ONE'S OWN

Many fans feel freer in fandom than outside of it to express themselves, ask
questions, and discuss alternative viewpoints. Teresa commented on what
have been for her the benefits of participation in the slash community.

> I still find it incredible writing to people and being able to talk
> about "slash" and use all those words that polite Catholic girls are not
> supposed to know (you know the ones—penis, cock, fucking)—as a
> Catholic, I knew Sodom existed as a town, but didn't dare ask what
> Sodomy was.[. . .] I think the reason I like slash fiction has more to do
> with the emotion in the story than the act itself. Our house was emo-
> tionally very cold. Any emotion had to be hidden—I grew up feeling
> embarrassed if I looked happy in public let alone if I cried in public. I
> like the emotional romances that just don't seem to exist outside of
> slash fiction. Mind you, I like the pure sex ones as well. [1] People like
> Leslie Fish and M. Fae have taught me so much about the human
> body and also about the human mind. The ideas bound up in some of
> these stories about what constitutes male/female good/bad accept-
> able/unacceptable sex have opened my eyes to the way society forces
> its ideas on us. [2] (Hehir, 1992, Winter/Spring; 1993, August)

What many slash fans enjoy is the sense of creating their own culture, of participating in the emergence of a new genre that more perfectly
expresses their own social visions and fantasies.

What I love about fandom is the freedom we have allowed our-selves to create and recreate our characters over and over again. Fanfic rarely sits still. It's like a living, evolving thing, taking on its own life, one story building on another, each writer's reality bouncing off another's and maybe even melding together to form a whole new cre-ation. A lot of people would argue that we're not creative because we build on someone else's universe rather than coming up with our own. However, I find that fandom can be extremely creative because we have the ability to keep changing our characters and giving them new life over and over. We can kill and resurrect them as often as we like. We can change their personalities and how they react to situa-tions. We can take a character and make him charming and sweet or coldblooded and cruel. We can give them an infinite, always-chang-ing life rather than the single life of their original creation. We have given ourselves license to do whatever we want and it's very liberat-ing. (Bannister, K., 1993, May)

The multiple perspectives of fandom on the same set of characters allow us to do one thing better than virtually any other form of con-temporary literature; they allow us to know one set of characters with tremendous depth. People are not as simple as even the most complex literary character in a single presentation. Any breathing human being is really many people, many of whom are contradictory. Reading overlapping versions of Ray Doyle, for example, leads to an under-standing that is in many ways more real for its breadth and depth, detail and yes, even its contradictions. I do not think it is coincidental that so many fans have been or are drawn to mainstream literary uni-verses consisting of multiple retellings of the same sets of stories by different authors—Arthurian myths and the Robin Hood legends spring immediately to mind as two other "evolving" universes. How is what we do different? (Jenkins, C., 1993, August)

I think part of what makes slash so alluring is not so much that it's taboo, although that does give it an extra edge, but that *we* create it, our community, unhindered by all the rules of creative writing profes-sors, of publishers and of marketers. We create the fiction we want to read and, more importantly, we allow ourselves to react to it. If a story moves or amuses us, we share it; if it bothers us, we write a sequel; if it disturbs us, we may even re-write it! We also continually recreate the characters to fit our images of them or to explore a new idea. We have the power and that's a very strong siren. If we want to explore an issue or see a particular scenario, all we have to do is sit down and write it. It gets read and instantly reacted upon in a continuing dia-logue among fans. You can't do that very often in the "real" world. For me, that's one of the strongest callings of slash in particular and fan-dom in general. (Bannister, K., 1993, August)

I certainly do agree with you that fanfic of any type allows for a "much wider range of use of sexuality." Well hell—it's not commercially oriented in the usual sense, and when you have to subscribe to commercial concerns and mores then you immediately restrict and censor yourself. Heaven forfend (as the wee Scot [M. Fae] always says) that fanfic should ever want to go aboveground. Fanfic's greatest strength is that it *is* underground and alternative. I rejoice in a system of government which tolerates this freedom of expression, this grassroots explosion of communication! Marginal our efforts and our writing may be considered, but an explosion it is and it is vast. (Nancy, 1991, November)

SUMMING UP

What has sustained this discussion for years is the complex set of questions that slash poses and the absence of easy, satisfying answers. Morgan and Barbara examine what they see as the power and the "paradox" of slash.

Slash makes you think. It presents you with scenarios and situations that confront and transgress our nicely constructed ideas of the "norm." It flat refuses to swallow the party line about who has what emotions in what circumstances. It is produced, mainly by women, in an effort to search through questions and answers about ourselves and our constructed sexuality/identity. In slash, we do what is unthinkable, we put the "wrong" people in bed, in the "wrong" situations. In a world that creates the individual's identity in terms of sexuality, we respond by challenging, rearranging, that sexuality, that identity. (Morgan, 1993, November)

Paradoxes surround slash literature. Slash has been confusing everyone including its creators for years. But isn't this because it's an expression of the hopelessly confusing and contradictory world women live in, and the confused and contradictory view society has of sex? [. . .] Slash is defined and shaped by women, and if it seems contradictory, or seems to tell more than one kind of story at times, maybe there's a reason. The writers aren't following anyone else's guidelines; they're writing, as best they can, what they feel. (Tennison, 1990, November)

REFERENCES

Anestopoulo, C. (1990, August). Darkling zine. *Terra Nostra Underground*, No. 3.
Bacon-Smith, C. (1992). *Enterprising women: Television fandom and the creation of popular myth.* Philadelphia: University of Pennsylvania Press.
Bannister, K. (1993, May). Untitled. *Strange Bedfellows*, No. 1.

Bannister, K. (1993, August). Desert blooms. *Strange Bedfellows*, No. 2.

Boal, N. (1990, May). Lavender lilies. *Terra Nostra Underground*, No. 2.

Boal, N. (1990, November). Lavender lilies. *Terra Nostra Underground*, No. 4.

Boal, N. (1991, May). Lavender lilies, addendum. *Terra Nostra Underground*, No. 6.

Boal, N. (1991, August). Lavender lilies. *Terra Nostra Underground*, No. 7.

Carnall, J. (1992, Winter/Spring). Not Cat's darkling zine. *Terra Nostra Underground*, No. 9.

Dery, M. (1993, Fall). Glossary. In M. Dery (Ed.), Flame wars: The discourse of cyberculture. [Special issue]. *South Atlantic Quarterly*.

Frame-Gray, N. (1991, February). Wonderframe. *Terra Nostra Underground*, No. 5.

Glasgow, M.F. (1991, November). Two heads are better than one. *Terra Nostra Underground*, No. 8.

Glasgow, M.F. (1992, May). Two heads are better than one. *Terra Nostra Underground*, No. 10.

Glasgow, M.F. (1993, May). Two heads are better than one. *Strange Bedfellows*, No. 1.

Glasgow, M.F. (1993, August). Two heads are better than one. *Strange Bedfellows*, No. 2.

Glasgow, M.F. (1995, May). Two heads are better than one. *Strange Bedfellows*, No. 9.

Green, S. (1990, May). For the world is hollow and I fell off the edge. *Terra Nostra Underground*, No. 2.

Green, S. (1991, November). For the world is hollow and I fell off the edge. *Terra Nostra Underground*, No. 8.

Hehir, T. (1992, Winter/Spring). To be announced. *Terra Nostra Underground*, No. 9.

Hehir, T. (1993, August). To be announced. *Strange Bedfellows*, No. 2.

Hereld, S. (1991, November). But t-shirt slogans are intellectual discourse!! *Terra Nostra Underground*, No. 8.

Hereld, S. (1992, November). T-shirt slogans *are* intellectual discourse. *Terra Nostra Underground*, No. 12.

Jenkins, C. (1993, August). *Menage a deux*. Strange Bedfellows, No. 2.

Jenkins, C. (1993, November). *Menage a deux*. Strange Bedfellows, No. 3.

Jenkins, H. (1992). *Textual poachers: Television fans and participatory culture*. New York: Routledge, Chapman and Hall.

Jenkins, H. (1993, May). Confessions of a male slash fan. *Strange Bedfellows*, No. 1.

Katherine, S. (1992, November). Writing from the margins. *Terra Nostra Underground*, No. 12.

Katherine, S. (1993, February). Writing from the margins. *Terra Nostra Underground*, No. 13.

Lamb, P.F., & Veith, D.L. (1986). Romantic myth, transcendence and *Star Trek* zines. In D. Palumbo (Ed.), *Erotic universe: Sexuality and fantastic literature.* New York: Greenwood.

Morgan, A. (1990, August). Criminal love. *Terra Nostra Underground,* No. 3.

Morgan. (1993, November). A different eye. *Strange Bedfellows,* No. 3.

Nancy. (1991, November). Two heads are better than one. *Terra Nostra Undergound,* No. 8.

Penley, C. (1991a). Brownian motion: Women, tactics, and technology. In C. Penley & A. Ross (Eds.), *Technoculture.* Minneapolis: University of Minnesota Press.

Penley, C. (1991b). Feminism, psychoanalysis and the study of popular culture. In L. Grossberg, C. Nelson, & P. Treichler (Eds.), *Cultural studies.* New York: Routledge, Chapman and Hall.

Resch, K. (1992, November). I used to be trek monogamous, but now I'm a media slut! *Terra Nostra Underground,* No. 12.

Russ, J. (1985). *Magic mommas, trembling sisters, puritans and perverts: Feminist essays.* Trumansberg, NY: Crossing Press.

Shell, L. (1994, May). W.H.I.P.S., women of Houston in pornography. *Strange Bedfellows,* No. 5.

Tennison, B. (1990, May). Strange tongues. *Terra Nostra Underground,* No. 2.

Tennison, B. (1990, August). Strange tongues. *Terra Nostra Underground,* No. 3.

Tennison, B. (1990, November). Strange tongues. *Terra Nostra Underground,* No. 4

Tennison, B. (1991, May). Strange tongues. *Terra Nostra Underground,* No. 6.

Tennison, B. (1992, Winter/Spring). Strange tongues. *Terra Nostra Underground,* No. 9.

Tennison, B. (1992, August). Strange tongues. *Terra Nostra Underground,* No. 11.

Tennison, B. (1993, November). Strange tongues. *Strange Bedfellows,* No. 3.

Tomorrow, A. (1990, August). Notes from tomorrow. *Terra Nostra Underground,* No. 3.

Tomorrow, A. (1993, May). Notes from tomorrow. *Strange Bedfellows,* No. 1.

Viegener, M. (1993). Kinky escapades, bedroom techniques, unbridled passion, and secret sex codes. In D. Bergman (Ed.), *Camp grounds: Style and homosexuality.* Amherst: University of Massachusetts Press.

Willard, L.S. (1992, Winter/Spring). Wellington's womblings. *Terra Nostra Underground,* No. 9.

▶II

FANDOM AND THE SOCIOLOGY OF CULTURE

A Sociology of Television Fandom

Cheryl Harris
New School for Social Research

Aesthetic intolerance can be terribly violent.—Bourdieu (1984)

Television is arguably our most pervasive representation of a shared "cultural space" within which the allocation of social value is negotiated. At the same time, the ability to overtly influence television content is severely limited. Still, audiences are generally oriented toward protecting and enlarging representations that resonate with them—few media scholars would accept the characterization of audiences as "couch potatoes." We *do* something with media content, if only in the expression of cultural preferences. That some of us are more active than others is clear: We call some active social groups "activists" or advocates, others are labeled "fans." For all of us, though, the process of asserting one's social values and "tastes" within the television programming structure or within our culture as a whole is highly politicized and class-driven. Fans and activists are simply very visible instances of this process. Because they are so visible, we can learn from a close examination of these subcultures something about the entire social contract a culture makes with its cultural industries, and the very real contribution to social identity the products of these industries provide for us. In this chapter, these issues are explored within the context of a 5-year study of a national fan group known as *Viewers for Quality Television.* Moreover, fandom is reconceptualized as a spectrum of practices engaged in to develop a sense of personal control or influence over the object of fandom in response to subordinated social status. In addition, varying degrees of involvement in fan practices is found to be associated with unexpected outcomes.

BACKGROUND

Over the past two decades, social science literature has demonstrated an emergent interest in the ability of the individual to resist mass culture (Fiske, 1989a, 1989b: Hall & Jefferson, 1976; Morley, 1986; Newcomb & Hirsch, 1983). This has been meaningful in that it reflects a move away from the preexisting dominant paradigm of the "passive audience" or the helpless (and hapless) audience vulnerable to direct effects from message exposure. At the base of these new concepts is the possibility for a struggle over cultural meanings and cultural space, whereby individuals and social groups negotiate their own insertion into the message and language systems of the culture.

This process challenges the boundaries of "appropriate" and "inappropriate" meanings; sanctioning what is defined as "good" and working to retain and encourage symbols, messages, and other cultural products that fit a collective set of criteria and "resonates" with a defined social identity. If this is so, it is important to know how individuals and groups construct a social identity (or identities) that then becomes enacted in a system of evaluative criteria ("taste") which is applied to a symbol system of cultural products, such as television programming. Using a sociology of culture perspective, I explore in this chapter how the seemingly amorphous and class-based notion of "taste" arises and becomes politicized when applied to cultural products by social groups with competing interests (Bourdieu, 1979, 1984, 1989, 1986; de Certeau, 1984).

If social groups do successfully challenge or "resist" culture and insert their own meanings in place of those offered, what might be the outcome? Some have theorized that the reward for resistance is personal and social "empowerment" in the face of a fragmented and anomic society. "Empowerment" is seen as a function and possibility of participation in popular culture (Amesley, 1989; Ang, 1985, 1991; Cohen, 1976; Fiske,

1989a, 1989b; Gans, 1974; Grossberg, 1984; Jenkins, 1988, 1992; Radway, 1984).

The concept of empowerment is suggested by the early Birmingham school work on subcultures (Hebdige, 1979; McRobbie & Nava, 1984; Willis, 1977) in which certain subcultures or well-delineated social groups appeared to have the ability to resist or challenge dominant ideologies, a concept notably at odds with earlier effects models (Blumer, 1933; Gerbner, 1971; Lasswell, 1927) and critiques of mass culture advanced by Frankfurt school theorists (Adorno & Horkheimer, 1972; Marcuse,1964). This resistance appeared to provide group members with a sense of empowerment in the face of seemingly monolithic or hegemonic forces. I suggest in this chapter that fan or pressure groups may similarly find empowerment in their consumption of popular culture, specifically television programs. Because many (some might say most) fans are women or girls, gender and its implications have also been important considerations in developing theories of fandom.

At the same time, it is impossible to ignore the extent to which media industries may be said to engage in an attempt to economically *disempower* fans by encouraging heavy spending on artifacts and merchandise, which to fans represent a kind of "capital accumulation" (Fiske, 1987).

Although the focus of this chapter and the book as a whole is on *audiences*, the texts to which audiences respond are inevitably part of the equation, and for quite some time now, researchers across the discipline have expressed renewed interest in how television constructs and circulates certain images, interpretations, and portrayals that may potentially influence aspects of our perceptions and beliefs as a culture. Certainly, this issue is an implicit feature of such theoretical perspectives as cultivation, but it also exists as a part of many other models in communication research. Much of what we take for granted in our theoretical framework as a field rests on the implied association between media imagery and our collective social construction of reality.

In examinations of popular culture in general and television in particular, the "stakes" may at first glance seem trivial. It is, after all, "just" TV, just the "boob tube." Yet if one looks deeper, it seems sensible to suppose that any medium that draws millions of people to it around the clock and around the globe, persists, and has formulated and assiduously maintained a specific structure, probably is one with "stakes." Television is our most pervasive representation of a shared "cultural space." Television's role, then, in circulating meanings with which we regularly engage in the course of everyday life, is a fairly important one. It has been suggested that in American society, our knowledge and experience of the outside world is increasingly available only from mass media, and predominantly from television. Further, our heterogeneous society is simply too complicated to know or experience directly, and so we must rely on television not only to represent our world to us but also to represent ourselves to the world (Carey, 1989; Cooley, 1919/1983). Interest in how individuals or social groups make use of the meanings television offers drives the work of some influential figures in our field such as Morley (1986), Fiske (1989a, 1989b), Gerbner (1971), and others.

An emerging problem, however, is the way in which we also may participate in the creation of meaning other than at the point of reception—ways in which audiences provide feedback or direction to those responsible for the technical production of cultural texts. Television, for example, is often thought of as an insular and one-way transmitter, beaming its signals out across the void to land in our living rooms. Yet, television producers, programmers, and other industry personnel do not create in a vacuum. There are a few feedback mechanisms that are expected to provide some indication of audience preferences. However, many of these mechanisms, such as the Nielsen ratings system, have largely been criticized for their relative insensitivity in measuring the appeal of programs or viewer satisfaction with them (Beville, 1985; Gitlin, 1983). One problem is that Nielsen ratings tend to skew "downscale" (rural and poor) to those who are more attracted to the slim incentive payments offered (Harris, 1992). In addition, the system is also known to exclude minorities and other significant populations (Gitlin, 1985).

This leaves us with a problem: One comes to realize that the issue of "what's on television" is associated with very high stakes at the same time that one realizes it is difficult to influence programming directly. Thus, it is not surprising that there is a long history of audience segments who organize themselves into lobbying groups in order to influence programming outcomes. The first television activist groups arose in the early 1950s (Montgomery, 1989) and proliferated throughout the 1960s and 1970s. Although a number of court decisions in the 1970s increased the power of activist groups to influence programming, the deregulation of the broadcasting industry in the Reagan area reversed these gains. According to Montgomery (1989) and Turow (1989), networks also developed a number of strategies for defusing and limiting the power of such audience-based groups (such as recasting the groups as "special interests," "incorporating" key members, and treating them as "fans"—all ways of marginalizing potentially threatening movements).

In any case, if we accept that television is an important cultural resource, then it should not be surprising that some audiences have had a history of fighting for their preferences in terms of the meanings and representations featured in television programming. Social groups who perceive real or imagined slights in their treatment on television have protested vigorously: African Americans, Latinos, gays and lesbians, Arabs, women, and many others. Generally, activist groups seek to redress their wrongs by asking that television "look like the real world" in terms of statistical proportions (11% of all characters on television should be African American, for example, in order to meet "real-life" percentages; Montgomery, 1986). Occasionally, groups will ask a show's writers to upgrade their characterizations beyond their "real life conditions" in the hope that that will influence the viewing audience to reconstruct their stereotypes. The power that these groups wield is usually associated with their threatened ability to boycott the products of sponsors who advertise on offending shows. The common thread is that all ask for a redistribution of the cultural space which television maps out. Williamson's (1986), Bourdieu's (1984) and Fiske's (1989a, 1989b) work suggests that consumption of anything—whether good, service, or idea—is inherently political and involves the subject in cultural work. This is a sophisticated version of the often-repeated maxim "the personal is political."

FAN PRACTICES

Activist and fan practices are simply intensified, more visible instances of everyone's everyday struggle over cultural meanings and cultural space in a battleground of commodified culture that is managed and represented most prominently by television (Fiske, 1987, 1989b). We *must* attend to it because not to do so is to risk being marginalized, even symbolically annihilated. Seen this way, each of us adopt and implement, sometimes in concert with others, a series of coping mechanisms to both evade, resist and change cultural meanings that are centrally distributed (Fiske, 1989a). Bourdieu argued that debates over the value of cultural artifacts (which images and ideas should be emphasized and which marginalized) are highly political in nature (Bourdieu 1980a, 1980b, 1980c, 1984). This is so because the perceived worth of cultural symbols (as represented in television narrative, for example) is closely aligned with the "social" worth of various individuals and groups in the culture and defines their position in the social structure. Thus, fighting for "cultural space" into which a symbolically defined group may insert themselves may be seen as a feature of everyday life, part of an ongoing struggle in which we all must engage to establish, maintain, and repair our own sense of ourselves. If, as has been argued, television is a centralized system of cultural representation and negotiation—typically controlled by a very few whose interests cannot be counted on to perfectly reflect our own—then its ability to construct a social reality in which differential amounts of "cultural capital" are conferred must be seen as very powerful.

The notion of culture as a site of perpetual struggle is a relatively recent one. British and American cultural studies of the last decade have regarded cultural materials as anything but self-contained (Fiske, 1987; Hall & Jefferson, 1976). Rather, their position has also been that approaches to texts depend on the position of the social interpreter, who is capable of activation in a wide variety of ways. Although cultural studies and subcultural studies have been criticized for their broad pluralism, which tends to leave large atheoretical or untheorized gaps (Cagle, 1989), this body of work, along with Bourdieu, provides the primary evidence for the concept that class and social position tends to determine one's reception of culture. In turn, this differential positioning also lays the foundation for popular cultures, in that different social segments will seek to represent themselves in different ways.

A Case Study: Viewers for Quality Television

Many scholars and theorists who have written about fans vehemently argue that it is impossible to understand fandom from the "outside;" one must be a fan and enter into its ethos fully in order to develop models that reflect the social realities of fans themselves (Jenkins, 1992.) An important part of this writing seems to be the "confession" of one's own fandom, along with the recounting of one's subsequent marginalization in the academy as a result of daring to write about something so stigmatized or trivial as fan behavior. I would have to say my experience is not different. My interest in fandom came about as the result of a 5-year involvement (1985-1990) with a group known as Viewers for Quality Television (VQT). This group, while headquartered in Virginia, grew from its grassroots beginnings to become a kind of national umbrella group for fans. This group operates both as an interpretive community (to share and discuss fan issues with other like-minded fans) and as an institution to challenge media industries if content they wish to protect is threatened. Organized in 1984 by a Virginia homemaker, Dorothy Swanson VQT has been instrumental in returning a number of canceled or marginalized programs to the air when they were threatened by low ratings (*Cagney & Lacey, Designing Women, China Beach, Beauty & the Beast, Alien Nation, Quantum Leap*, etc.) Skilled at positioning the group as an important "quality demographic" of use to networks, Swanson, throughout the mid 1980s, became "the housewife the networks can't ignore" (Ryan, 1988).

Like many fan groups, VQT generates a massive amount of data: newsletters, conventions, surveys, public relations materials, member experiences, and testimonies. All of these are interesting moments of institutionalized fan practice.

"QUALITY" AND FAN TASTE

However, the group is relatively unique in fandom because its interests are not centered around a star, text, or genre, but is concerned with the survival and endorsement of many different types of television programming—as long as they meet the group's collectively defined notion of "quality." That the term "quality" relates fairly directly to issues of social identity is quickly seen by a perusal of the group's monthly newsletters. Members, primarily women, negotiate readings of their favorite texts every month in the newsletter. Member letters and commentary form the lion's share of newsletter content, in which members offer their interpretations of shows and characters in great detail. Members often challenge individual episodes as being at odds with their perceptions of the show's overall meaning system. This exercise is repeated so often that it seems to be critical to group function. After all, "identity is about belonging, about what you have in common and what differentiates you from others . . . at the center are the values we share or wish to share with others" (Weeks, cited in Rutherford, 1990, p. 90).

Because the group defines itself as standing for "quality" television, the notion of quality itself deserves examination. The aesthetic standards brought to bear on cultural materials are "mediated through . . . concepts like 'quality' or 'taste'" (Hebdige, 1988, p. 106), which are not readily understood by those not sharing the class position of the critic. This is important, because the term "quality" is often narrowly interpreted as somehow synonymous with "high culture" definitions of excellence. However, looking at the thematics of programs which VQT has supported and campaigned for since 1985, the common thread appears to be that the "quality" VQT members and fans admire is actually a series of qualities that express *emotional* realism (as in "believability," "problems similar to my own life," etc.) but not necessarily physical realism.

Naturally, one's social membership (and conversely, sense of "difference" from others), in filtering all impressions of the environment, influences perception generally and consequently, consumption decisions (Schroder, 1987). Products, as Williamson has asserted, "speak social identities." She argues that in our society the conditions of production (meaning working life) are ones over which people have little or no control. However, consumption offers a way to cope with the frustrations of capitalist conditions by seeming to provide an escape from control. Capitalism, in this view, posits ownership as the only form of legitimate control in our culture and products the only way to control expressed meanings and social identities (Williamson, 1986).

Also important to the VQT agenda is an ongoing challenge to the Nielsen ratings as a presumed arbiter of taste. Fans find this measurement system to be a sort of systematic disenfranchisement—a "mainstreaming" effect. The promise of being able to assert one's cultural preferences within the framework of a national culture industry is VQT's primary offering, and perhaps, that of all fan groups. In doing so, an implicit benefit of membership becomes the "distinction" that Bourdieu insists is crucial to the formation and maintenance of social identities, a process that an anomic contemporary social system contributes to but poorly.

INVOLVEMENT AND FANDOM

How do fans define themselves and how does this self-definition ultimately relate to the practice of fandom? In a survey of 1,100 VQT members, virtually all (95%) readily admitted that they considered themselves to be "fans." Yet, when I looked at what fans say they actually do in pursuit of their fandom, there were enormous differences in levels of participation, in recognized fan activities (letter writing, co-viewing and/or discussions with other fans, newsletter participation, collecting artifacts, etc.). The data on participation in fan practices taken as a whole suggested that several underlying variables affect level of participation and that "fandom" should properly be conceived as existing on a continuum. *It is not a unified concept.* This finding becomes important because the extent to which one is involved in a range of fan activities seems to be strongly related to an achieved sense of control over the object of one's fandom—arguably perhaps the point of fandom itself and its ultimate pleasure.

Involvement in activities (taking into account frequency, type, and duration) also seems to predict satisfaction, enjoyment of television, sense of belonging, and a host of other variables *regardless of whether or not the objective of the involvement was achieved* (such as returning a cancelled show to the air). In attempting to explain these associations, it is likely that the more active fans are, the more power and control they feel they have. Fans come to see themselves as "owners" of texts (be they stars, shows, books, etc.) and believe that they contribute to the production of the text over time.

Interestingly, the more active VQT fans were the more likely they were to feel that they personally exerted influence over the industry or the object of their fandom but less likely to feel that VQT exerted influence (see Table 3.1). Also, the more one felt able to influence the television industry, the more enjoyment one had from television (again, whether or not the objective was achieved; perception is everything). When these same variables were re-examined by applying controls (in order to remove the possible influence of education, income, TV exposure, and length of VQT membership) the correlations were not significantly weakened or strengthened (see Table 3.2).

Table 3.1. Pearson Correlations for Dependent and Independent Variables and Control Variables ($N = 966$).

	Fandom	Overall Influence	Personal Influence	VQT Influence	Enjoyment of TV
Fandom	--	.11**	.14**	.03	.12**
Overall Influence	.11**	--	--	--	.28**
Personal Influence	.14**	--	--	.36**	.22***
VQT Influence	.03	--	.36**	--	.23**
Enjoyment of TV	.11**	.28**	.24**	.23**	--
Length of Membership	-.02	.06	.09*	.00	.05
TV Exposure	.00	.12**	.07	.13**	.29**
Education	-.05	-.10**	-.05	-.13**	-.10**
Income	-.11**	-.07*	-.03	-.11**	-.15**

Note: Fandom: Degree of involvement in fan activities; personal influence: Perceived personal influence over TV industry; VQT Influence: Perceived VQT influence over TV industry; Overall influence: Summated scale of perceived personal and VQT influence.

$* p < .05$; $** p < .01$; $*** p < .001$

The upshot is that speaking of fans, even the same group of fans, as homogeneous is almost certainly incorrect. They are probably distinct from other fans in special ways due to the object of their fandom; yet they are similar and differentiated from each other within the same group due to the degree of immersion in fan practices.

A MODEL OF FAN PRACTICE

As a result of several years of close study of the VQT (measures included focus groups, an elaborate survey of the memberships, personal interviews, and textual analysis of written materials) I was able to piece together a preliminary model of how a social group begins the process of contesting the allocation of social space. In doing so, I was also able to test other notions related to issues of "taste" and cultural politics such as the function and practices of fandom.

In my analysis, I kept returning to the notion of fandom within a sociology of culture perspective as a phenomenon in which members of

Table 3.2. Pearson and Partial Correlations for Dependent and Independent Variables.

	Fandom	Overall Influence	Personal Influence	VQT Influence	Enjoyment of TV
Fandom					
Pearson	--	.11**	.14**	.03	.12***
Partial	--	.11***	.14***	.02	.10***
Overall Influence					
Pearson	.11**	--	--	--	.28**
Partial	.11**	--	--	--	.26**
Personal Influence					
Pearson	.14**	--	--	.36**	.22***
Partial	.14***	--	--	.36**	.23***
VQT Influence					
Pearson	.03	--	.36**	--	.23**
Partial	.02	--	.36**	--	.19***
Enjoyment of TV					
Pearson	.11**	.28**	.24**	.23**	--
Partial	.10***	.26***	.23**	.19***	--

Note. Partial correlation coefficients control for education, income, average daily hours of television exposure, and length of membership. Degrees of freedom range from 987 and 1007.

*$p < .05$; **$p < .01$; ***$p < .001$

subordinated groups try to align themselves with meanings embodied in stars or other texts that best express their own sense of social identity (Dyer, 1986). More importantly, my experience with fans led me to conclude that just as audiences are not unified, these "extreme" audiences are not unified in their motivations or rewards for fandom. Here I part company with much of the previous fan literature, which tends to focus on the remarkable similarities between fan practices but is unable to dig deeper. On the contrary, when I examined the frequency and type of fan practice with a complex of attitudes toward these practices, the overwhelming finding was that there are widely varying degrees of involvement in fan practices oriented toward this alignment, and this variance is associated with different outcomes. The most important outcome for fans is that the more involved one is in fan practices, the more one comes to feel one has personal influence or control over the object and fandom (and the industry in general).

As mentioned earlier, interestingly, this is regardless of whether or not one's efforts to influence or control the object of fandom have been successful or unsuccessful in the past. The activity of fandom itself appears to lead to a stronger sense of influence and control, perhaps "empowering" viewers in the face of a monolithic industry in what may be the only possible way (short of being a member of a network president's immediate family). Because empowerment has been discussed in cultural studies literature as the desirable result of "cultural resistance," it is plausible that this is one manifestation of resistance to culture—a phenomenon that has been difficult to observe empirically and is theoretically slippery at best. Is this why fans are "fanatics"?

Empowerment has been described as the ability to resist and challenge "hegemonic or dominant pressures, and consequently obtain pleasure from what the . . . cultural system offers" (Brown, 1990). It is important to note, however, that I am not describing some kind of populist overthrow of the television industry. Audiences retain a kind of parasitic relationship with television for a chance to play in the game of cultural politics. The contest has an unusual mutual payoff: Fans help the culture industries recoup their marketing costs for stars and texts in return for its limited access. Real control of the industry remains in the hands of the few.

Throughout this chapter I suggested that audiences make some choices about what messages (and programs) they will consume and that those choices are political because they contribute to one's social identity. The discussion of Viewers for Quality Television is meant to illustrate one way in which audiences may perform cultural "work" by challenging the system of representation and asking for a range of images that will be resonant with their collective social identity. In making this assertion it is impossible to ignore the ways in which the social construct of "taste" becomes politicized and class-driven. What audiences want to see depends on their "tastes," which, in turn, depends on how they were socialized. The ways in which people are socialized are through the family, educational institutions, the church, and the state. The forms which these socializing influences take are dictated by access to economic and, especially, cultural capital. In life, we tend to try to protect and enlarge the social space bounded by our cultural capital—our complex of "taste" which becomes so natural it is basically invisible. People come to television as members of different social groups sharing differential cultural capital and, therefore, tastes.

The ultimate payoff for fans has less to do with whether or not they get the ostensible goals they have articulated and more to do with the activity of being a fan—again, the more involved one is in a spectrum of fan activities the more likely one is to feel he or she influences television (whether or not one really does). Feeling a sense of influence over the

medium appears to be associated, in turn, with how much one enjoys television, as opposed to it being a source of negative emotions such as guilt,
fear, or depression. This is the root of power for fans, and it is intrinsic to
the maintenance of fan social identities.

REFERENCES

Adorno, T., & Horkheimer, M. (1972). *The culture industry: Enlightenment
    as mass deception. The dialectics of enlightenment.* New York:
    Herder and Herder.
Amesley, C. (1989). How to watch Star Trek. *Cultural Studies, 3*(3), pp.
    323-339.
Ang, I. (1985). *Watching Dallas.* New York: Methuen.
Ang, I. (1991). *Desperately seeking the audience.* New York: Routledge.
Beville, H.M. (1985). *Audience ratings: Radio, television and cable.*
    Hillsdale, NJ: Erlbaum.
Blumer, H. (1933). *The movies and conduct.* New York: Macmillan.
Bourdieu, P. (1979). Symbolic power. *Critique of Anthropology, 13/14,*
    77-85.
Bourdieu, P. (1980a). The aristocracy of culture. *Media, Culture and
    Society, 2,* 225-254.
Bourdieu, P. (1980b). The production of belief: Contribution to an econo-
    my of symbolic goods. *Media, Culture and Society, 2,* 261-293.
Bourdieu, P. (1980c). *Qualifications and jobs.* (Stencilled Occasional
    Paper #46). Birmingham, England: Centre for Contemporary Cultural
    Studies (CCCS).
Bourdieu, P. (1984). *Distinction: A social critique of the judgment of taste.*
    Cambridge, MA: Harvard University Press.
Bourdieu, P. (1986). The forms of capital. In J. Richardson (Ed.), *Handbook
    of theory and research for the sociology of education.* Westport, CT:
    Greenwood Press.
Bourdieu, P. (1989). Social space and symbolic power. *Sociological
    Theory, 1*(7).
Brown, M. E. (Ed.). (1990). *Television and women's culture: The politics of
    the popular.* Beverly Hills, CA: Sage.
Cagle, Van M. (1989). The language of cultural studies: An analysis of
    British subculture theory. In N. Denzin (Ed.), *Studies in symbolic
    interaction.* Greenwich, CT: JAI Press.
Carey, J.W. (Ed.). (1989). *Communication as culture.* Boston: Unwin
    Hyman.
Cohen, S. (1976). *Escape attempts: Theory and practice of resistance to
    everyday life.* London: Allen Lane.

Cooley, C.H. (1983). *Social organizations*. New Brunswick, NJ: Transaction Books (Original work published 1919)

de Certeau, M. (1984). *The practice of everyday life*. Berkeley: University of California Press.

Fiske, J. (1987). *Television culture*. London: Methuen.

Fiske, J. (1989a). *Understanding the popular*. London: Unwin Hyman Press.

Fiske, J. (1989b). *Reading the popular*. London: Unwin Hyman Press.

Gans, H. (1974). *Popular culture and high culture: An analysis and evaluation of taste*. New York: Basic Books.

Gerbner, G. (1971). Violence in television drama: Trends and symbolic functions. In G. Comstock & E. Rubinstein (Eds.), *Television and social behavior, Vol. 1: Media content and control*. Washington, DC: U.S. Government Printing Office.

Gitlin, T. (1983). *Inside primetime*. New York: Pantheon Books.

Grossberg, L. (1984). Another boring day in paradise: Rock and roll and the empowerment of everyday life. *Popular Music, 4*, 225-257.

Hall, S., & Jefferson, T. (Eds.). (1976). *Resistance through rituals: Youth subcultures in post-war Britain*. London: Hutchinson.

Harris, C. (1992, May). *The raters berated: A history of the Congressional investigation of audience measurement techniques in television broadcasting*. Paper presented at the 1992 Broadcast Education Association Conference, Las Vegas.

Hebdige, D. (1979). *Subculture: The meaning of style*. London: Methuen.

Hebdige, D. (1988). *Hiding in the light*. London: Comedia.

Jenkins, H. (1988). Star Trek rerun, reread, rewritten: Fan writing as textual poaching. *Critical Studies in Mass Communication, 2*(5), 85-107.

Jenkins, H. (1992). *Textual poachers: Television fans and participatory culture*. New York: Routledge.

Lasswell, H. (1927). *Propaganda technique in the world war*. New York: Knopf.

Marcuse, H. (1964). *One dimensional man*. London: Routledge and Kegan Paul.

McRobbie, A., & Nava, M. (Eds.). (1984). *Gender and generation*. London: Macmillan.

Montgomery, K.C. (1989) *Target: Primetime*. New York: Oxford University Press.

Montgomery, K.C. (1986). The political struggle for prime time. In M.G. Cantor & S. Ball-Rokeach (Eds.), *Media, audience and social structure* (pp. 214-225). Newbury Park, CA: Sage.

Morley, D. (1986). *Family television: Cultural power and domestic leisure*. London: Comedia.

Newcomb, H., & Hirsch, P.M. (1983, Summer). Television as a cultural forum: Implications for research. *Quarterly Review of Film Studies*, pp. 45-55.

Radway, J. (1984). *Reading the romance: Feminism and the representation of women in popular culture*. Chapel Hill: University of North Carolina Press.

Ryan, M. (1988, April 17). The housewife the networks can't ignore. *Parade Magazine*, p. 6.

Rutherford, J. (Ed.). (1990). *Identity: Community, culture, difference*. London: Lawrence & Wishart.

Schroder, K. (1987). Convergence of antagonistic traditions: The case of audience research. *European Journal of Communication, 2*, 7-31.

Turow, J. (1989). Pressure groups and television entertainment: A framework for analysis. In Rowland & Watkins (Eds.), *Interpreting television: Current research perspectives*. Beverly Hills, CA: Sage.

Viewers for Quality Television, Inc. Newsletters. February 1985-present.

Williamson, J. (1986). *Consuming passions: The dynamics of popular culture*. New York: Marion Boyars.

Willis, P. (1977). *Learning to labor*. New York: Columbia University Press.

▶4

Collecting Comic Books:
A Study of the Fan and
Curatorial Consumption

Jonathan David Tankel
Indiana University-Purdue University Fort Wayne
Keith Murphy
Fort Valley State College

INTRODUCTION: WHY ARE THINGS COLLECTIBLE?*

As often happens with popular usage, the adjective collectible has come to be used as a noun: We are urged by sellers of all sorts to acquire for ourselves and our posterity a whole range of items because they are *collectibles*. This term has come to mean an artifact that is acquired because its presumed monetary value will increase over time. Artifacts such as plates, commemorative coins, and ceramic dolls are offered for purchase

---

*An earlier version of the study was presented to the 1992 Annual Conference of the International Communication Association at Miami, FL. The authors acknowledge the participation of James Smead in the original study. The authors thank the proprietors and patrons of Broadway Comic Book and Baseball Card Shop and Books, Comics and Things in Fort Wayne, IN.

not because of any inherent artistic or aesthetic value, but because someone else at some future date will take it off your hands for your profit. It is
important, however, to recognize that acquisition and possession of artifacts can be a defining component of being a fan. For the fan, the potential
for profit at some future date, while always present as in any economic
transaction, is often overshadowed by the value created by the ownership
of the artifact in the present, whether it is the poster of your favorite star of
Beverly Hills 90210 hanging from the ceiling or the *Star Trek* medallion on
display on the mantlepiece.

By interrogating the fan as collector it becomes possible to determine the ways in which the intentionally ephemeral becomes collectible,
as opposed to those artifacts that producers manufacture to be *collectibles*.
From this perspective on theorizing the fan, the process of acquisition is
viewed as the primary activity of the fan, although in many contexts of fandom, acquisition of artifacts is a subsidiary activity, for example, collecting
posters of rock stars because you are a fan of their music. In this view of
fandom, the interplay between the attainment of pleasure in the present
and the potential for profit in the future affords us a window on understanding the dynamics of fandom over time. The creation of value for the
collector of popular culture artifacts such as comic books, recordings,
movie posters, antique cars, and so on, is a complex *pas de deux* between
the personal and the social, an expression of fandom as both psychological
and cultural practice. Collecting comic books is therefore an appropriate
activity to investigate in order to theorize how fandom may manifest itself
as a material process that we describe as *curatorial consumption.*

REVIEW OF SCHOLARLY LITERATURE ABOUT
COMIC BOOKS

The published literature specifically about comic books is limited, unlike
the comic books themselves. The available literature seems to fall into
three categories. First are the "how-to" manuals that serve to inform current and potential collectors of the mechanics of collecting and preservation (e.g., see Leiter, 1983). Second are descriptive works that deal with
the comic book as text in terms of both specific comic book series and
comic books in general (e.g., see Inge, 1990; Perry & Aldridge, 1991).
Finally, there are the few scholarly attempts to use the methodologies of
communication research to investigate various aspects of comic books and
their readers. Most notable is the scholarly study *The Many Lives of the
Batman: Critical Approaches to a Superhero and His Media* (Pearson &
Uricchio, 1991), which appeared at the apex of the Batman revival in the
early 1990s fostered by the success of the film *Batman* and the recontextu-

alizing of comic book Batman as the "Dark Knight" by, among others, Frank Miller. While some of the chapters in this book touch on the issues raised in this study, no general study has yet examined the collection process itself and the value perceived by the comic book collectors that motivates their activities.

Given the paucity of literature concerning comic books and their collectors,[1] the authors looked to Radway's (1984) study of the romance novel industry and romance novel readers to provide a perspective that is helpful in studying the comic book collector. Unlike many critical theorists who had determined by textual analysis alone that romance novels only reified patriarchy, Radway offered romance readers the opportunity to "speak" for themselves through surveys and focus groups and, therefore, offered to the scholarly community a more textured interpretation of the role of romance novels in the lives of their readers and more generally about the uses of popular culture in everyday lives.[2]

WHY STUDY COMIC BOOKS AND THEIR COLLECTORS?

The comic book can be considered the quintessential product of the mechanization and industrialization of graphic reproduction. The first comic strip (the forerunner of the comic book) was the eponymous Yellow Kid which appeared in 1897 as a byproduct of the Pulitzer-Hearst Yellow Journalism circulation wars.[3] Any study of the comic book industry must begin with reference to concerns about the changing nature of "the work of art in the age of mechanical reproduction," as identified by Benjamin (1933/1969, p. 217). Although comic books were no doubt outside Benjamin's consideration in 1933, his ambivalence about the ultimate consequences of mechanical reproduction is central to the issues raised by comic book collecting. Benjamin observed that reproducibility altered the

---

[1]There are two works, although not from a scholarly perspective, that deserve mention: *Comics* (Eisner, 1992) and *Understanding Comics* (McCloud, 1993). Each is an insightful and important work in the understanding of comic books.

[2]In an examination of various ethnographic approaches to the study of media consumption, Bird (1992) places Radway's theoretical and methodological practices in the context of recent concern over privileging idealized audiences over empirical studies (see Carragee, 1990; Evans, 1990; Gitlin, 1990). The authors place this current study in the Radway model, in that the collection of comic books is viewed as part of an overall cultural practice, although this study focuses only on curatorial behavior.

[3]It was reported recently that 11 original drawings of the Yellow Kid were found in Syracuse University's Bird Library. They had been donated in the 1960s, but had been overlooked until a staff member discovered them while indexing library materials ("Yellow Kid" comic uncovered, 1992).

value that individuals derived from possessing works of art. Although the separation of art from various forms of ritual, primarily religious, created new contexts for artistic expression, mass reproduction trivialized the unique character of art. Benjamin concluded that mass produced art is divorced from authenticity based in the unique character of the specific work of art and that to "an ever greater degree the work of art reproduced becomes the work of art designed for reproducibility" (p. 224).

His conclusion applies directly, if not intentionally, to the production and acquisition of comic books, an art form that is only made possible by the technologies of reproduction. Comic book collectors determine value through a complex set of criteria structured by the reproduction and distribution process. Comic book collectors identify unique qualities in those comic books that are deemed valuable, qualities that permit differentiation among a range of mass-produced artifacts. Therefore, the value of mass-reproduced cultural artifacts such as comic books is determined by the consumers of such artifacts, who are able to recognize what is unique from what is, by Benjamin's determination, uniform. This capacity to see value where others see repetition and banality, for many, describes an essential component of fandom.

CURATORIAL CONSUMPTION

Concerns such as Benjamin's have been updated by Ewen (1988) and others. These critics see mass consumption as integral to consumer capitalism and observe that this type of consumption is fueled by planned obsolescence both in image and in artifact. From this perspective, consumption is encouraged continually in order to replace that which is no longer functional. In other words, consumption is intended to be evanescent, creating voids that need to be filled constantly. This perspective, however, is not adequate in and of itself to describe the fan as collector. The process of collecting for the fan can be viewed as a personal strategy that allows the fan to participate in and embody the contradictions of consumer capitalism. In other words, those products designed for obsolescence are preserved and valuated in such ways as to bring pleasure and possibly financial reward to the consumer rather than the producer. The process of collecting comic books, then, confronts the widely accepted view of mass production and consumption.

In effect, those who create value by making artifacts such as comic books *collectible* are engaged in a form of capital formation. The initial providers, in this case the comic book publishers, distributors, and retailers, offer their product at a set price, but the valuation of the product over time is determined by the collector as individual in terms of psychological value and as entrepreneur in terms of resale/exchange within the networks of other collectors. Whether it is comic books, used sound recordings, or antique cars, the collector valuates artifacts based on utility to the collector rather than traditional criteria such as production and distribution costs. Collectors, then, value possession and preservation in the present, while deferring financial gain.

In order to differentiate this type of consumption from the ephemeral consumption usually associated with mass production, we employ a concept originated by McCracken (1988) in his study of the relationship among cultural representation, consumption and social change. In his presentation of the story of Lois Roget, described as the "keeper of her family's possessions" (p. 44), McCracken observed the curatorial nature of her patterns of consumption. Her possessions included many artifacts that derived from the history of her family. Each piece seemed to be described not by function but according to the meaning each artifact evoked from its usage in that family's history. These artifacts were not simply things, but conveyors of personal and social history. McCracken termed this type of consumption as curatorial, in that possession, preservation, and orderly succession of ownership superseded the immediate use dictated by industrial production.

McCracken concluded that this type of consumption has all but vanished in a world of mass production and consumerism. The curatorial consumer is concerned with the utility of the product acquired in both immediate and long-range contexts. The curatorial consumer is concerned with meanings that derive from the purchase and preservation of the product acquired. The personal investment in artifacts that typifies McCracken's notion of *curatorial consumption* seems similar to cultural practices associated with fandom. While he may be correct as pertains to the long-range familial archiving he describes, the basic concept is useful in defining the process of collecting comic books and other artifacts of mass-produced popular culture.

THE COMIC BOOK INDUSTRY

Before examining the curatorial behaviors of the fan as collector, it is clear that the production and distribution of comic books *is* a process of mass production and consumption. The comic book industry has taken an ancient narrative form and turned it into a multimillion dollar industry. Today the revenues realized from this ancient narrative form total in the millions (Stewart, 1991). In fact, the sheer volume of comics sold since their inception in the mid-1930s is staggering. According to Benton (1989), "More comic books have been printed, read, and sold than all the

Top 10 best selling books of the last 50 years combined" (p. 11). According to Goulart (1991), comic book publishers have exceeded $400 million in annual retail sales. Further, in order to buy one copy of every comic released in a month would cost in excess of $1,000.

THE VOICE OF THE FAN: A SURVEY

In order to determine whether fan behaviors can be accurately described as *curatorial,* the authors designed a study modeled on Radway's ethnography of romance readers. A survey questionnaire was administered to comic book collectors in a midwestern city (population 165,000). The city has two primary stores that engage in, among other activities, advanced comic book orders. This service for comic buyers ensured that respondents to the survey were not casual buyers and that the sample would contain a sufficient number of collectors. The two stores are in different sections of the city and that geographic difference allows for demographic diversity.

The questionnaire was modeled on the final questionnaire used by Radway (1984, pp. 231-240). Fifty questionnaires were distributed as follows: 5 for student volunteers, 20 for one store, and 25 for the other. Thirty eight questionnaires were returned, although not all questionnaires were answered completely. The discrepancy between stores occurred because one of the authors is an employee of that store and could recruit more respondents. Although some might question the reliability of this "auto-ethnography," the problems encountered are not so different from traditional ethnographies (Hayano, 1979) and, in addition, the other author had little contact with the comic book stores per se. The results of the survey form the basis for the following discussion of comic book collecting as a form of *curatorial consumption.*

WHO ARE THE COLLECTORS?

The most striking and expected demographic characteristic of the comic book collectors surveyed is that 100% are male. Despite the small sample size and despite the fact that Kim Thompson, president of comic book publisher Fantagraphics Books, told one of the authors, "any publisher who does offer you such figures [audience demographic] is probably lying through his teeth, or utterly deluded" (personal communication, November 1991), the overwhelming male dominance of comic book collecting is consistent with industry and personal experience over time. DC Comics, in their most recent demographic package, characterized their readership as 91.5% male (Mediamark, 1993).

Therefore, the most obvious of question is: "Why is collecting comic books a predominantly male activity?" This remains true despite the effort that all the major publishers put into winning the readership of females. One tactic over the past few years has been to introduce a large number of female heroes. One of the most popular comic books, *The Uncanny X-Men*, features a team of heroes led by a female character named Storm (Stewart, 1991). As explained in *Marvel Comics' Internal Correspondence Special: 1992 Editorial Plan*: "Female readers. Possibly the most elusive consumer in the direct market. Marvel continues to experiment with efforts to attract the other 50% of the demographic base to comic book stores" (Stewart, 1991, pp. 174). These industry concerns suggest that the lack of female interest in comic book collecting over time has been due to the dominance of male heroes and action-oriented themes, rather than any inherent gender skew in curatorial behaviors in general.

One explanation of the male skew in comic book collecting may rest on the origins of the curatorial behaviors. The following is a breakdown by age group of when respondents began to buy comic books:

5-8 years	27% (10/37)
9-12 years	35% (13/37)
13-16 years	22% (8/37)
over 17	16% (6/37)

Given that the mean age of the collector is 26.4 years old (the youngest is 10 years old and the oldest is 42 years old), it is clear that comic book buying begins at an early age and stays with the collector into adulthood. The fact that most comic book collectors are male results from the early age at which the curatorial relationship begins. This conclusion is supported by the attempts by Marvel to attract young female consumers by continuing its series of Barbie comic books (Stewart, 1991, p. 174). Perhaps this comic, based on the popular toy, will serve as a gateway character into the "Marvel Universe." As one respondent mentioned, G.I. Joe served as just such a gateway character for him. Both Marvel and DC have used children's toys[4] as gateway characters in the hope that once introduced to comic books through a different curatorial object, the consumer will transfer that need for acquisition to currently available publications. In other words, young females do display curatorial instincts but not for comic books.[5]

---

[4]The list runs from Marvel's highly successful *G.I. Joe* and *The Transformers* to the less than successful *Sectaurs*.

[5]Females do collect Barbie dolls and accessories, as evidenced by the current booming market for adult collectors.

Curatorial consumption requires disposable income for the purchase of the comic book and the paraphernalia of curatorship. Income statistics from the survey showed that while median personal income was in the $10,000-14,999 bracket, median family income was approximately $25,000. This indicates that for both married and single respondents, the individual was not the sole source of income for the household. Of the respondents, 71% were single or divorced, 60% were employed full time, and 42% were students (the University in this city targets returning and part-time students). The availability of excess income is a requirement for curatorial consumption, which would account for the middle-class status of most collectors.

It is clear from the study and the supporting industry data that comic book collectors tend to be white, middle-class males who became interested in comic books during their adolescence and teens. The income requirements are obvious and the male dominance seems to be tied to the content of the comic books themselves, as discussed below. The pleasure derived by the typical collector can be traced to the early age at which comic books were introduced into their cultural lives. First the content, and then the comic books themselves, started to fulfill needs and desires of young males by becoming part of their cultural and imaginative lives. In this way, the entry into and continuation of curatorial consumption hinges on how the artifacts fulfill emotional needs, not just the needs of the comic book industry.

WHY DO THEY COLLECT?

The needs of the comic book collector are, therefore, recognized by the comic book industry. In all other forms of mass media, the product is tailored for a specific audience. Although this is true for comic books as well, the audience takes an active role in the direction and maintenance of the product. Through the letter pages and fan-produced magazines, the fan is in a position to determine the direction of plot and who will write or draw specific titles. More importantly, according to DC Comics editor Michael Eury (1992), the fans share a special sense of togetherness through this textual community: "You see, we comics fans share a very special language all our own. We talk about continuity, meta-humans, and indicia, things most people have never heard of. . . . We're almost like a club of readers who share a marvelous secret, that secret being just how spectacular the world of comics truly is" (n.p.).

Thus, the readers and collectors of comics converge symbolically as they share similar reactions to the dramas played out in the narrative. In many ways the messages played out in the narrative form of the comic books shape the reality of the readership (Littlejohn, 1989). Bormann (1982) called these messages *fantasy themes* and the larger continuation of these messages and their characters and plotlines he called *rhetorical visions.* It is through the sharing of these themes that the individual is drawn into and begins to identify with the group reality and can be said to have symbolically converged with the group. "The sharing of fantasies within a group or community establishes the assumptive system portrayed in the common rhetorical vision and contributes to the special theory [symbolic convergence] associated with the community's communication style" (p. 293).

The surveys support the notion of comic book collectors as members of an interpretive community by providing insight into the motivations for starting to collect comic books. In response to the question, "What first motivated you to buy comics?", influences clustered in four areas: art, family or a friend, specific characters, and plots. Some respondents mentioned art, especially cover art, as the primary reason for first becoming a collector. "I used to enjoy drawing the characters—trying to match the pictures in the books." When directly asked, "Is the art an important factor in choosing your comic books?", virtually all respondents answered affirmatively. For the collector, the comic book as art is a strong factor in establishing the collectibility of the artifact. Because it is obvious that the art is part of the artifact and not intended directly to make the comic book a *collectible,* it is clear that collectors see value in the inherent qualities of the comic book as a form of expression.

A few respondents said that family members provided the impetus for their collection, whereas four other respondents gave this credit to friends and peers. Collectors remarked, "Kept me busy while Mom shopping," and "A friend told [sic] me." These reasons for beginning to become interested in comic books supports a social context for the entry into curatorial behaviors.

Some collectors started with an interest in aspects of content: specific comic books or characters, the stories, the action, and the obvious escapist nature of comic book narratives. "*Amazing Spiderman, #58.* I liked the story and I identified with the main character." Character preference also bore out the relationship between age and curatorial behaviors. Of the 32 respondents who claimed to have a preference for specific characters, 18 (57%) preferred the traditional "super boy scout" hero or heroine.[6] The remaining 44% seemed to prefer the "violent vigilante."[7] Of the 32 individuals who stated a preference for specific characters, the mean

---

[6]A list of traditional heroes would include those who capture the villains and let the courts and police departments take care of punishment. Such characters would include Superman (DC), Batman (DC), Captain America (Marvel), and The Fantastic Four (Marvel).

[7]A list of the "violent vigilante" would include Lobo (DC), The Punisher (Marvel), Deathstroke the Terminator (DC), Wolverine (Marvel), Cable (Marvel), and Judge Dredd (Fleetway). These characters serve as judge, jury, and executioner when dealing with villains. For a graphic example of this character type, read Lobo's *Paramilitary Christmas Special* (DC Comics).

age was 26.2. Of those who chose the traditional character, the mean age was 32.6 years of age. This compares to a mean age of 19.7 years for those who chose violent vigilantes as their favorite characters. Once again, age of the collector correlated with the types of comic books prevalent when they were first exploring the pleasures of collecting.

These various reasons for collecting comic books provide various textures to the emotional and psychological basis for curatorial behaviors. The age discrepancy in terms of comic character attractiveness is further support for the conclusion that curatorial behaviors develop at a young age. Social context also seems to provide a gateway to collecting. Finally, the aesthetic pleasures of art and story support the notion that collecting fulfills psychological needs and desires distinct from ephemeral consumption.

Perhaps the most intriguing answers about motivation came from two questions dealing with pleasure and self-image. When asked if "comic book collecting was a means to feel good," most answered yes. When asked the open-ended question, "What do you think your collection says about you?," the collectors felt that their collection said things about their economic or financial status. Those responses included, "I am a good buyer," "I spend too much on it," and "I make too much money," They also felt that their comic collections said something about their notion of right and wrong. "The characters of my collection are good and it associates me with good things," hence, their collection said that they were imaginative and young at heart.

COMIC BOOK COLLECTING AS CURATORIAL CONSUMPTION

The comic book as the object of curatorship is a relatively recent phenomenon. By curatorship, we mean the conscious planning of acquisition and preservation. The so-called "fanzines" did not begin publication until the shortlived *EC Fan Bulletin* in 1953 (Overstreet, 1994). Preservation materials were not available to the general public until the advent of direct market comic book stores in the 1970s. Today, the comic book collector is well armed with information about the hobby. A trade press has evolved that keeps the collector up to date on all aspects of the hobby. Publications such as *Wizard, Hero, The Comic Book Collector, Comics Value Monthly, The Overstreet Guide to Comics,* and *Triton* provide comic book enthusiasts with a sneak peek at upcoming projects, investment picks, and retail price guides that allow the comic collectors to gauge the value of their collection. In addition, publications like *The Comic Buyer's Guide* serve as an information clearinghouse and a marketplace for the collector. This, when combined with the innumerable comic

book interest forums on computer networks, allows the comic book curatorial consumer to be among the most discriminating of buyers.

More than two-thirds of the collectors defined regular buying as
every week. Comic book publishers release their product on a weekly
schedule, so it is evident that consistent attention to that release schedule
is an important part of the collectors' habits. The comic book readers who
composed the sample population were not impulse consumers. Rather,
they planned their purchases. This planning process is called "pre- ordering."[8] Pre-ordering begins as much as six months before the consumer
receives the comic book. Industry publications like The Comic Shop
News, Advance Comics, and Direct Current announce "coming attractions," which provide plot sketches, explain character crossovers, and
highlight special "gimmicks" that may make a particular issue more collectible than normal. This information is available to the customer through
direct sales or in-store promotions. Approximately eight weeks before the
comic books are due to be released, "pre-order" customers receive an
order form from their retailer. This order form contains such information as
character crossovers and plot sketches. At this time, the "pre-order" customer carefully chooses the comic books he wishes to receive and provides a down payment to insure that a copy of each comic book ordered is
reserved for him. Thus, the "pre-order" customer tends to be much more
informed about the product than does the "impulse" or point-of-purchase
shopper. In addition, because the "pre-order" requires a commitment from
the customer, he tends to be more dedicated to archiving the comic books
once he has purchased them.

The vast majority of respondents in our study, with the exception
of some who failed to answer this question, indicated that they practiced
at least some curatorship with their comic books. This preservation is seen
as essential as the materials that go into the production of the comic books
degrades rapidly if exposed to sunlight, high humidity, changes in temper-
ature, and even during the handling of the books while they are being
read. Despite the fragility of the "near mint" condition of a comic book, it
is rare for a comic book in other than "near mint" condition to be considered collectible. Thus, most collectors attend to at least minimal preservation practices.

The cost of even minimal preservation practices is staggering. The
bare minimum is to place the books in plastic or mylar sleeves, and then to
place the sleeved comic in a specially constructed, acid-free cardboard box.
For this minimum of protection, the collector pays, on average, $8 to pre-
serve 100 books. This cost rises to $15 per 100 when acid-free backing

---

[8]Some stores call this "comic club membership." This practice is also prevalent
among mail order comic book companies.

boards are inserted into the sleeves with each book. This is the level of preservation granted to new books of current negligible investment value.[9] For books that have higher investment values, collectors can invest in hundreds of dollars of restoration or preservation measures for each comic. In this survey, collectors estimated their average annual expenditure on curatorial supplies to be $70.90. That expenditure can be broken down as follows:

Item purchased	Percentage purchasing item
comic bags	84% (32/37)
comic boxes	60% (24/37)
backing boards	36% (14/37)
mylar sleeves	21% (8/37)
title dividers	13% (5/37)
labels	10% (4/37)
other items named by less than 10% of respondents	

This expenditure is directly aimed at preserving the comic book;[10] allowing the fan to go past the point of being a consumer focused on the acquisition of artifacts of only fleeting interest.

The comic book collector should be described as a *curatorial consumer*, a curator, an archivist, and a preservationist for artifacts that have meaning for their cultural lives. The financial investment in preserving these artifacts does not represent any rational cost/benefit ratio if viewed only in a monetary sense. The value received from these artifacts is measured in terms not usually mentioned in the course of mass production and consumption; that is, in aesthetic pleasure and personal satisfaction derived despite, and not because of, the low esteem in which they are held by those who do not recognize the respect with which these artifacts are viewed by the knowledgeable collector.

CONCLUSIONS

The acquisition, collection, and preservation of comic books resembles the activities of museums and libraries more than the purchase and use of disposable artifacts of mass culture. Although the objects of acquisition are products of mass-produced culture, they are simultaneously the basis for this *curatorial consumption*. By this, we mean the process by which indi-

---

[9]In fact, one of the authors of this paper has an entire eave of his house filled with long white "acid-free" cardboard boxes.

[10]Both the federal government and museums use mylar sleeves to protect important documents from degradation.

viduals invest artifacts with social and psychological value and the behaviors that determine and preserve those values. This form of consumption turns the ephemeral nature of modern popular culture into fulfilling and lasting cultural practice. Recognition of this transformation of the trivial into the valuable is important in providing a textured theoretical framework for understanding the dynamics of fandom.

The motivations for *curatorial* behavior, as for fandom in general, do not derive from qualities uniquely inherent in the artifact, but rather from the value received from the collectors' interactions with the artifacts and, equally, the curatorial behaviors themselves. To return to where we started, the process of *curatorial consumption* specifically, and the act of fandom generally, have taken on the ritual qualities that Benjamin (1969) recognized in earlier uses of art and artistic expression, albeit secularized. *Curatorial consumption* and fandom permit the individual, alone and in community, to find pleasure and satisfaction from the products of mass culture. *Curatorial consumption* and fandom are strategies of resistance that recognize the futility of modern life, while simultaneously offering the possibility of finding personal meaning in an impersonal world.

REFERENCES

Benjamin, W. (1969). The work of art in the age of mechanical reproduction. In H. Arendt (Ed.), *Illuminations: Essays and reflections* (pp. 217-252). New York: Schocken Books. (Original work published 1933)

Benton, M. (1989). *The comic book in America.* Dallas: Taylor.

Bird, S. E. (1992). Travels in nowhere land: Ethnography and the "impossible audience". *Critical Studies in Mass Communication, 9,* 250-260.

Bormann, E. (1982). Colloquy I. Fantasy and rhetorical vision: Ten years later. *Quarterly Journal of Speech, 68*(202), 288-305.

Carragee, K. (1990). Interpretative media study and interpretive social science. *Critical Studies in Mass Communication, 7,* 81-96.

Eisner, W. (1992). *Comics and sequential art.* Tamarac, FL: Poorhouse Press.

Evans, W. (1990). The interpretive turn in media research: Innovation, iteration, or illusion? *Critical Studies in Mass Communication, 7,* 147-168.

Eury, M. (1992). Direct currents. *Outlaws, 8,* n.p.

Ewen, S. (1988). *All consuming images: The politics of style in contemporary culture.* New York: Basic Books.

Gitlin, T. (1990). Commentary: Who communicates what to whom, in what voice and why, about the study of mass communication?. *Critical Studies in Mass Communication, 7,* 185-196.

Goulart, R. (1991). *Over 50 years of American comic books.* Lincolnwood, IL: Publications International.

Hayano, D. (1979). Auto-ethnography: Paradigms, problems, and prospects. *Human Organization, 38,* 99-104.

Inge, T. M. (1990). *Comics as culture.* Jackson: University Press of Mississippi.

Leiter, M. (1983). *Collecting comic books.* Boston: Little, Brown.

Littlejohn, S. W. (1989). *Theories of human communication* (3rd ed.). Belmont, CA: Wadsworth.

McCloud, S. (1992). *Understanding comics.* Northhampton, MA: Tundra/Kitchen Sink Press.

McCracken, G. (1988). *Culture and consumption: New approaches to the symbolic character of consumer goods and activities.* Bloomington: Indiana University Press.

Mediamark Research, Inc. (1993). *A survey of young upwardly mobile men: Conducted for DC Comics.*[In-house publication]

Overstreet, R. (1994). *Overstreet comic book price guide.* New York: Avon.

Pearson, R., & Uricchio, W. (Eds.). (1991). T*he many lives of the Batman: Critical approaches to a superhero and his media.* New York: Routledge.

Perry, G., & Aldridge, A (1971). *The Penguin book of comics.* London: Penguin.

Radway, J. (1984). *Reading the romance: Women, patriarchy, and popular literature.* Chapel Hill: University of North Carolina Press.

Stewart, T. (1991). *Internal correspondence special: Marvel 1992 editorial plan.* New York: Marvel Comics.

"Yellow Kid" comic uncovered at Syracuse University (1992). T*he Chronicle of Higher Education,* April 29, p. A5.

▶III

STRATEGIC FANDOM

▶ 5

Redeeming Values: Retail Coupon and Product Refund Fans

Steven Classen[*]
California State University-San Bernardino

If industry reports are correct, well over 300 billion manufacturer-issued coupons are distributed across the United States annually, and nearly 80% of the nation's households have used coupons within the past month (Manufacturers Coupon Control Center, 1989; NCH Promotional Services, 1993). Coupons and manufacturer refund offers have become pervasive promotional tools, part of the commonplace consuming experience for most Americans—used so commonly that industry abstractions tell us that

---

[*]An earlier version of this chapter was presented at the 1991 meeting of the International Communication Association, as part of a Popular Communication panel addressing "the nature of popular communication outside the traditional mass media."

Because fan permission to use specific periodical excerpts could not be secured (due to a lack of access to complete names, or addresses and phone listings) all references to contributor names and addresses have been either changed or omitted. This editorial choice should not be read as suggesting that coupon/refunding fan activities are necessarily secretive or mandate such privacy measures.

during the next month you and I will likely cash in at least a few, or perhaps even a dozen or two, coupons and refund offers.[1]

However, a relatively small population, who call themselves "coupon queens" and "refund fans," defy what the promotions industry defines as normative consumer activities. They regularly claim not only large savings but substantial profits from their ventures, and exchange hundreds of promotional items monthly. In short, they are couponers and refunders who are "excessive"—consumers who, according to conventional expectations, have taken a good thing too far. As cultural theorist John Fiske (1989a) explained, it is this quality of excessiveness that defines the "fan," as well as an "active, enthusiastic, partisan, participatory engagement with the text" (pp. 145-146).

This chapter describes and analyzes the practices and meanings produced by those using coupons and refund offers to "excess"—couponing and refunding "fans." Empirically this project relies primarily on an examination of the letters, editorials, and other correspondence published in a national, subscription-funded fan periodical titled *Refunding Makes Cents* (RMC) over an approximately 9-month period. Comments volunteered by a half dozen local self-identified coupon and refunding fans in response to the topic of this project also provided important insights.

During the early 1990s, RMC claimed approximately 12,000 subscribers and was one of the largest circulation refunding and couponing bulletins available in the United States. In this study, and particularly in the first section of this chapter, the information gained from perusal of RMC issues is placed alongside contemporary industrial and scholarly periodical treatments addressing consumer behavior and the use of coupon and refunding promotionals.

Theoretically this chapter places a focus on the productivity and potentials of consumption—what cultural theorist Michel de Certeau (1984) described as the rich and multilayered art of consumers using those products produced and imposed on them by others in meaningful ways. The industrial products or texts discussed here—retail coupons and refund materials—have not been considered in discussions of media fandom, and in themselves may seem to offer little in the way of semiotic or linguistic opportunity. But as such materials are put into circulation, the art of consumption is very much in evidence.

---

[1]The statistic of "nearly eighty percent" is based on shopper self-reports. In a major 1988 survey conducted by the Manufacturers Coupon Control Center (1989), 77% of households' principal grocery shoppers said they saved and redeemed coupons (p. 5). A 1992 report from NCH Promotional Services, a leader in coupon processing and promotion information management, made the claim that nearly 80% of households use coupons on a yearly basis. Among 1992 survey respondents who claimed coupon use in the past month, the average number of coupons used was 26 coupons per month (p. 8).

In practice, the culture of self-proclaimed couponing and refunding "fans" seems to, at least partially, parallel other fandoms.[2] Couponers and refunders possess particular forms of cultural production, constitute a base for consumer activism, and offer alternative social communities (see Jenkins, 1992, pp. 277-287). And, as I show, they delight in the concrete profits and pleasures that their excessive practices supply. From the vantage point of social and cultural investigation, it can be seen that the practices of "excessive" couponing and refunding are not so much trivial as trivialized and have important intersections with notions of community, gender politics, and economics.

Within the dominant conceptualization of business and marketing research, the consumption of coupons as well as other products comfortably signifies an "end" which invites little inspection in itself as long as it is achieved. Consumer science research on coupons and refunds, ostensibly designed to privilege consumer rather than industrial interests, offers further insight but often evidences a scientistic distancing of itself from the practices and explanations of the everyday (e.g., abstract cost-benefit analyses of coupon use presupposing or prescribing high levels of consumer rationality; see Levedahl, 1988). The categories and taxonomies of such studies most frequently conform with those of industry and administration.

However, a less abstract, socially contextualized examination of coupon users and refunders avoids some of these functionalist pitfalls. And it allows for a better understanding of the varied, creative meanings and practices of consumption, as well as of everyday life.

STRATEGIES–THE INDUSTRIAL MODEL

The billions of coupons and rebate offers distributed annually make the varied practices of couponing and refunding possible. In the United States, since 1986, manufacturers have annually placed over 200 billion coupons in a variety of print media (Campanella, 1987; "Coupon clutter," 1989). And the all important "redemption", that only consumers can bring, remained relatively constant for most coupon types in the late 1980s and early 1990s, ranging from 2%-4% (Campanella, 1987; "Coupon clutter," 1989; NCH, 1993, p. 17). For example, in 1992, 7.7 billion manufacturer-distributed coupons, or approximately 2.5% of the total 310 billion coupons distributed, were redeemed.

---

[2]Henry Jenkins (1992) identified "five levels of activity" that mark the television fandom of his study. Some of the characteristics and activities that Jenkins articulated in this discussion seem to carry as much descriptive power for couponing and refunding fandom as they do for the alternative culture he detailed.

Even what might appear to be a relatively low rate of redemption should not be considered insignificant in light of a volume of hundreds of billions. Several billion coupons are "cashed in" annually, adding up to billions of dollars in savings or revenue for consumers. According to Nielson Clearing House estimates, consumers redeemed nearly $4.5 billion worth of coupons in 1992 (NCH, 1993, p. 16).

Product manufacturers and the marketing industry have an understandable fixation on these redemption rates and are consistently attempting to assess the promotional value of the coupon and refund campaigns. Coupons are generally discussed and budgeted under the industrial category of promotions, separate from budgeting for other forms of media advertisement, although it is not unusual for major manufacturers of certain products, such as prepared foods, to allocate more money for promotions than advertising. Marketers design promotional efforts to introduce consumers to new brands and products as well as encourage brand and product loyalty. Theoretically, increased brand loyalty means decreased consumer price sensitivity. Once brand loyalty is established, manufacturers hope to maintain relatively high prices on the retail level, offering occasional incentives as needed to keep sales up.

This is the industry's model, untouched by consumer hands. In practice, couponing and refunding are not nearly so unproblematic or unidimensional. Arguing from an industrial profit-based perspective, trade literature expresses corporate doubts regarding the attractiveness of continued high investments in couponing. Some industrial players claim to feel trapped, forced to maintain costly coupon distribution programs to remain competitive with other manufacturers, while admitting that further investments in coupon promotions are of questionable effectiveness (Kessler, 1986).[3] Coupon redemption rates have remained relatively level since

---

[3]To provide just one relatively recent example of these corporate concerns, in April 1994, General Mills Incorporated, the nation's second-largest maker of cereals, announced it would bring down prices on several of its most popular breakfast foods, but also cut back on the number of cents-off coupons it distributes to promote cereals and lower their value (Gibson, 1994). According to *Advertising Age,* "General Mills Chairman-CEO Bruce Atwater . . . dropped some amazing numbers on analysts: Cereal marketers distributed more than 25 billion coupons in 1993, up 6 billion in three years. Despite the huge increase, the number of cereal coupons redeemed stayed at 500 million—a redemption rate of less than 2% . . . [and] promotion spending ultimately rose to 28% of General Mills cereal sales, up from 20% in 1991" (Liesse, 1994). Although the ultimate direction or consequences of such a corporate strategy are unclear, it does call attention to the investments at stake within promotional spending and the corporate anxiety that accompanies such activities. For dedicated coupon fans, the GM move might be disappointing but would most likely prompt many of them to look for bargains elsewhere, given their motto of "forget brand loyalty" and primary allegiance to bargains over brands.

1986, with the exception of a 13% jump in 1991, and a minority of relatively unattractive (i.e., shrewd) coupon users seem responsible for a large
share of the redemption that occurs.

As stated earlier, a majority of Americans claim to use at least a few
coupons or refunds each month, yet it is a relatively small proportion of the
shopping population that redeems a majority of coupon and rebate offers
(Antil, 1985; Kingsbury, 1987; McQuade, 1983). Studies indicate that over
half of what are termed "low value" coupons (generally under 50 cents) are
redeemed by "heavy" users of coupons and refunds (Kingsbury, 1987).[4]

In 1983, when A.C. Nielson reports stated that the "average" consumer used about 70 coupons during that year, or approximately one per
supermarket trip, McQuade (1983) offered a corrective, noting that such
numbers were "like the statistic which claims the average American drinks
a case of beer a week. In couponing, as in beer drinking, an avid core of
enthusiasts keeps the average extremely high" (p. 33). Against the Nielson
"average" McQuade (1983) juxtaposed the numbers for a "typical member
of the 100,000-strong American Coupon Club"—11 coupons per shopping
trip, 800 annually, and 13 refund offers per year (p. 33). Clearly, there are
"excessive" couponers and refunders—enthusiasts whose practices are
often marked by reactive comments of observers regarding their "obses-
sive" behavior or "warped" lifestyles. Coupon and refund zealots have
taken the respectable activities, techniques, and materials of the cultural
mainstream and employed them in what some consider an "excessive"
fashion.

DISASSEMBLING THE INDUSTRIAL MODEL

Industrial managers have long recognized that coupons and couponers
present problems of inefficiency within the context of the retail outlet. In
1979, the Food Marketing Institute estimated the cost of coupon handling
ranged from slightly over five cents to about nine cents per coupon, and
that approximately 25% of this expense was due to the extra time—
approximately five seconds—spent by the checker and the bagger in

---

[4]"Heavy" users are people like "Pam" from Nebraska, who carry the moniker of
couponer and/or refunder and express their commitment to their "hobby" in autobio-
graphical notes and letters to refunding and couponing club periodicals. She writes:

> I ALWAYS shop with coupons, and on double coupon days. I also work
> ahead on refunds, not just the current month's offers. . . . My hubby and
> two kids are great to save labels for me, and are very supportive of my
> hobby. Hubby's only complaint is the amount of space my "junk" takes up
> in HIS garage! I doubt if I'll ever quit refunding! It's just too much fun!
> (RMC, July 1990, p. 46).

accepting the coupon (Gallo & Hamm, 1982, p. 16). Of course, the Institute's data are industrial abstractions, constructing average shoppers and checkout times that scarcely do justice to the couponing fan notorious for her or his disruption of an otherwise smooth-flowing checkout line.

Coupon and refund club literature reveals that club members often discuss checkout cashiers in adversarial terms, believing that these cashiers represent an industrial efficiency that threatens to dilute their personal gains. Holding to a popular skepticism regarding the intentions of such industrial representatives, and complaining that cashiers are consistently wrong in their calculations, coupon fans often demand extra time at the counter to check their cash register slips and records regarding product prices and coupon use. In such a context, the model of the coupon as an efficient mechanism of marketing is disassembled. In this situation and many others, the couponing fan disrupts normative consumer activities and expectations.

The practice of fraud also disrupts the efficient industrial model. Due to the covert nature of such activity, no definitive data is published or even possible, yet industrial estimates state that losses due to fraud are in the hundreds of millions annually and illegitimate redemption rates run from 10%-25% of all coupons redeemed (Campanella, 1987; Varadarajan, 1985). Industry income contingent on legitimate coupon redemption is particularly vulnerable to fraud because the latter can take place at several points during the major stages of printing, distribution, and redemption of coupon promotions. Although the major losses to fraud are attributed to organized efforts among retailers, counterfeit rings, and other industrial players, some individual consumers also engage in what might be considered fraudulent practices to increase their personal earnings or savings.

This is not to say that most coupon and refunding fans embrace such practices or simply ignore the various ethical concerns that accompany their activities. To the contrary, newsletters and club bulletins frequently serve as forums on ethical practice, addressing an assortment of "grey areas" and pragmatic problems. And, at least in my sampling of club materials, most coupon and refund enthusiasts seem quite circumspect regarding activities that might be deemed unethical or illegal. Still, given the ethical murkiness that surrounds many industrial promotions and strategies, it is not surprising that some fans have definitions and notions of fraud that differ substantially from those of industry.

In contradiction to scientific and industrial claims that coupons actually entice the consumer to pay higher prices, buy more, or at best, result only in slight savings, many coupon and refunding hobbyists regularly declare not only savings, but substantial profits. For example, a Deerfield, MA woman wrote to RMC, "I saved $57.74 with coupons! I was a celebrity for the day as I stood by the front door of the store having my picture taken with people coming in and staring. It was a lot of fun" (RMC, Special Mini-edition, p. 7). Along the same lines, a San Bernardino, CA, enthusiast also wrote, providing a refunding primer in her description of her recent activities:

> For example, one of the stores in my area had the 72 oz. box of Tide on sale for $2.99. I had 30 $1 coupons that the store doubled, making my cost for each box only 99 cents. Then I took the net weights off [for proof of purchase] and sent for the $2.99 refund. My friend will buy the extra boxes, and I can trade the extra refund offers with other refunders.
>
> I just bought a new 1989 Ford Aerostar with the money I made refunding and selling my free and almost free products. Refunding really MAKES CENTS for me. (RMC, Special Mini-edition, pp. 7-8)

Although these testimonies are used as promotionals and are particularly dramatic, refunding bulletins regularly publish letters from readers claiming to make profits of hundreds of dollars monthly.

THE POPULAR PLEASURES OF CONSUMPTION

Even given the importance of the economic gains claimed by refunders and couponers, it must be noted that explanations and motivational analyses rooted exclusively in economics are probably as misleading as they are helpful. Such motivations and explanations must be examined in light of specific, local practices and situations.

As Janice Radway's work and other cultural studies scholarship has convincingly argued, the popular pleasures of consumption stray far from any simplistic linkage to economic benefit. In *Reading the Romance,* Radway (1984) concludes that a group of primarily middle-class women, many of whom work exclusively within the home, read romantic fiction productively—in their consumption addressing such needs as independence and excitement that most likely would not be satisfied in their predominantly patriarchal living environment.

Similarly, Fiske's (1989b) analysis of shopping women foregoes any focus on microeconomic benefits, instead discussing the pleasures women receive from crossing back and forth, and consequently blurring the lines, between the domestic and private space of the home and the public space of the mall or shopping center. He observes that shopping, "while apparently addressing women precisely as disempowered domestic consumers, may actually offer opportunities [for women] to break free" (p. 24) from meanings that patriarchy has inscribed on such activities, as well as blurring or dismantling the structure of binary oppositions that produces such explanatory schemes.

Interestingly, both industrial and academic demographic research repeatedly indicates that couponing and refunding is common among those that might enjoy, but do not have the greatest need for, the extra income such activities might provide. Industrial studies suggest that couponing is most prominent in households earning more than $25,000 annually ("Coupon clutter", 1989, Manufacturers Coupon, 1989). Again, such industrial averaging may be helpful, but in its abstraction it loses any strong claims to representation of the nonaverage—that is—the marginalized coupon zealot. Fan club membership and correspondence would indicate that such coupon and refunding enthusiasts are not unlike Radway's romance readers—they are primarily female, and many of them work exclusively within the home.

Although demographic data suggest an increasing number of men use coupons, the percentage of women who use coupons has been considerably larger. Over 80% of women who claim the role of "household's principal grocery shopper" also say they use coupons (MCCC, 1989, p. 5). Not surprisingly, the majority of what the industry terms "heavy" users are also women.[5]

Coupon use and refunding are activities strongly linked to shopping, and today, just as they did 20 years ago, demographics indicate that women, especially those defined as traditional "housewives," still invest considerably more of their time in shopping than men (Gusso, 1987; Robinson, 1989). Perusal of industrial surveys and reports on coupon use reveal that industrial interests believe that women, rather than men, hold the household coupon capital (Babakus, Tat, & Cunningham, 1988).

Informed by the above theoretical framework and observations, the balance of this chapter turns to an examination of the practices and reflections of women who call themselves coupon and refund "hobbyists" and who correspond with RMC.[6] RMC consistently encourages fan correspondence as well as the "excessive redemption" of coupon and refunding materials. It provides personal profiles, letters, and notes from members of the club, in addition to volumes of information helpful to the coupon and refund enthusiast. Also, it clearly targets a female audience. Over 90% of the profiles and letters printed in the bulletin are from women—a large proportion of whom, according to self-description, work exclusively in the home.

---

[5]In their 1989 research summary, the Manufacturers' Coupon Control Center arrived at a "profile of the typical coupon user." This user is female, age 45, has a weekly grocery bill of $74, and probably has at least a high school education, perhaps some college. Her household of three members has an annual income of $29,000 (MCCC, 1989, p. 8).

[6]A 1990 *U.S. News and World Report* article estimated that over 100,000 such hobbyists were involved in couponing or refunding through affiliation with one or more widely circulated refunding newsletters ("Coupon criminals," 1990, p. 19).

TACTICS–THE PRACTICES OF EXCESSIVE REDEMPTION

A coupon collector from Madison, WI, intervened early on as I offered a very cursory outline of my research interests. Anticipating that I would try to define or explore her activities as economically motivated, she interrupted, "But I don't do it (use coupons) for the money. I do it because I feel like I am getting away with something. . . . I feel like I am beating them at their own game." Offering a similar explanation for her enthusiastic involvement with food coupons, a California woman writes, "I began refunding as a means to stretch food dollars and tide the family over lay off periods. While I no longer need to do this anymore I keep at it because of the joy of walking out of a market paying less than the person behind me. It's like I have some kind of secret code that allows me a discount" (RMC, August 1990, p. 64).

Neither of these women use coupons or refunds out of economic necessity, nor do they represent their activity as financially centered. Rather, both refer to their activity as something akin to covert action, a secret advantage to enjoy as they work within the places of a larger system.

Such activities align themselves with de Certeau's (1984) representation of consumption as characterized by ". . . its clandestine nature, its tireless but quiet activity, in short by its quasi-invisibility, since it shows itself not in its own products, but in an art of using those imposed on it" (p. 31). Using the products and processes of a dominant economic order intended to discipline and control consumer behavior, shoppers exhibit an everyday creativity, or "art," that is frequently contrary to institutionalized marketplace norms. And it is this creativity, always local and specific, that is at the heart of de Certeau's theorizing on everyday life and the tactics of consumption.

As couponing and refunding are played out on the terrain of the manufacturer, the marketer, and the grocer, the practices of the excessive couponer or refunder resonate with de Certeau's explication of "tactics." He explains:

> The space of the tactic is the space of the other. Thus it must play on and with a terrain imposed on it and organized by the law of a foreign power. . . . It must vigilantly make use of the cracks that particular conjunctions open in the surveillance of the proprietary powers. It poaches in them. It creates surprises in them . . . (p. 37)

Although the consumer may, and does, use industrial spaces in varied and often unanticipated ways, she or he cannot lay final claim to it as her or his territory. Rather, the shopper transiently "makes do" with what the marketplace provides. To be more theoretically precise, de

Certeau's writing on space and place argues that space, as opposed to the dominant's place, is what the weak make within and out of the places of the dominant. It follows that the space of consumption is constructed within time and exists only in its moments of practice. Using this theoretical frame, the coupon and refund fan is construed as constantly on the lookout for windows of opportunity, "cracks" open to exploitation, even as they stay within the places and larger systems of commercial institutions.

de Certeau's differentiation between the strategies of the dominant and the tactics of the dominated is played out well in the example of refunders and their dependence on cash register tapes (CRTs) for refunding success. Whereas past manufacturer refund offers simply required some proof of purchase be returned, more recent refund offers require that a proof of purchase and the original cash register tape itemizing that product be remitted. As RMC's editor explains, this has become the "overwhelming pet peeve of refunders." She explains to her readers that by asking for the tapes, manufacturers are engaging in a industrial strategy known as slippage—"the phenomenon that occurs when someone buys a product intending to send for the refund on it, but loses the tape and never mails for the refund" (RMC, August 1990, p. 4). Faced with such exigencies, she suggests it might be appropriate for refunders to engage manufacturers tactically. Realizing that she faces a corporate strategy that she cannot change, she "makes do." The editor writes:

> The impact of slippage is much greater than the impact of refunds submitted by refunders. For this reason I feel no guilt in picking up a cash tape from the parking lot of the grocery store and using it with a proof of purchase cut from the package. Manufacturers are hoping I WON'T send in for my refund. I'm making sure that I will . . . (RMC, August 1990, p. 4)

Along the same lines, some fans get product code numbers from stores or refunding publications and manufacture their own cash register tapes. Because such tactics are numerous, varied, and locally situated, attempts to provide exhaustive accounts of fan tactics are inevitably futile, as are industrial efforts to eliminate them. Such activity is "tireless yet quiet." Coupon fans incessantly trade and/or sell batches of dozens or even hundreds of coupons, despite the numerous warnings, often stamped in bold print on the coupons themselves, against their sale or transfer to others prior to store redemption. Refunders, recognizing the rules say "one refund per household," offer multiple, sometimes fictitious, mailing addresses in their returns, or enlist the cooperation and addresses of other friends, family, and refunders.

After stocking up on free or nearly free items that they have carried from the store, couponers sometimes also resell their bounty in a "grey market" activity that offers an ironic inflection of "free enterprise." Selling out of their garage or basement stockrooms, these entrepreneurs offer goods that they have acquired at little or no cost—"for free"—to local neighbors and friends with discounts designed to soundly beat the retail market. In doing so they construct their own economy—one that is admittedly vulnerable to larger economies and enjoys little autonomy, but nevertheless momentarily positions the consumer as the seller in a distinctive second-level sphere of shopping and marketing that derives its resources almost entirely from first-level industrial interests. As one fan put it, in her description of the pleasures that she receives from "surplus stock sales":

> People love my sales. When they see me out at other places they always ask, "When is your next sale?" I have a few people that buy from me regularly. It helps to get those refunds on stuff I normally wouldn't buy.
>
> I know some people don't think people should resell groceries. But I get such positive comments from the people who come to my sales. They appreciate it so much. Some of the people are on a very limited income and my prices beat the stores by a long shot. (RMC, August 1990, p. 58)

Another refunder writes:

> We just had our first garage sale. I had 256 boxes of soap, 112 shampoo & conditioners, 50 deodorants, 21 toothpastes, some food and lots of pine cleaners and waxes all bought with double coupons . . . . People were thrilled to get them, sold all but a few deodorants, all at my price after doubling . . . . I overheard one lady tell another that it was against the law for me to sell health/beauty items and food so I butted in and told her I paid cash and taxes and the food all had seals and I wasn't forcing anyone to buy. She left. (RMC, September 1990, p. 48)

The negative reactions received by these women are commonplace and are expected by any excessive fan. Negative reactions come from neighbors, onlookers, and, not infrequently, from their husbands.

TRASHY PLEASURES

In a regular and very popular RMC column titled "Trashy Confessions," dozens of different women write with considerable relish and good humor

about their regular habits of digging through trash dumpsters and contain-
ers, as well as other ill-mannered behaviors, all in their search for cash
register receipts, proof of purchase seals, and other refunding materials.
The humor in this column is self-reflexive. The letter writers frequently use
the opportunities such columns afford to laugh at themselves and their
predicaments within the context of a reading community that understands
their enjoyment and embarrassment. Their enjoyment in writing about
these exploits seems to center on the juxtaposition of presumably
respectable—"middle-class" women—with the less respectable—those
who pilfer and search through refuse. Slightly embarrassed by their linkage
to such unsavory practices and elements, they offer their somewhat
cheeky "confessions" to those who would likely empathize. The level of
embarrassment and humor often rises when they are "caught in the act" by
outside observers, including family members and friends, who are not
coupon/refund fans and have no understanding of, much less appreciation
for, their "hobby."

For example, one woman writes:

> My husband and I were on the way to the supermarket when I spotted
> a heap of trash bags piled on the walk. A 25 lb. Tide box was sitting
> alongside it. I jumped out, grabbed the Tide box, when a lady came
> out and said, "Hey, there's more garbage in back if you're that desper-
> ate." I got into the car and fled the scene. (RMC, June 1990, p. 46)

Similarly, a refunder from California "confesses":

> We were on vacation and my husband and I were walking down the
> sidewalk when we happened to pass an open garbage can. I saw a
> Benson & Hedges carton. I quickly stopped and my husband said,
> "Oh no!" I grabbed the B&H carton and there was another, and anoth-
> er, and then a whole pile more of great cigarette cartons! I kept grab-
> bing and saying, "Wow, there's more!" My husband said, "But we're
> on vacation." People were starting to stare and I was halfway into the
> garbage can. I ended up with a pile of great garbage and we carried it
> all the way back to our room while the other tourists stared. (RMC,
> August 1990, p. 70)

Finally, a Wisconsin woman provides one example of the activities of
those enthusiasts who don't wait for packaging to be discarded or defined
as refuse before appropriating it.

> I was caught in a public restroom removing the UPCs [Universal
> Product Codes—used for proof of purchase] from toilet tissue stacked
> on a shelf. Felt like a fool until the gal said she was also a refunder.
> We shared the UPC's. (RMC, September 1990, p. 59)

Although some women state that such public embarrassment and disapproval curbs their "trashy" activities, just as many write in to proudly declare their persistence. This persistence is not insignificant, especially as it is considered in the context of familial and spousal disapproval. Letters to the refunding bulletin indicate that husbands often trivialize or discourage their wives' couponing or refunding activities, particularly as the women demonstrate the "excessiveness" of their ways.

Not unlike Radway's romance readers, women who coupon and refund sometimes express guilt regarding the amount of time that their "hobby" consumes—time that the voice of patriarchy would tell them should be devoted to the nurture of family and maintenance of the domestic sphere. Couponing "steals" time from the appropriate "housewife" activities of washing clothes and food preparation. As one refunder exclaims, "My family knows it's [refunding newsletter] day when they get microwaved hot dogs and chips for dinner" (RMC, September 1990, p. 52). Or as another puts it, "I love refunding . . . it's my favorite hobby, and I spend a lot of time on it. I also read alot, do counter-cross-stitch, play Bridge, and have loads of house plants. This doesn't leave much time for housework, but who needs that" (RMC, August 1990, p. 55).

As Radway (1984) has put it, a woman's guilt in such situations

> is the understandable result of . . . socialization within a culture that continues to value work above leisure and play. . . . Guilt arises, then, as a result of the reader's own uneasiness about indulging in such an obviously pleasurable experience as much as it does as the consequence of other's disapproval. (p. 105)

Still, guilt rooted in disapproval is very evident, especially when the negative reactions come from within the family. In correspondence to the newsletter, complaints from husbands were represented as revolving around two concerns. First was the embarrassment that men felt in their connection to women and mother-recruited children who engaged in less-than-respectable social activities. One refunder offers these words from her husband, "If you must continue this hobby . . . and I use the term loosely, can't you do it in another state? I have the reputation of the family to think about" (RMC, August 1990, p. 70).

The second, and perhaps more interesting category of complaints, revolved around their wives' collections of trash, which in its clutter and overabundant heaps appropriated male territory—"the husband's space." Coupon and refund fans often claim garages and entire rooms in homes, as well as a variety of shelves, tables, and floors in their efforts to accumulate, store, and organize large quantities of materials. Couponing and refunding is a hobby that rewards volume, and volume demands space. As the hobbyist increases her collection, it encroaches on the space of others.

For example, one coupon fan writes that although her "hubby" is supportive of her couponing and refunding, his only complaint is that her "junk" takes up too much space in "HIS garage" (see note 4). Parallel to this, a woman from Kentucky writes that her husband "doesn't like the look" of her label collections but "tolerates it because he knows how well I do." She also explains that she has annexed a desk that her husband planned on using but has since relinquished. "He still refers to it as his desk but we both know he'll be waiting for a LONG time before he ever gets it back" (RMC, June 1990, p. 45).

Certainly in gender politics as well as the politics of economy, the regulation and use of areas and space is a central concern. And to better understand the political dimension of everyday life it is important that challenges to the control and definition of space be acknowledged, even if such challenges are not immediately or necessarily linked to larger social change. As de Certeau theorizes, and couponing fans demonstrate, an important yet often invisible creativity exists as "spaces" are made within and out of the "places" of the dominant. In the examples provided above, the women make a point of nominating the properties and spaces as male-controlled, yet for that very reason they take a special pleasure in an admittedly temporary occupation of that space. They express no explicit desire to dismantle the environment in which they live and define themselves, yet they manifest a paradoxical pleasure in making their own spaces within the places of patriarchy.

CONCLUSION

It should not go unnoticed that the refunding/coupon club newsletters examined in this research have a primary function of linking coupon and refunding fans to other individual fans, as well as a larger, predominantly female community. Newsletters print names, addresses, and phone numbers of local contacts and clubs, and dedicate large portions of their contents to personal ads offering coupon swaps, information exchanges, and other deals between individual correspondents. Cooperation and interaction are encouraged as a means to, among other things, even greater economic reward.

Through participation in their "hobby," coupon and refund enthusiasts construct social networks in which women can receive the encouragement, support, and nurture of other women, both on the local neighborhood and national organizational levels. The practices of couponing and refunding need not be socially cooperative, and, in fact, industrial interests attempt to thwart cooperative components such as trading and selling that produce increased benefits for the consumer. The industrial scheme, often metonymically stamped on the coupons themselves, prescribes individualistic use. Yet, coupon fans, realizing the multiplicity of benefits accrued from social interaction, often step outside of the normative consumer model and disregard such industrial directives.

Undeniably, a prominent pleasure derived from such community and cooperation is centered on the economic. Although cautions against economistic analysis of the pleasure fans derive from their activities are appropriate and necessary, the practices of the coupon and refund fan suggest that the importance of microeconomic benefit cannot be ignored. The act of economic exchange is central to the surrounding activities of couponing and refunding. It is at the checkout counter that the fans' excessive redemption of coupons subverts or even inverts a mechanism of marketing, allowing them to receive a product for little or no charge, or in some cases, actually to profit from the "purchase" or "consumption" of products. This moment suggests that although recent theory regarding popular culture and consumption has fruitfully addressed the limitations of economistic analyses, it should be careful not to dismiss the economic as abstract or uniformly oppressive, but instead articulate the ways in which the microeconomic and the processes of purchasing and acquiring are often intertwined with popular semiotic and social pleasures.

The sense of pleasure that the "housewife" derives from a successful couponing or refunding foray is complicated and paradoxical. The unpaid "housewife" emerges as a significant economic contributor while often remaining within the role prescribed by dominant male culture. The sense of accomplishment that she may feel in regard to her economic contribution is frequently bound up with a patriarchal value system that privileges paid, rather than unpaid, domestic labor and disciplined thrift.

Yet, to recognize these paradoxes is not to argue patriarchy's invincibility any more than it is to declare coupon fans as victors over a dominant economic system. Rather, such recognitions remind us of the contradictory and vulnerable social constitution of patriarchy and the ideologies that inform it. As Radway's work has demonstrated, consumers within patriarchy resist or alter ways in which mass-produced, ideologically laden objects are used or understood. Such is the case with coupons. Their fans continue in productive, "tireless, yet quiet" activities, finding moments of empowerment and pleasure in the multi-accented redemption of consumption.

REFERENCES

Antil, J. (1985). Couponing as a promotional tool: Consumers do benefit. *The Journal of Consumer Affairs, 19*(2), 316-327.

Babakus, E., Tat, P., & Cunningham, W. (1988). Coupon redemption: A motivational perspective. *The Journal of Consumer Marketing, 5*(2), 37-43.

Campanella, D. (1987). Sales promotion: Couponamania. *Marketing and Media Decisions, 22*(6), 118-122.

Coupon clutter lowers redemption. (1989). *Marketing Communications, 14*(3), 42-43.

Coupon criminals, please cut it out. (1990, February 12). *U.S. News and World Report,* p. 19

de Certeau, M. (1984). *The practice of everyday life.* Berkeley: University of California Press.

Fiske, J. (1989a). *Understanding popular culture.* Boston: Unwin Hyman.

Fiske, J. (1989b). *Reading the popular.* Boston: Unwin Hyman.

Gallo, A. (1982, Spring). Coupons: Part 1. *National Food Review,* pp. 11-15. Washington, DC: United States Department of Agriculture, Economic Research Service.

Gallo, A., & Hamm, L. (1982, Summer). Coupons: Part 2. *National Food Review,* pp. 12-16. Washington, DC: United States Department of Agriculture, Economic Research Service.

Gibson, R. (1994, April 5). General Mills to slash prices of some cereals. *The Wall Street Journal,* p. A6.

Gusso, J. (1987). The fragmentation of need: Women, food & marketing. *Heresies, 21,* 39-43.

Jenkins, H. (1992). *Textual poachers: Television fans and participatory culture.* New York: Routledge.

Kessler, F. (1986, June 9). The costly coupon craze. *Fortune,* pp. 83-84.

Kingsbury, S. (1987). Study provides overview of who's redeeming coupons—and why. *Marketing News, 21*(1), p. 56.

Levedahl, J. (1988). Coupon redeemers: Are they better shoppers? *The Journal of Consumer Affairs, 22*(2), 264-283.

Liesse, J. (1994, April 11). Cheerio to $180M in cereal promos. *Advertising Age,* p. 3.

McQuade, J. (1983, May-June). Clipping coupons: A boom for whom? *Consumers Digest,* pp. 33-34.

Manufacturers Coupon Control Center (MCCC). (1989). *The impact of coupons on consumer purchase decisions.* Clinton, IA: Author.

NCH Promotional Services (1993). *Worldwide coupon distribution and redemption trends* (Vol. 27). Lincolnshire, IL: Author.

Radway, J. (1984). *Reading the romance: Women, patriarchy, and popular literature.* Chapel Hill: University of North Carolina.

Robinson, J. (1989, September/October). The shopping days of our lives. *Utne Reader,* p. 68.

Varadarajan, P. (1985). Coupon fraud: A $500 million dilemma. *Business, 35*(3), 23-29.

▶ 6

"Lookit That Hunk of Man!": Subversive Pleasures, Female Fandom, and Professional Wrestling*

Chad Dell
Monmouth University

As America's service personnel returned home from World War II, the country began to negotiate the economic transition from wartime to peacetime, and the ideological shift to the culture of the cold war. During that transition, the exploits of such characters as Wladek "Killer" Kowalski, Maurice "The French Angel" Tillet, Hans "The Horrid Hun" Schmidt, and Ivan "The Russian Hangman" Rasputin became known in households across the country, as did the activities of Mrs. Eloise Patricia Barnett of

*Earlier versions of this chapter were presented at Console-ing Passions: Television, Video and Feminism, Los Angeles, April 1993; and the American Studies Association conference, Boston, November 1993. The author wishes to thank John Fiske, Julie D'Acci, Michele Hilmes, the graduate students of the telecommunications section of the Department of Communication Arts at the University of Wisconsin-Madison, and conference participants for their helpful suggestions on various drafts of this chapter, and Anne-Britt Orlik for her invaluable help and support, editorial and otherwise.

the Bronx, better known in the press as "Hatpin Mary." Heroes and villains of World War II perhaps? Not likely. The men were all emerging postwar stars of professional wrestling in the United States, and Hatpin Mary and many others like her were endemic of the genre's rapidly increasing popularity among the nation's women. By most accounts, wrestling drew more women than men to both the box office and the television screen, where wrestling programs quickly became a nightly occurrence.

This chapter examines the dramatic rise in female fandom of professional wrestling at that particular historical juncture, utilizing a cultural studies approach to speculate about popular readings and uses of wrestling by female fans. Following a historical sketch of the period, with particular emphasis on the ideological frame of domesticity, the status of cultural taste is discussed, invoking Pierre Bourdieu to consider the perceived "habitus" of the fans. Employing Mikhail Bakhtin's work on the carnivalesque and Michel de Certeau's notions of strategy and tactic, the "transgressive" behavior of wrestling's attendant female fans is considered as a tactic to temporarily evade patriarchy and redefine the notion of "appropriate" female behavior.

The research material for this chapter is drawn largely from mainstream press accounts of the phenomenon, which, of course, were written predominantly by men. In utilizing these sources, I recognize the difficulty in finding and considering evidence of female voices situated within texts written by male authors, evidence which I consider within what Gaye Tuchman (1978, pp. 1-8) and others described as its larger "frame;" as female voices spoken or often reinterpreted within a larger masculinist context. Although I bracket much of this debate, it is a subject to which I return in order to consider why a female phenomenon of this type garnered such male attention and to analyze the explanations offered for such seemingly inexplicable behavior.

WORLD WAR II AND BEYOND

During America's participation in World War II, the nation adjusted to a workforce increasingly drained by military needs by encouraging women to "get a war job" and fill the office and factory positions required to support the war effort. Images of "Rosie the Riveter" and her ilk were persistent reminders to women of the pressing needs of the military effort. However, the war's end put six million people out of work in America, 60% of them women (Byars, 1991; Walsh, 1984). Furthermore, with the conclusion of the war came yet another redefinition of the idealized role of women in American society, one that emphasized a return to domesticity. Lynn Spigel (1990) argues that women were told to return to their homes and reassume their "natural" roles as housewives and mothers, an image regularly reinforced and reproduced by the media.[1] Numerous popular entertainment forms demonstrate the persistence of these images: from the discomforting cinematic portrayal of the independent woman in *film noir* to a veritable "cult of domesticity" represented in magazines, films, and later in television situation comedies, the role of women in society was being renegotiated (though not entirely successfully) to better suit the needs of postwar patriarchal capitalism.[2]

WRESTLING AND TELEVISION: A MATCH MADE . . .

By the mid-1940s, professional wrestling was in the midst of a decade-long decline in audience interest and attendance, due at least in part to the war effort.[3] However, the industry's fortunes would soon soar with the postwar resurgence of the newest manifestation of the electronic media: television. Wrestling had been included in NBC's earliest programming experiments when television was publicly introduced in 1939; by 1945 the first weekly wrestling program had its debut on KTLA in Los Angeles (Powers, 1984). Shot on a Paramount sound stage, the program was so successful that within two years it was moved to the 10,096-seat Olympic Auditorium, where the program enjoyed a 36-year syndicated television run.[4] By 1948, wrestling was a weekly feature on three of the four television broadcast networks (Brooks & Marsh, 1988).[5]

Wrestling was a seemingly "natural" genre for the then-emergent television broadcasters: The action took place in a limited space that could easily be shot with one or two cameras. Moreover, wrestling is a staged theatrical event. Unlike a boxing match, which can easily end in a first round knockout, leaving numerous commercial messages unplayed and

---

[1]Cf. May (1988) for a more lengthy discussion of the subject.

[2]Cf. Haralovich (1992). Byars (1991), Walsh (1984), and others argue that most women did not return to work exclusively in their homes, but rather maintained at least some form of employment outside the home.

[3]Professional wrestling had experienced a rise in popularity in the late 1920s with the introduction of an increasingly theatricalized performance style (though nothing comparable to today's wrestling styles). However, the industry's fortunes waned in the late 1930s, due in part to its characterization by news magazines as a vulgar and unrefined form. Cf. "Baba & behemoths" (1936) and Liebling (1954).

[4]Joe Jares (1974) notes that the Olympic Auditorium matches were kinescoped and rebroadcast in 57 markets nationwide.

[5]In 1948, ABC, NBC, and DuMont each sponsored at least one weekly wrestling program; CBS joined the fray in 1950.

sponsors unfulfilled, a wrestling program can be manipulated to satisfy the needs of commercial television.[6]

If television benefited in its relationship with professional wrestling, the reverse was also true. Estimated annual attendance at professional wrestling events in the United States surged 800% in eight years—from three million in 1942 to 24 million in 1950—and insiders attributed the new-found prosperity to television (Farrell, 1942; Shane, 1950). *Business Week* reported in 1950, "even the top wrestling promoters will tell you that television is directly responsible for this lush success" ("It pays," p. 25). However, the journal probed further, asking: "What made wrestling such a big TV feature? Mainly it was due to the fact that its most ardent fans are women. One big eastern promoter estimates the home wrestling audience to be 90% women" (p. 25). In 1950, NBC estimated the number of "television households" at roughly 3.9 million; four years later the figure stood at 26 million (*Television Factbook*, 1950, 1954; cited in Sterling & Kittross, 1978). That year, *TV Guide* published a story entitled "Lo, The Lady Wrestling Fan!" which further investigated the phenomenon of female fandom of professional wrestling:

> To the female American television fan there is apparently nothing quite so beautiful as a 350–pound wrestler swan-diving into the ropes. At least that's the impression 30,000,000 American husbands, brothers and sons must have after watching their womenfolk ogle the big fellows two or three times a week on TV. Hundreds of disgruntled males can testify that this year alone wrestlers received thousands of upside-down cakes, shoo-fly pies, bouquets of flowers and marriage proposals from supposedly normal schoolgirls, housewives, maiden aunts and grand-mothers. (De Blois, 1954, p. 18)

Its mildly deprecating tone aside, this text underscores the popularity of the form among women and, I contend, the power these women exercised in regularly—and successfully—choosing to watch this television program type at a time when the power to choose likely rested predominantly with males.[7]

---

[6]It was revealed in the press at the time that a series of signals were often exchanged between the TV announcer and the wrestlers, a practice that is still in evidence at World Wrestling Federation events. One wrestler explained: "When the announcer picks up a piece of paper we know its time for the commercial and we go into a slow stall on the mat—the sponsor's gotta live, too." Fay (1948, p. 6).

[7]Many recent studies have demonstrated that the power to make program choices rests primarily with males in most domestic contexts. I have little doubt that these results have a correlation with the practices of family set owners in the 1940s and 1950s (cf. Gray, 1992; Morley, 1986).

WRESTLING, BOURDIEU, AND CULTURAL TASTE

The tone of the earlier extract could be interpreted in a variety of ways—disapproving, puzzled, flippant, or perhaps simply curious. The male author was attempting to account for a phenomenon that, as he describes it, was unfolding in front of the (disbelieving) eyes of husbands, brothers, and sons in family rooms across America. After all, he queried, what was it about a 350–pound wrestler that women—"*their* womenfolk"—found appealing? This article may simply be an attempt at understanding their behavior. Yet arguably there is a judgmental undercurrent apparent in the text, one that positions itself—and its masculinist audience—above the seemingly curious cultural taste and inexplicable behavior of otherwise "normal" women.

Pierre Bourdieu's meticulous work in the area of economic and sociocultural differentiation is useful here. Bourdieu (1984) maintains that "taste, the propensity and capacity to appropriate (materially or symbolically) a given class of classified, classifying objects or practices, is the generative formula of lifestyle, a unitary set of distinctive preferences" (p. 173). However, although taste is a marker of social differences, Bourdieu argues that the dominant class disguises these social distinctions in terms of natural differences, simultaneously naturalizing and privileging the practices of the ruling class over those of the dominated or working class. In this way, Bourdieu argues, social and economic hierarchies are justified in nature.

Among the distinctive oppositions frequently raised as differentiating the dominant from the dominated class are the notions of "form" over "function" and "distance" over "participation." Bourdieu maintains that these oppositions are especially apparent in the expression of popular and bourgeois art and entertainment forms:

> The most radical difference between popular entertainments—from Punch and Judy shows, wrestling or circuses, or even the old neighborhood cinema, to soccer matches—and bourgeois entertainments is found in audience participation. In one case it is constant, manifest (boos, whistles), sometimes direct (pitch or playing-field invasions); in the other it is intermittent, distant, highly ritualized, with obligatory applause. (pp. 487-488)

These oppositions are also evident in each group's conceptualization of the body, which Bourdieu argues is the most indisputable materialization of class taste.

Typically, then, dominant class taste privileges the formal properties of art while denying its functionality, demanding a distanced relation to the content of the work in favor of its form. Preferences in cultural performance forms tend toward theater, ballet, and the like, and are marked by a critical distance between audience and performers. The bodies of both are carefully controlled; the appearance and motion of the performers' bodies are rigidly disciplined, emphasizing through formal characteristics the properties of health, restraint, and control. Correspondingly, the bodily response of the audience is marked as well by restraint and control, with appreciation valued over participation. Participatory engagement is muted, tempered, and usually limited to light applause.

Conversely, working-class taste generally privileges the functionality of the art work, preferring content over form. Similarly, preferences in performance genres tend toward the participatory and the spectacular; rock concerts, sports events, and professional wrestling all invite intensive vocal and bodily audience involvement and participation. Finally, the working-class conception of the (male) body emphasizes strength, physicality, and plentitude; as John Fiske (1989b) points out, the typical wrestler's body is simply an exaggeration of these norms (a subject I return to shortly).

It is this active, participatory engagement of wrestling's performers and fans that is viewed disparagingly by the excerpt cited earlier. The article begins by subtly questioning the attraction women find in a "350-pound wrestler *swandiving* into the ropes" (De Blois, 1954, p. 18; emphasis added). Given Bourdieu's schema of class concept of the body, the weight reference is an easy marker of working-class values; a 350-pound body is conceptually outside middle-class ideals. Further, the image of a wrestler "swandiving" into the ropes betrays more than a modicum of sarcasm. The dichotomy between the sport of diving and a wrestling performance is clear: The former, a generally middle-class activity, with its emphasis on lithe bodies executing controlled movements, is antithetical to the latter, which emphasizes precisely the opposite qualities, namely, the body physically and often performatively out of control.[8] By conflating the two disparate images, the writer establishes the perceived working-class positioning of wrestling's performers and its female fans.

CATEGORIZING FEMALE FANS

Class taste is not the only marker in evidence in this excerpt. It seems simplistic to say the article is an attempt to locate the fan with regard to both gender and class, but the article is quick to identify not simply *female* fans, but particular *categories* of women: "supposedly normal school girls, housewives, maiden aunts and grandmothers." Each of the four categories is first modified by the qualifier "supposedly normal," thereby questioning

---

[8]Wrestling performers often give the *appearance* of being performatively out of control. However, such performances are usually carefully rehearsed and performed to avoid injury. For the purposes of this argument, I am more interested in the appearance given during performance.

the veracity of the members of each group. Furthermore, each category is suspect in one manner or another: schoolgirls are not yet adults, and thus not yet women; maiden aunts are not yet (and not likely to be) married, and thus are not "truly" women; and grandmothers are elderly (and thus enfeebled) and presumably know better than to be attracted to such indecorous entertainment. The category of housewives is perhaps the most threatening of the four; their marital status and occupation mark their participation as highly questionable, not to mention unnerving, given the context. Thus, the collectivity of women being described is subtly disparaged from the start.

Finally, the response of these women to professional wrestlers is berated. The writer argues that none of these women has any business acting amorously toward these burly performers, who, the author reports, have received "thousands of upside-down cakes, shoo-fly pies, bouquets of flowers and marriage proposals." Certainly the least eligible women mentioned are the housewives, arguably the primary area of concern for both the article's author and the millions of "husbands and sons" whose descriptive titles define their domestic relationships to these women, and whose wives and mothers have been actively pursuing wrestling's performers while transgressing their domestic roles.

Bourdieu (1984) offers a schema for considering the socioeconomic positioning of members of these various class fractions which replaces the notions of subject and subjectivity with "dispositions of thought"—what he calls the "habitus" (p. 208). For Bourdieu, habitus is a generative formula that translates economic necessity into a particular lifestyle. However, the concept can be broadened considerably to incorporate an amalgam of ideas: It is at once *socio-geographical—where* we live, the physical and social place we inhabit, our habitat; *behavioral—* involving both how we inhabit our habitat and habituated ways of behaving; and *conceptual—*involving habits of thought. Habitus is both a schema for plotting space and a means of moving through it.

Thus, in many ways the article I have cited is an attempt to situate these female fans, to identify their habitus, their practices and behaviors, as a means of understanding those practices and simultaneously *categorizing* the practicing women in order to dispense with them, marking them as "not us." The enthusiasm with which these women respond, the assertiveness of the act of looking in which they engage (as they "ogle the big fellows"), and their spirited pursuit of the wrestlers with gifts and proposals mark these women as members of a working-class fraction with the requisite tastes, practices, and allegiances, which are thus outside desirable dominant norms.

A CARNIVAL OF BODIES

The world of professional wrestling is a world of *bodies*. A veritable sea of fannish bodies surrounds the ring, urging on the often excessive bodies of the performers contained within. Although the bulk of academic study has concentrated on wrestling's performers rather than its fans, I consider some of the academic approaches to these bodies in motion to better understand the body of female fans gathered around the ring.

Much of the scholarly attention paid to professional wrestling has focused generally on the wrestling performance (cf. Ball, 1990; Mazer, 1990; Morton & O'Brien, 1985) and specifically on the transgressiveness of the wrestler's body, beginning with Roland Barthes's (1986) seminal essay originally published in 1952 and continuing in the work of Fiske (1987, 1989b), Freedman (1988), Jenkins (in press), and others. Fiske (1989b) points out the similarities between Barthes's work on wrestling as popular spectacle and Mikhail Bakhtin's theory of carnival, which Fiske argues was developed to account for the disparity between the life proposed by the disciplined social order and the repressed pleasures of the subordinate, of which carnival is perhaps the quintessential expression. Carnival, according to Bakhtin (1984), is based on a foundation of inversion, on the logic of the "inside out" (p. 11). Carnival effects a (temporary) inversion of the world, a shifting from top to bottom, from front to rear, one that provides "a parody of extracarnival life" (p. 11).

Fiske (1989b) points out that bodies are a central focus of carnival, utilized as an expression of the materiality of life: "It is a representation of the social at the level of materiality on which all are equal, which suspends the hierarchical rank and privilege that normally grants some classes power over others" (p. 83). Bakhtin (1984) maintains that this bodily principle in carnival is manifest in terms of what he calls "grotesque realism," an expression of the bodily element that is "deeply positive" (pp. 18-19). In this context, the body represents the collectivity, the *social* body, characteristically and exaggeratedly expressed in terms of fertility, growth, and abundance. Further, the essence of grotesque realism is degradation—a "bringing down to earth"—the lowering of all that is high and spiritual to a material, earthy level.

It is perhaps because of this emphasis on the body that professional wrestling has been pointed to as an archetypal expression of subordinate or "popular" culture. Fiske (1989b) argues that televised wrestling is "television's carnival of bodies, of rule breaking, of grotesquerie, of degradation and spectacle" (pp. 83-84). The element of spectacle is present both in the event itself—in the exaggerated bodies and performances of the wrestlers—and, Fiske maintains, in the spectator and his or her pleasure in looking: Because the object is pure spectacle, it works only on the physical senses, on the body of the spectator. Thus, wrestling evokes a physical pleasure in the attending fan.

CARNIVAL AND FANDOM

Despite apparent contradiction, parallels can be drawn between the roles of the participant in carnival and the spectator in wrestling. Bakhtin (1984) insists that in carnival there can be no separation between actors and spectators; to erect footlights would obliterate that which marks the event as carnival. Instead, the foundation of carnival lies in its location within *the people*, where *all* are participants, and where the individual is replaced by the collective, social body. Conversely, the basis of official culture lies in the production or reinforcement of hierarchical relationships—between rich and poor, powerful and powerless—and in differentiated relationships—between priest and congregation, patron and artist, and, in a theatrical context, between actor and audience.

Wrestling straddles these two schemas, drawing from both. Like so many other modern performance genres, professional wrestling events are held within a variation of a theatrical or sporting context. Unlike the carnival context, in which the entire area in use is marked as a performance space and all within it are marked as performers, most contemporary performance contexts attempt to control and prioritize the activities of the participants involved by marking an area as either "performance" or "audience" space, thus demarcating the roles of the participants into (active) performer and (passive) audience.[9]

Despite this separation, the participatory character of an audience is not defined simply by the layout of the area but also by the expectations implied by the event organizers and the genre (though these expectations in no way guarantee audience adherence). Lawrence Levine's (1988) study of Shakespearean theater in 19th and 20th century America illustrates this point: He notes that two separate theatrical contexts existed (not entirely happily) in America in the 19th century, bifurcated primarily along socioeconomic lines. Such a division closely replicates Bourdieu's schema of

[9]Areas are also marked for different uses at different times. Contemporary Shakespearean theater companies (such as American Players Theater in Spring Green, WI, and the Royal Shakespeare Festival in Stratford, Ontario), using versatile performance models based on the Globe Theater, often make use of areas other than the stage, such as the aisles, which are normally "reserved" for audience use. However, audiences are frequently warned not to move to or from their seats during the performance and are prevented from using spaces such as the aisles, thus reinforcing the spacial hierarchy.

cultural taste: working–class Shakespearean acting styles were boisterous, exaggerated, spectacular. They were described by contemporary critic George William Curtis in 1863 as "the brawny art; the biceps aesthetics; rant, roar, and rigmarole" (cited in Levine, p. 57). Likewise, working-class audiences were active participants in the performance, rather than simply observers. Levine maintained:

> to envision nineteenth-century theater audiences correctly, one might do well to visit a contemporary sporting event in which the spectators not only are similarly heterogeneous but are also . . . more than an audience; they are participants who can enter into the action on the field, who feel a sense of immediacy and at times even of control, who articulate their feelings vocally and unmistakably. (p. 26)

In this theatrical context, the audience was free to request (or demand) that songs be sung, participating in and at times charting or altering the diegesis as they saw fit.

Not surprisingly, given my earlier discussion of Bourdieu's argument, 19th-century ruling-class audiences were marked by restraint and control. Offering a comparison of working- and ruling-class theater experiences, Curtis wrote that with regard to the latter experience:

> The difference of the spectacle was striking. The house was comfortably full, not crowded. The air of the audience was that of refined attention rather than that of eager interest. Plainly it was a more cultivated and intellectual audience. (quoted in Levine, 1988, p. 59)

These two examples illustrate the very different roles audiences can (and are encouraged to) play in a theatrical context. Although professional wrestling is similarly situated within a theatrical performance space, with areas demarcated for performers and audience members, the importance of the participatory role of the audience—so essential to the event—speaks to the similarities between wrestling and 19th-century working-class theater experience, and between wrestling and carnival. Although Bakhtin (1984) maintained there can be no distinction between performer and spectator in carnival, I believe nonetheless that nonhierarchical distinctions were made between the various *roles* carnival participants played. One example of such role playing is the function of the *mask* in carnival, from which Bakhtin argued such manifestations as parodies, caricatures, and comic gestures—foundational elements of carnival—were derived. Masks afford the wearer an opportunity to transcend both human and natural boundaries, to play a new, distinct, and specifying role in the ongoing diegesis.

Arguably, all who attend a wrestling event are offered specific participatory roles to play. In contrast with the experience of attending either the theater or a motion picture, where the audience is invited to *observe* the performance, wrestling audiences are encouraged to transcend their customary specular capacity and *participate* in the event, engaging the body as well as the mind.

THE TRANSGRESSIVE FEMALE FAN

Although the transgressiveness of the male wrestling body has been a central (and productive) scholarly focus, I believe the notion of transgression is applicable as well to the female wrestling fan of the 1940s and 1950s. I argue many of the same pleasures described earlier were operable for the fans in question. For in an era when an increasingly conservative, patriarchal definition of femininity was regaining currency (among those in positions of power, if not among women themselves), professional wrestling events offered female audiences a context in which to rebel against this definition and in which to create their own. For Bakhtin (1984), carnival "celebrated temporary liberation from the prevailing truth and from the established order," and as such allowed for the creation of "special forms of speech and gesture, frank and free . . . from norms of etiquette and decency imposed at other times" (p. 10). Much as carnival constructs a "second world and a second life outside officialdom" (p. 6), in Bakhtin's words, these female fans of wrestling built a temporary world outside the reach of patriarchy, although as I discuss below, not beyond its view.

One frequent cultural observer of the time, *The New York Times,* reported at some length about the behavior of female fans at wrestling events, as these excerpts illustrate:

> A wrestling show doesn't reveal a great deal about wrestlers, but it does reveal a very great deal about their audience. People burst out in real anger as the villain of the piece apparently is crunching the hero's neck to bits. Women who would be as gentle as lambs shake their fists and cry out wild curses at wrestlers. Others mutter at them as they enter or leave the ring.
>
> Women, for some strange reason, often go berserk and stick pins in a wrestler who comes within the reach of their soft, white hands. The villain especially is in danger and women specialize in taking off high-heeled slippers and beating the poor man heavily about the head. Or sometimes they just yank out his hair.
>
> Women flock to wrestling matches, and of course many more watch them on TV. They get to recognize their favorites and when they see them in public places often come up to them, ardor burning in their eyes. (Boal, 1949, pp. 24-31)

As these observations demonstrate, the women in attendance were able to transcend behavioral expectations and engage in conduct that was "out of control." Much like the excessive, out-of-control body of the male wrestler, these female fans chose to abandon the demure, deferential, "gentle as lambs" role to which they had been assigned and act aggressively—both verbally and physically. In his analysis of the parallels between carnival and wrestling, Fiske points out that "billingsgate"—verbalized and gestured curses and oaths—is an active component of both forms and is engaged in by both wrestlers and spectators. Billingsgate, Fiske (1989b) writes, is "oral, oppositional participatory culture, making no distinction between performer and audience" (p. 89). The newspaper extract clearly illustrates this type of engagement: By shaking their fists, cursing, and crying out, these women are clearly participating in the diegesis, simultaneously breaking with the domesticated role that society—represented in this instance by the disbelieving author—has suggested for them. For some fans, such actions may have represented a moment of carnivalesque freedom; for others, this sort of unfeminine—or arguably *anti-feminine*—behavior suggests an explicit break with normative constructions of the role. These women were not simply exercising freedom from control, they arguably were creating actions *against* the constricted gender norms that were utilized to control them.

PHYSICAL CONFRONTATION . . .

Beyond the verbalized and gestured actions lies another form of aggressive response in evidence in the article. Utilizing the tools of femininity—the "soft, white[10] hands" and the "high-heeled slippers" described in the article—some female fans chose to *physically* engage the wrestlers, participating in the performance in a more direct, heightened manner. Perhaps the best example of this behavior was provided by the most infamous fan of the period, a Bronx native named Hatpin Mary, whose actions were no doubt the inspiration for many female fans, and who both baffled and amazed the press corps:

> Everyone seems to want to get into the act. Women like Hatpin Mary (recently enjoined) will sit at ringside and prod any portion of a protruding anatomy which carelessly presents itself. When [wrestler

---

[10]Not surprisingly, the quote betrays the racist attitudes of the time and assumes an exclusively white audience. In fact, African Americans and Hispanics were active both as wrestlers and fans during the 1950s (cf. "Wrestlers," 1950; Daly 1957; "Negro Wrestlers," 1962; "Rocca the magnificent," Zimmerman, 1962).

Gorgeous] George has landed in the seats, women have pulled his hair and clubbed him about the curls with their spiked heels. Others have showered him with bottles. (Shane, 1950, p. 71)

Hatpin Mary and fans like her took the performance to new levels, physically accosting the villainous male wrestlers with the symbols of domesticated, civilized femininity: high heels, hat pins, and soft, white hands. It is as though these women were gleefully throwing the emblems of femininity back into the face of patriarchy, temporarily suspended and momentarily vulnerable: exacting payment, drawing blood, these female fans drew pleasure from violent disorder and bodies out of control.

... AND ASSERTIVE SEXUALITY

Another form of participatory pleasure engaged in by these fans was, if not the reverse of violence, perhaps the other side of the coin: passion. If the image of physically aggressive women was troubling to both male reporters and wrestling's villains, then aggressive female sexuality was perhaps as troubling to wrestling's heroes. Assertive sexual behavior was at this historical moment almost exclusively a male prerogative; only "loose" women conducted themselves in such a manner. Yet decades before specifically female-targeted male strip shows became commonplace, genres such as professional wrestling provided the context for women to publicly exhibit sexual desire, whether real or feigned—or at least freedom from the disavowal of desire—and transgress the norms of "acceptable" female sexual behavior.

This sort of behavior was manifest in numerous ways. Much like the women who verbalize their desire at a Chippendales performance,[11] female wrestling fans were often equally forthcoming, as this male writer for *Cosmopolitan* observed:

It is obvious from the kind of sentiment expressed by many of the women in the heat of a match that their psyches are responding to something besides the purely dramatic aspects of wrestling. "Lookit that hunk of man!" is a common cry. "What a build! How would ya like to date that one. C'mon, Superman, bust him one for me!" (Kobler, 1953, p. 126)

[11]The Chippendales are one of many popular, all–male dance revues.

Although *Cosmopolitan*'s explanation of this behavior focused on the "romantic thrill" these women received from seeing "large, lusty males in violent contact," I believe much of the pleasure involved had more to do with the act of participation itself than the supposed "object" of their affections. Most of these expressions take wrestlers as the object but are intended specifically to be *shared* with other audience members. Yelling out the phrase "Lookit that hunk of man!" may be an expression of desire, but it is also a confirmation of the speaker's ability to publicly express sexual desire within a specific social community, while transgressing the role prescribed by patriarchal society. Arguably, then, a significant aspect of the pleasure in these exclamations comes from the sharing of this transgressive behavior with other women.

This is not to discount the role of sexual desire in these women's fandom, nor the apparent threat it poses. The point was aptly expressed in the *TV Guide* (De Blois, 1954) essay discussed earlier, which described the thousands of gifts and proposals sent to "disgruntled" wrestlers from adoring female fans, or, as was expressed in *The New York Times* article (Boal, 1949), the way in which some women would approach wrestlers with "ardor burning in their eyes." Many women would take their passion beyond the arena, as the *Times* article went on to illustrate: "Often wrestlers sleeping peacefully in hotel rooms are awakened by a phone call from a dulcet-voiced girl murmuring, 'Oh, Mr. Ape Man, I just think you're so—'" (p. 30). The article reassuringly concluded that the wrestlers "properly" responded with "horror."

SOCIALLY "TROUBLING" BEHAVIOR AND POPULAR MUSIC

The public expression of female sexual desire is by no means unique to wrestling; on the contrary, it brings up illuminating parallels with other performance genres. One such example is popular music: It is not uncommon for women (or men, for that matter, though usually they respond somewhat differently) to react strongly to certain performers, and their reaction is frequently considered to be socially "troubling." Current performers regularly experience the rush of screaming young (and not so young) women at concert appearances, a phenomenon that was familiar to succeeding generations of fans of performers such as young Frank Sinatra, Elvis Presley, The Beatles, and Michael Jackson (cf. Ehrenreich, Hess, & Jacobs, 1992). Moreover, each generational phenomenon was of concern to certain vocal members of society, who reacted strongly and punitively to such public expressions of female desire—*young* female desire—and thus young female bodies seemingly "out of control"—certainly out of *their* control.

Attempts to gain power over individuals by gaining control of their bodies has long been a familiar tactic in human history, as the work of Michel Foucault has so aptly illustrated. Foucault (1980) detailed elaborate Victorian–era efforts with regard to the human body—and particularly the female body—in order to bring it under (male) control, through the deployment of medical and educational institutions, prisons, and so forth. As Foucault points out, the "discovery" of the specifically female disease "hysteria" is but one particularly relevant example of attempts to assert power over the female body. Much the same sort of effort was made in the 1940s and 1950s to control the "loose" bodies of the female fans of Sinatra and Elvis. The public expression of female sexual desire ran counter to the image of the domestic(ated) woman so prevalent at the time.

Like Frank Sinatra and Elvis Presley, professional wrestling attracted its share of passionate female fans during the 1940s and 1950s, much to the consternation of certain sectors of society. *The New York Times* observed the phenomenon with no lack of disbelief, wondering

> how could anyone over the age of twelve believe in such a figure as Gorgeous George with his platinum hair . . . or Mr. America, a nobly handsome youth who is now the current favorite of the bobby-soxers, who find wrestling almost as good, and considerably more personal, than Sinatra or Mel Torme. It is reported of Mr. America . . . that more young girls have swooned on meeting him than any other wrestler, a statistic that might be more interesting to a sociologist than to a man in the box office. (Boal, 1949, p. 24)

Whether one is analyzing the phenomenon of Luke Perry, who, as I write this, must be airlifted in and out of shopping malls amidst the crush of female fans, or Frank Sinatra, whose every movement, reporters in the 1940s noted, would make "young girls faint and old women scream" (reported in Kelley, 1986, p. 74), or wrestlers like Mr. America, whose "beauty and brawn makes bobby-soxers swoon" (Boal, p. 24), the phenomenon of the defiant female body "out of control" was and is arguably a significant and powerful transgression of prevalent gendered norms.

THE NEWS ORGANIZATION

It is appropriate to pause and consider the context within which the stories told here are being written. All the evidence drawn on for this essay was written by a particular group of people within a specific industrial context: the news organization. Gaye Tuchman's work on the news industry is useful here. Briefly, Tuchman (1978) argues that news is first and foremost a social institution and as such is tied to the social context, which I have explored at some length. Further, the news industry considers itself one of a select group of loosely allied legitimated institutions (including government, business, education, religion). Consequently, news organizations legitimate the authority of those that hold power: bureaucrats, politicians, social and business leaders, and so forth. Because news organizations are institutionally linked to other facets of the power–bloc, they are generally committed to reproducing social mores.

Following accepted institutional news practices, newsworkers strive to turn occurrences into discernable events, using "frames" to organize and transform everyday reality into news stories (Tuchman, 1978, p. 192).[12] By limiting the kind and amount of information told within a story, and by framing that information in a purposeful way, newsworkers create meanings that reinforce social institutions and social norms. Thus, when considering the type of evidence presented in this chapter, one must take into account not only the voices of the women cited, but the frame within which their voices are placed. For that matter, the reader must also take into account my own position as the male author of this chapter, for I, too, am presenting evidence and framing female voices in a deliberate way, though arguably with very different intentions. Newspaper writers at the time were almost exclusively male, as were most professional members of news organizations. Arguably then, the framing device used to "make sense" of these women's stories was based at least partly in patriarchal assumptions about the role of women in contemporary society.

"FRAMING" FEMALE FANDOM

The fact that the news industry was dominated by men begs the question of why these male reporters would take notice of women's interest in professional wrestling, even if the answer seems clear. For in a time when women were being asked to give up their jobs, leave the workplace and return to their homes, husbands, children and domestic roles and responsibilities, the sudden, widespread rise in interest in professional wrestling—a debased entertainment form to begin with—coupled with the types of transgressive behavior exhibited by these women both in public and in the

---

[12]Erving Goffman is often associated with "frame analysis," though he did not coin the term. Goffman defines a frame as "the principles of organization which govern events—at least social ones—and our subjective involvement in them" (cited in Tuchman, 1978, p. 192).

privacy of homes across the country, no doubt was cause for some concern for these men, as it was for the "30 million American husbands, brothers and sons" (De Blois, 1954, p. 18) across the country.

Nearly all the articles studied made some attempt to explain the behavior of these women, calling on psychologists, promoters, or other "experts" to rationalize these seemingly bizarre actions. *Cosmopolitan* (1953) mused that perhaps the appearance of "raw masculinity" was the appeal for some women, whereas for others the sight of an "ugly" wrestler would make the woman's husband or date appear attractive by comparison.[13] However, the magazine concluded that it was the "women in need of letting off steam" who benefited most, the "suppressed, overworked, underappreciated, elderly housewives, who probably get the deepest satisfaction out of watching wrestling" (p. 126). Even though *Business Week* argued the most "common" explanation was that watching wrestling gave women a "mental release for some kind of sexual frustration," they concluded by citing the opinion of "psychiatrists" who contended instead that "little girls are brought up to control their hostility and to be ladies at all costs. Watching wrestling—and especially siding against the villain—lets them release their aggressive feelings" ("It pays," p. 25). As these articles demonstrate, in most cases the press argued that women needed a venue in which to vent frustrations, to release the pent-up aggravations that are a side effect of their daily routines as *housewives*.[14] No doubt such diversions are acceptable (more or less) so long as a woman's primary task— her *raison d'être*—is adequately fulfilled.

Nonetheless, the tenor of these articles suggests that the behavior exhibited by these women was at least a little bizarre; tolerable, perhaps, but hardly something to be encouraged. The amount of speculation in which the authors indulge regarding the pleasure women derive from wrestling is, I argue, evidence of the degree of distress or alarm felt by men regarding this phenomenon. Clearly, explanations were called for and served a key function: to categorize and rationalize the women's behavior, isolating it as one might isolate a virus, so as to disarm it. Much as the ruling class during the Victorian era would identify as aberrant certain behavior (such as homosexuality) in order to suppress it (cf. Foucault, 1980), by nam-

----

[13]Sexual appeal was a commonly offered explanation for wrestling's appeal to women. One wrestling promoter suggested that "wrestling is done only by extremely well–built men, and it is just as natural for a woman to stare at a semi–nude wrestler as it is for you and me to stare at Betty Grable in sweater and shorts" (McPherson & Arnold, 1949, p. 76).

[14]Fiske (1989a) offers a persuasive discussion of what he sees as the inadequacies of the "safety valve" argument, which would diffuse the challenge to power such actions or pleasures represent.

ing these women's behavior, the writers (and, by extension, the multitude of concerned male readers) hoped to render it nonthreatening and thus contain it. The eras are different, but the strategies in use are much the same.

STRATEGY VERSUS TACTIC

Such attempts at containment are rarely totally successful, as the work of theorists such as Michel de Certeau (1984) clearly explains. De Certeau, for one, was noted for his careful analyses and insightful explication of the struggle between the powerful and the weak. In discussing such relationships, he offered the metaphors "place" and "space," and "strategy" and "tactic." The powerful, he argued, always operate from their own place of power, a base of operations from which they can identify targets or threats, and devise strategies for dealing with them. On the other hand, the weak do not control their own place of operation, and as such must carve out temporary spaces within the place occupied by the powerful. They do so through the use of tactics: fleeting, calculated actions that take advantage of whatever opportunities present themselves. Although the weak never confront the powerful directly, nonetheless the actions of the weak are always "within the enemy's field of vision" (de Certeau, pp. 36-37). Thus, as Fiske (1989b) maintains, "these tactics involve spotting the weak points in the forces of the powerful and raiding them as guerrilla fighters constantly harry and attack an invading army," in order to "maintain their own position within and against the social order dominated by the powerful" (p. 19).

These descriptive metaphors are useful in explaining the behaviors of both the male reporters and the female fans. The reporters are operating from within a place of power—the news institution—and are engaged in occupations that (generally) seek to maintain the status quo, which is, after all, their foundation of power. As I argued earlier, the process of writing and publishing stories that investigate—and typically deride—the behavior of these female fans is a strategic attempt to address (and, they no doubt hope, contain) these women's actions while preserving patriarchal privilege in the process. Although the act of writing about this subject does not directly prevent the behavior, it does draw attention to it, marking it as either the aberrant or quirky behavior of teens or grandmothers, or, at best, as the eccentric but necessary actions of frustrated housewives. The process of discursive identification is, as Foucault (1980) pointed out, the first step in formulating a strategy against it.

On the other hand, I believe that, whether intentionally or not, some female fans were using wrestling as a means of carving a space out of the place of patriarchy, both privately in the home and publicly in the arena. Within the context of the home (which, after all, was a man's castle), the *TV Guide* (De Blois, 1954) article illustrated how millions of women during the 1940s and 1950s occasionally but effectively held hostage both the television set and the family. Women successfully insisted on watching televised wrestling two or three times a week and then openly admired the parade of male bodies that filled the screen, transgressing the roles set out for them as wives and mothers, while disgruntled husbands and sons looked on. In doing so, they created a temporary space within the home, employing tactics that allowed them to supplant the normative domestic, demure, caregiving role expected of them with an assertive, self-gratifying, sexualized role.

FANDOM AS COMMUNITY

Likewise, within the context of the wrestling performance, female fans employed tactics that openly defied and, in the spirit of the carnivalesque, *turned upside down* the gendered role set out for them. In its place they offered up a new, playful model of the feminine, albeit fleetingly, but one they could create anew at the next opportunity. These fans, operating within a public place—a sporting arena that long has been the place of patriarchy—were able to carve out a space in which to employ the tactics of transgression and create a temporary, communal context where they could exchange these shared behaviors, all under the watchful eye of the powerful. When the event was over and the house lights were turned on, these fans melted away, returning to their daily lives with the knowledge of their resistance.

They also left with the knowledge of their membership in a community. One fundamental characteristic of fandom, Fiske (1989b) argues, is the activity of discrimination: Fans make careful distinctions between what they are fans of and of what they are not. Such textual discriminations, Fiske maintains, are often homologous of social discrimination:

> Choosing texts is choosing social allegiances and fans form themselves into a community much more explicitly than do the middle-class appreciators of highbrow art. The links between social allegiance and cultural taste are active and explicit in fandom, and the discrimination involved follows criteria of social relevance rather than of aesthetic quality. (p. 147)

Direct evidence of the tendency to form communal bonds among female wrestling fans does exist: Hundreds of wrestling fan clubs were started in the 1940s and 1950s, almost invariably founded by women. Every top wrestler had a national fan club, and the membership was almost entirely female (Kobler, 1953, p. 126). Nevertheless, I find the indirect evidence I have cited—the informal communities of women formed at the arena and at home—to be both compelling and suggestive. These women embraced wrestling, using it as means of resisting and defying—albeit temporarily—the confinement of patriarchally bound roles. The huge surge in female attendance at matches, the transgressive behaviors exhibited, and the communal nature of the behavior all speak to the social allegiances being formed around this performance genre. Furthermore, I would argue, the social relevance of creating an assertive female community contra the demands of patriarchal expectation was arguably more significant for these female fans than any criteria of aesthetic quality. These women could enjoy the pleasure of defiance—of shared public defiance—and, in the domestic context, the momentary pleasure of male disapproval and male inability to alter such behavior. In each instance, these women found tactics for evading the pressure of male expectation and experienced the ephemeral assertion of renegotiated female characteristics shared by other female fans across the country. Even women isolated at home watching matches on television could find evidence of this rebellious community by reading the discomfort expressed in the articles that appeared in magazines and newspapers across the country.

Finally, there is the possibility, however fleeting, that some men might actually have benefited from this phenomenon, gaining new insights into the women around them by coming into contact with such fandom. One man demonstrated such a transformation after reading the *Cosmopolitan* article in 1953: "Vastly enjoyed amazing experience of reading your article. I begin to think I understand my wife"—E.C. Struthers, New York, New York ("The last word", p. 131).

No doubt this can be seen as proof that for some there is still hope.

REFERENCES

Baba & behemoths. (1936, May 18). *Time, 27*, p. 56.

Bakhtin, M. (1984). *Rabelais and his world.* Bloomington: Indiana University Press.

Ball, M. R. (1990). *Professional wrestling as ritual drama in American popular culture.* Lewiston, NY: Edwin Mellen Press.

Barthes, R. (1986). The world of wrestling. In S. Sontag (Ed.), *A Barthes reader* (pp. 18-30). New York: Hill and Wang.

Boal, S. (1949, November 20). Big boom in the grunt and groan business. *New York Times Magazine*, pp. 24-31.

Bourdieu, P. (1984). *Distinction: A social critique of the judgment of taste* (R. Nice, Trans.). Cambridge, MA: Harvard University Press. (Original work published 1979)

Brooks, T., & Marsh, E. (1988). *The complete directory to prime time network TV shows: 1946-present.* New York: Ballantine.

Byars, J. (1991). *All that Hollywood allows: Re-reading gender in 1950s melodrama.* Chapel Hill & London: University of North Carolina Press.

Daley, A. (1957, November 27). Pantomime flimflammery. *New York Times,* p. 34.

De Blois, F. (1954, September 11). Lo, the lady wrestling fan! *TV Guide,* pp. 18-19.

de Certeau, M. (1984). *The practice of everyday life* (S. Rendall, Trans.). Berkeley: University of California Press.

Ehrenreich, B., Hess, E., & Jacobs, G. (1992). Beatlemania: Girls just want to have fun. In L. Lewis (Ed.), *The adoring audience: Fan culture and popular media* (pp. 84-106). London and New York: Routledge.

Farrell, E. (1942, December). Lady wrestlers. *The American Mercury, 55,* pp. 674-680.

Fay, B. (1948, May 1). Collier's sports. *Collier's, 121,* p. 6.

Fiske, J. (1987). *Television culture.* London and New York: Methuen.

Fiske, J. (1989a) *Reading the popular.* Boston: Unwin Hyman.

Fiske, J. (1989b) *Understanding popular culture.* Boston: Unwin Hyman.

Foucault, M. (1979). *Discipline and punish: The birth of the prison* (A. Sheridan, Trans.). New York: Vintage. (Original work published 1975)

Foucault, M. (1980). *The history of sexuality volume I: An introduction* (R. Hurley, Trans.). New York: Vintage. (Original work published 1976)

Freedman, J. (1988). *Drawing heat.* Windsor, Ont., Canada: Black Moss.

Gray, A. (1992). *Video playtime: The gendering of a leisure technology.* London and New York: Routledge.

Haralovich, M. B. (1992). Sitcoms and suburbs: Positioning the 1950s Homemaker. In L. Spigel & D. Mann (Eds.), *Private screenings: Television and the female consumer* (pp. 111-141). Minneapolis: Minnesota University Press.

It pays to sponsor television corn. (1950, October 7). *Business Week,* pp. 25-26.

Jares, J. (1974). *Whatever happened to Gorgeous George?* Englewood Cliffs, NJ: Prentice-Hall.

Jenkins, H. (in press). "Never trust a snake": WWF wrestling as masculine melodrama. In A. Barker & T. Boyd (Eds.), *Gender, race and sports.* Bloomington: Indiana University Press.

Kelley, K. (1986). *His way: The unauthorized biography of Frank Sinatra.* New York: Bantam.

Kobler, J. (1953, December). Where grandma can yell "bum." *Cosmopolitan, 135*, pp. 120-127.

Levine, L. W. (1988). *Highbrow/lowbrow: The emergence of cultural hierarchy in America.* Cambridge, MA: Harvard University Press.

Liebling, A. J. (1954, November 13). A reporter at large—From Sarah Bernhardt to Yukon Eric. *The New Yorker, 30*, pp. 132-149.

May, E. T. (1988). *Homeward bound: American families in the cold war era.* New York: Basic Books.

Mazer, S. (1990). The doggie doggie world of professional wrestling. *The Drama Review, 34*(4), pp. 96-122.

McPherson, C. L., with Arnold, O. (1949, October 29). What gives in "rasslin". *Collier's*, pp. 30-31, 75-76.

Morley, D. (1986). *Family television: Cultural power and domestic leisure.* London and New York: Comedia/Routledge.

Morton, G. W., & O'Brien, G. M. (1985). *Wrestling to rasslin: Ancient sport to American spectacle.* Bowling Green, OH: Bowling Green State University Popular Press.

Negro wrestlers. (1962, May). *Ebony, 17*, pp. 43-46.

Powers, R. (1984). *Supertube: The rise of television sports.* New York: Coward-McCann.

Shane, T. (1950). Gorgeous George the wrestler. *The American Mercury, 71*, pp. 64-71.

Spigel, L. (1990). Television in the family circle. In P. Mellencamp (Ed.), *Logics of television: Essays in cultural criticism* (pp. 73-97). Bloomington and Indianapolis: Indiana University Press.

Sterling, C., & Kittross, J. (1978). *Stay tuned: A concise history of American broadcasting.* Belmont, CA: Wadsworth.

Struthers, E. C. (1954, February). The last word [Letters to the editor]. *Cosmopolitan, 136*, p. 131.

Tuchman, G. (1978). *Making news: A study in the construction of reality.* New York: The Free Press.

Walsh, A. S. (1984). *Women's films and female experience, 1940 to 1950.* New York: Praeger.

Wrestlers. (1950, July). *Ebony, 5*, pp. 21-24.

Zimmermann, G. (1962, August 14). Rocca the magnificent. *Look, 26*, pp. 59-64.

▶IV

THE RHETORIC OF FANDOM

▶7

Talking About Soaps: Communicative Practices in a Computer-Mediated Fan Culture

Nancy K. Baym
Wayne State University

In the last decade, fans of many popular media have moved their discussions to computer networks, a move which in many ways enhances the social potential of fandom while simultaneously making these aspects of fandom far more accessible to scholars. This chapter explores one of the first and most successful computer-mediated fan groups: Usenet's *rec.arts.tv.soaps* (r.a.t.s.), a group established in 1984 to discuss soaps online.

R.a.t.s. challenges stereotypical conceptions of soap opera fans as "inferior to more prestigious audiences . . . morally questionable and an enthusiastic consumer" (Brown, 1994, pg. 48). Although the "typical" soap fan is seen as home-bound, isolated, and uneducated, r.a.t.s. fans are educated, employed, and computer-literate. Of the thousands of participants, almost three-quarters are female. Most are in their 20s or 30s and are computing professionals or students. Others are scientists, secretaries, nurses, and other professionals who participate while at work. They sometimes watch the soap operas live, but they generally prefer videotape. Watching on tape allows them to time shift until work is over, but also to "FF" (fast-forward) through advertisements and characters they do not like.

R.a.t.s. also challenges gender stereotypes of computer users and Usenet groups because it is populated primarily by women. Given the centrality of social interaction in soap opera enjoyment it is hardly surprising soap fans have appropriated a network, albeit a traditionally male-dominated one, in order to discuss soaps. Scholars from a number of traditions have found that soap opera fans love talking to each other about soaps. Quantitative survey work within uses and gratifications (e.g., Babrow, 1987, 1989; Cantor & Pingree, 1983; Compesi, 1980; Perse & Rubin, 1989; Rubin, 1985) has found that the chance to interact with other viewers is one of the genre's main appeals. College students who expect to be able to socialize during and after watching soaps are more likely to look positively on the viewing experience (Babrow, 1987, 1989). College students also cite social utility, the opportunity to interact with others, as a motivation for viewing soaps more than other television genres (Rubin, 1985). Using the language of uses and gratifications, but the qualitative method of interviewing, Whetmore and Kielwasser (1983) argue that postviewing and previewing interaction are as important as the actual viewing. With the soap audience ethnographers Hobson (1989, 1990) and Brown (1994), Whetmore and Kielwasser demonstrate that people often start watching soaps so they can participate in the soap-talk communities in their homes and at work. There is no question that talking about soaps is an integral part of becoming and being a soap fan.

However, in almost 50 years of work on soap operas and their audiences, most of which notes the importance of fan talk, very little has directly observed fan discussions. Notable exceptions include Lemish's (1985) participant-observation study of soap opera viewing in a public gathering place, Hobson's (1990) interview study of a group of coworkers, Williams's (1992) own discussion with one fan, and Brown's (1994) ethnographic interviews and observations of several small groups of soap opera fans. These researchers have begun to demonstrate the range, complexity, and importance of such talk, but have been limited by the small size of the groups observed and the short time over which groups were observed or interviewed.

It is not just soap opera fans who enjoy discussing their genre. Fandom is generally defined as an intrinsically social phenomenon in which a person becomes a fan, in part, for the social connections or community that fandom entails (Fiske, 1992; Jenkins, 1992). Many social theorists, including Bourdieu (1977), argue that the locus of community or culture is in the ordinary practices of its members. It is their habitual ways of acting that support, maintain, and continually recreate a group's norms, values, and belief systems. Bourdieu, like many practice-oriented theorists, argues that practices are always motivated by purposes. The question then becomes what purposes the communicative practices in r.a.t.s. and fan groups more generally serve.

Although it is not exactly "talk," a point to which I return below, r.a.t.s. and other computer-mediated fan groups allow direct access to more fan interaction than previous researchers have been able to observe. Because online discussions are electronically recorded and transmitted, one can collect and examine a wide range of naturally occurring interaction over an extended period of time. I show how the interactions in r.a.t.s. can be seen as a set of distinctive practices that reveal a complex set of implicit and interwoven goals. Those goals include the enhancement of interpretive resources, the creation of a performance space with the potential status and recognition that entails, and perhaps most provocatively, the opportunity to engage in public discussion of normally private socioemotional issues. These findings raise questions about the functions implicitly served by the frequently overlooked mundane interactions between fans.

USENET

To understand r.a.t.s., one needs a basic understanding of the network that hosts it. Usenet runs primarily through the Internet, linking tens of thousands of sites, including universities, computer-related companies, telecommunication companies, government laboratories, and increasing numbers of individuals. R.a.t.s. was one of over 5,000 Usenet discussion groups (newsgroups) that span an enormous and ever-increasing range of topics from the grave to the absurd. Since this research was conducted, r.a.t.s. has been divided into three groups—rec.arts.tv.soaps.abc, rec.arts.tv.soaps.cbs, and rec.arts.tv.soaps.misc.

The contents of newsgroups are electronic letters (posts), identical to e-mail, which are sent by users from their sites and automatically distributed to each Usenet site receiving the group. Prior to its subdivision, r.a.t.s. was one of Usenet's most prolific groups, generating hundreds of new messages each day. Each of the offspring groups now carries as many messages as the single group then carried. As many as 40,000 people worldwide may be reading the r.a.t.s. groups (Reid, n.d.).

Newsgroups for many shows and media have been successful on Usenet. In July 1993, for example, 9 of the 25 most prolific newsgroups were fan groups (Reid, 1993). They discussed baseball, basketball, and soccer; movies; Rush Limbaugh; and Star Trek; as well as soaps. In that month alone those nine newsgroups wrote 31,488 messages. These nine represent only a tiny fraction of the fan groups organized on Usenet and other computer networks such as Prodigy and American Online. The processes taking place on r.a.t.s., therefore, while helping to illuminate soap opera fandom, also provide a window into a phenomenon of enormous consequence to all scholars interested in fan culture.

COMMUNICATIVE PRACTICES IN R.A.T.S.

I have been a participant in r.a.t.s. as well as a researcher. My initial involvement with the group, in September 1990, was as a fellow soap fan, eager to discuss the shows and read others' perspectives. After spending an hour a day reading and posting to r.a.t.s. for nearly a year, I decided to write about it. I had begun to see that as participants discussed the soaps, they created an engaging community, and I started approaching r.a.t.s. as an ethnographer and discourse analyst. I announced my intentions to the group and began collecting data. In October 1991, I saved one month's posts, collected survey responses from several participants, and held e-mail discussions with others. In February 1992, I began saving all the messages. When I stopped doing this 10 months later, I had collected a corpus of 32,308 messages. This constituted 93% of the total public discourse during those months, and (at that time) approximately 40% of the total public discourse since the very first post to r.a.t.s.

I shared my analyses with r.a.t.s. participants, who were extremely supportive. I participated in r.a.t.s. on and off through 1993. By that time the traffic had grown so much that I could no longer afford the time that keeping up demanded. Furthermore, I had stopped enjoying *All My Children*, which had been the show whose net discussion I most enjoyed (though I have remained a loyal *General Hospital* viewer).

In this chapter, I focus on four communicative practices in r.a.t.s.—informing, speculating, criticizing, and reworking—in order to show how fan talk transforms and enhances the pleasures of soap viewing and creates new social pleasures. Each of these practices represents a broad category which organizes interaction and culture on r.a.t.s. Although most r.a.t.s. messages involve at least one of these practices, these four are intended to exemplify rather than exhaust the range of activities in r.a.t.s. I illustrate each practice with typical excerpts of posts from the 10-month r.a.t.s. corpus.

A few features of the examples need noting. They appear in a mono-space font in order to best retain the look and feel of the original messages. For the same reason, I retained misspellings and grammatical errors. Many of these messages respond to previous messages. When this is the case, the quoted message is marked by ">" in the left margin, as it appears on screen. Also, all the examples here discuss *All My Children*. The practices they show, however, are common to discussions of all the soaps. Several posts refer to "Pine Valley" or "PV." This is the fictional Pennsylvania town where *All My Children* is set.

Finally, as the examples make clear, these posts are not oral, face-to-face, or synchronous. The relationship between asynchronous Usenet interaction and face-to-face conversation is too complex to summarize here. My intention is not to suggest that this interaction is identical to fan talk in face-to-face conversations. Indeed, the issues of similarities and differences between the two kinds of fan interaction are thus far unexplored. I use the word "talk" to describe r.a.t.s. interaction, in part, because participants themselves do, as seen in these two women's descriptions of what r.a.t.s. offers them:

> Although I like to watch the show alone, I enjoy having some people to talk about the show with. It is great since I just moved to CA and I don't know that many people, that I know some already who I can chat about GH with. (survey response, Nov. 27, 1991)
>
> Rats is the closest thing to actually watching the show in a group. . . . The more boring the show is, the more we seem to talk about it (survey response, Nov. 27, 1991).

In my survey data, participants use the word "discussion"—a word which connotes the face-to-face situation—more than any other in describing their interaction. As illustrated above, they also make explicit comparisons between their online and face-to-face interactions. Interestingly, although they do describe themselves as "reading" rather than "listening," they characterize their own messages as "sharing" or "expressing," never as "writing."

Informing

One of the most pervasive practices on r.a.t.s. is sharing information relevant to the soap opera. Fans share knowledge of the show's history, in part, because the genre demands it (Seiter, Borchers, Kreutzner, & Warth, 1989). Any soap has broadcast more material than any single fan can remember; most soaps have now shown thousands of episodes over periods of years. Furthermore, because soap operas are shown so frequently, many fans miss shows. Although the redundancy soaps use to compensate for this has been the source of countless parodies, the scripts are in fact selective in which history they emphasize, and often refer to a past that is not fully explained. This would be inconsequential, as it is in most other television genres, except that soaps continually draw and build on their pasts, weaving ever more convoluted narrative webs. Furthermore, as textual analysts have argued, soaps imply more meanings than they need to move the narrative forward (see Allen, 1983, 1985). The more information one has about the characters' histories and social networks, the more one can read into the current dramas (Allen, 1985; Kielwasser & Wolf, 1989; Whetmore & Kielwasser, 1983). Deep knowledge allows viewers to build richer interpretations of stories and find the resolutions more rewarding.

Such information often comes at the request of people who have missed a show, as is the case in this post (March 3, 1992), in which a fan who missed the most recent episode pleads to be filled in:

>Help.....I read Lance's awesome update..but am dying to know...did Haley
>marry Will.......I am just dying to know....and if she did wish I saw Uncle
>Pork Chops face when she announces there news....

Yes they were married. And the cliffhanger yesterday
was Will getting arrested at Nexus as Trevor walks in.

The information exchanged about the show often stretches into the show's past. In this post (February 25, 1992), for instance, one fan corrects another's foggy memory about two characters introduced to the show approximately three years earlier:

>I have been wondering about two of the newer characters: Dixie (Ditsie!)
>and Will. Back when they were in Pigeon Hollow and were played by other
>actors, I seem to recall that they were *not* brother and sister, but
>were MARRIED! When they moved to PV because of Adam's scheming, they

When Dixie and Will came to PV, if I remember correctly, for a very short
time, we didn't know what their relationship was. But it became apparent
soon after they WERE brother and sister. I don't recall ever thinking
they were married.

The retellings above are fairly straight reports; however, they are also quite personalized and affect-laden, creating a sense not only of the show, but also of the writers. In other words, in the process of telling less-informed fans what happened on the show, these fans are creating public identities. This is most clear in those informative posts that are virtuoso performances. The most stylized information-sharing practice is the "update." Updates are long messages written by designated participants to summarize a day's show. In this excerpt (March 1, 1992), an updater uses punctuation, selective embedding of dialogue and detail, and other stylistic techniques to liven up what could be reported only as "Erica's secretary, Joan, sold her shares of Erica's company to Dimitri. Erica felt betrayed:"

> Joan, pressed beyond temptation by Dimitri's double-offer to buy her (23)
> shares in Enchantement at 3x the market price, and to employ her brother
> (Eddie - the arc welder - "thinks beer is one of the major food groups") at an
> Italian design firm, sells-out. Erica: "How could you do this to me??! After
> all the warm cameraderie, the intimate lunches??" Joan: "Lunches?!" Erica:
> "...light lunches...coffee...Joan, did you betray me because the _meals_
> weren't large enough???!"

Using a very different style, involving capitalization and the embedding of
what she calls her "cynical (or insightful) comments," this updater also brings
a distinctive narrative personality to her retellings (February 25, 1992):

> Dimitri sees Nat and asks if she can forgive him and if they can
> have a life together. Nat says that she HAS forgiven him, but they
> can't have a life together because she doesn't love him. { I don't
> know - seems like a good reason to me. } She says that she NEEDED him
> and that she was dependent on him, but she never really LOVED him.
> Dimitri thinks she wants to get back with Trevor and such { DIM -- BUY
> A CLUE -- she don't LOVE you. } She says she needs to be
> self-sufficient { watch out Nat -- you're heading into very unfamiliar
> territory } . Later Dimitri is in the park and is thinking, maybe,
> just maybe, he needed to save someone and Nat needed to be rescued.

These informative posts allow fans who have missed shows to know as
much about them as those who saw the shows. They also provide plat-
forms for building public personas.

R.a.t.s. fans also draw on information beyond the soap operas'
texts to interpret soaps, often pooling information from soap magazines,
star appearances, commercial computer networks, and other sources.
These scoops include previews of what will happen on future shows and
personal news about the actors. Though the information originates outside
of the soap opera fiction, this kind of information also affects fans interpretations of the show, as this post (May 14, 1992) about two actors who
played the lovers Trevor and Natalie indicates:

> >I gotta know this: What is the story between James Kiberd and Kate Collins?
> >Don't they get along? (I need some juicy gossip here!) :)
>
> There have been lots of rumors about the fact that Kiberd and Collins
> don't get along. It all started WAY back when Collins found out that
> Nat's "new" love interest was going to be Trevor. According to the
> Soap Rags, she ran into her dressing room in tears.
>
> There hasn't been a lot said recently about this. I saw Jean LeClerc
> (Jeremy) at a Woman's Show last month, and he said eveyone on the set
> (including Collins and Kiberd) got along just fine. LeClerc also
> lavished praise on Collins for her recent performance of Nat/Janet.

> Someone who saw Kiberd last year said he hinted that Collins was a
> lesbian, but again, I heard LeClerc say he once had a "relationship"
> with Collins (now they are just friends), and she is currently
> "involved" with someone. Either way, it's her business and really
> has nothing to do with her ability to act.

> However, it *does* seem that the chemistry that used to be there
> between Kiberd and Collins (when they play Nat & Trevor) just isn't
> there anymore...They used to have a LOT more spark!

The more soap-relevant knowledge fans have, the richer their interpretations of the shows can be. A large group of fans can do what even the most committed single fan cannot: accumulate, retain, and continually recirculate unprecedented amounts of relevant information. Participants in r.a.t.s. pool their memories and external resources to provide all with an exceptionally rich knowledge base. R.a.t.s. participants collaboratively provide all with the resources to get more story from the same material, enhancing many members' soap readings and pleasures.

In addition to enhancing the soap opera's worth, talk about soaps also enhances participation in the group. Hobson (1989) claims that knowledge of the events that happened on the soaps are a form of cultural capital because it enables participation in the social groups that form around soap talk, a point elaborated by Fiske (1992). Soaps serve as the capital of the fan culture. People who do not watch the shows cannot participate in the debates of fan community (Jenkins, 1992). Talk that distributes information about the show thus functions not just to help the information-poor enjoy the soaps more fully, as is argued in most current work on soaps, but to help them participate in the fan community more fully as well. Talk does not just enrich the soaps, the soaps enrich the talk.

The updates quoted here show that the presentation of information about the show can be entertaining in its own right. Brown (1990) compares soap retellings to traditional orally transmitted narratives, suggesting that experienced retellers stylize their performances to provide entertainment to the listeners. Clearly this is the case on r.a.t.s.; updaters and others turn simple reporting into a creative art, making the messages entertaining beyond their referential value. These performative retellings are a transformation of the soap opera—here *All My Children* becomes a resource on which further entertainment can be built.

Fans not only enjoy gaining information about the show, but also enjoy giving it, as has been observed by Hobson (1982), Brown (1990, 1994), Geraghty (1991), and Jenkins (1992). According to Jenkins, the pleasure of retelling may lie in its ability to help sustain the emotional immediacy that attracted the fan to the show initially. In r.a.t.s. another, more social, pleasure surely lies in that fact that skilled retellings are rewarded with expressions of praise and gratitude.

Speculating

The fans on r.a.t.s. use many posts to speculate, treating the story like a game in which they try to discern what a character is like, what could happen, what should happen, what will happen, how it will happen, and what the ramifications throughout the soap community could be. Textual analysis (Allen, 1985; Brunsdon, 1983; Geraghty, 1991; Hobson, 1982) has shown that soaps encourage viewers to make such inferential leaps by resisting final resolutions and through other formulaic devices which I elaborate below. For example, each scene ends at the point of maximum suspense, creating, by the end of each episode, a set of "unresolved narrative puzzles to carry viewers across the time gap from one episode to another" (Geraghty, 1991, p. 10).

Soaps also encourage speculation through characters and thematic content. Central to all soaps are the dozens of richly interconnected characters. The viewers who have followed for some time, or read r.a.t.s., build rich understandings of the characters and their historical interconnections. This soap-based knowledge offers an entree into speculation on what feelings, beliefs, and concerns motivate characters' behavior.

Many of these scholars have also argued that speculation is encouraged by the soaps' reflection of the viewers' social world, which pushes them to draw on that knowledge to fill in story blanks and imagine story possibilities. The characters' experiences, although obviously exaggerated, are akin to viewers' own (Allen, 1985; Ang, 1985; Brown, 1994; Hobson, 1982; Livingstone, 1989). Soap stories revolve around intimate relationships, particularly the familial and romantic. Indeed, soaps are *about* emotionality in personal relationships. Though fans are quick to point out that the fictional circumstances may be outrageously contrived, they use their own experience and knowledge of emotion and intimate relationships to speculate on how characters feel. In this post (March 18, 1992) a woman draws on her knowledge of Livia and Terrance, and also her own and (vicariously) her mother's experiences, to speculate on why Terrance and his mother Livia behaved as they did when Terrance's long-lost father ("Breaker") showed up in town:

> >Livia didn't tell Terrance the truth abouth Breaker for 1 week, Terrance is
> >acting like a class A jerk.
>
> I disagree. I can understand your point of view because you're a single
> parent and all, but I think Terrance is acting like any normal teenager
> would. I was in a similar situation when my dad decided he wanted to a)
> meet me, and b) be a real dad after 12 years of non-support (and
> non-contact). My mother had never badmouthed my father *too* much, and I
> at least knew his name, etc. But having a total stranger tell me he's my

father was weird. I didn't react like Terrance because my mother never
tried to hide anything from me, although she admitted to feeling
slightly jealous at the thought of him being in my life now. Needless to
say, Breaker is a typical, (IMHO) black male. Livia was overeacting
because she was scared and felt threatened. She didn't want to lose
Terrance. Unfortunately she didn't consider how Terrance might react --
obviously. Ok, so Terrance doesn't have to be quite so rude, but the boy
is upset, confused, and hurt. I think he'll calm down soon (at least I
hope so), he and Livia can have a heart to heart, and everything will be
ok. It *is* kind of weird tho -- you'd think if anyone, Terrance would
be mad at Breaker.

Here, the responding poster is inferring the reasons for the characters'
behavior: Livia "was scared and felt threatened," Terrance "is upset, confused, and hurt." Both posters are also going beyond speculation on
Terrance and Livia's psyches; they are publically negotiating socioemotional norms. The characters become the "emotional representatives"
(Geraghty, 1991) through which fans can articulate these private experiences. In this case, a single mother and the daughter of a single mother
compare their sense of what behaviors are and are not appropriate for
children and parents in this kind of situation. By speculating together on
character perspectives fans are able to discuss socioemotional norms with
more ease than discussions between acquaintances usually allow. Brown
(1994) argues that the negotiation and discussion of social issues of concern to women is a form of resistant pleasure that accounts for why
women are so drawn to soap talk.

As the speculation that Terrance will calm down and he and Livia
will talk demonstrates, viewers often speculate on what will happen in the
show's future. Guessing what will happen is the most game-like practice
of soap fandom, and participants draw on several resources to make their
predictions. In the previous example, the fan relied on her own experience
to predict Terrance's. In this post (March 5, 1992), a fan uses her knowledge of the show's recent events concerning the just-raped Gloria and
Dimitri, past events between Dimitri and Nat(alie), and her sense of
Dimitri's character to predict that he will try to save (and presumably fall
in love with) Gloria:

Wait a minute. Dim just hired Glo to be Angelique's nurse during her
recovery. Glo is going to move into WierdWind. Glo has confided in
Dim about her upcoming rape trail..Dim is sympathetic. Does anyone
else think Dim is going to go into his "white knight to the rescue of
the poor troubled helpless blonde victim" act. It happened with
Nat, why not Glo?

Fans also take advantage of their knowledge of soap opera's
video-cinematic and formal codes (Allen, 1983) to predict what will hap-

pen. As Geraghty (1991) argues, "only soaps invite the audience both to enter intimately into a fictional world and to stand back and view with dispassion the formal conventions through which that world is constructed" (p. 10). Allen (1983) offers this example of how audiences use video-cinematic codes:

> A device such as the unmotivated camera movement, which would probably go unnoticed in the average Hollywood film, is such a departure from the norm in soap opera style that its use immediately privileges the content of the shot for the audience—the viewer "reads" this device as "something important is about to happen." (p. 100)

Other formal codes include the "soap opera's use of time and space . . . codes of acting . . . the use of multiple intersecting narratives . . . nondiegetic music" and many more (Allen, 1983, p. 100). Viewers read these internal conventions to predict future events. In this post (April 22, 1992), two fans draw on their knowledge of the narrative workings of "Soap-Land" to predict immanent doom for the happy couple of Jeremy and Ceara:

> >Isn't it about time that St. Jeremy and Sunset Ceara
> >parted ways? What happened to those two characters?
>
> On Tuesday's show, they were shown to be "blissfully" happy,
> all kissy-face and goo-goo eyed over each other. Which can
> only mean ONE THING in Soap-Land:
>
> The writers are setting us up. One of them will soon be
> gone, or a deep tragedy will occur to one/both of them. NO
> ONE can stay happy for long in Pine Valley...(remember when
> Angie and Jesse were SOOOOO happy? Then they killed Jesse
> off....remember when Greg and Jenny were SOOOOO happy? And
> Cliff and Nina....Tad and Dixie....)

Not long after this post, Ceara died tragically in an accidental shooting. Here, a woman picks up on a typical soap-operatic foreshadowing to predict a death:

> In Wednesday's episode Will said:
>   "Hayley I will love you until I DIE."
> Goodbye Will

It is clear, especially in these latter two examples, that the exercise of genre competence involved in speculation is pleasurable. Fans who are not involved in soap opera discussion networks can also guess at the show's outcomes and enjoy both the speculation and, as often happens, generating correct predictions. However, speculation is certainly more rewarding when there are others with whom to share those guesses. Like information one did not have, predictions one did not think of can enhance the meanings found in the show. Furthermore, guessing correctly in public shows others just how genre competent one is; hence, fans on r.a.t.s. are delighted and quick to point out when they were first to predict an outcome. This pride is encouraged by other participants who, upon seeing on the show what had been predicted on r.a.t.s., often extend congratulatory praise to those who called it in advance. As a result, a new, inherently social pleasure emerges: recognition for one's soap opera expertise. These posters' expert speculations on the soap are a resource for developing one's own genre competence. Speculation, when practiced collectively, offers the fans pleasure and pride beyond that which the soap writers could intend.

Criticizing

R.a.t.s. fans often find the soap opera aggravating, and many use their posts to criticize the show. Criticism involves evaluating the show at multiple levels including internal consistency and the quality of props, sets, acting, writing, and ideological content among other criteria. The information one has about the soap, one's understanding of the genre, and one's understanding of reality are used as criteria for continual assessment of the stories. Work in cultural studies has demonstrated how viewers assess the shows' messages, story construction, and, above all, realism (Ang, 1985; Hobson, 1989; Liebes & Katz, 1989; Seiter et al., 1989). Viewers also critique their own involvement with the shows, occasionally experiencing mixed feelings stemming from disapproval of the genre's perceived ideology, while enjoying the stories tremendously (Ang, 1985; Brown, 1994; Liebes & Katz, 1989). What is especially important is that criticisms are not just the limits that temper involvement. Criticism is a kind of involvement itself, one that can be just as pleasurable as noncritical involvement.

The most-criticized aspect of soaps in r.a.t.s., as previous research would lead one to expect, is realism. In this post (March 5, 1992), a woman draws on personal experience to criticize the credibility of the show's portrayal of the Immigration and Naturalization Service:

> This immigration thing is REALLY getting on my nerves. My husband and
> I had to go through immigration as he is a British citizen and needed
> to get a green card. No one EVER visited our house and it took
> forever to get an appointment (after they had lost the paperwork and
> we had to refile!). I'd say it took us a little under a year.

Another thing, Brian doesn't have a job that can support him and is
still in school. I find it very hard to believe that Immigration
would allow him to "sponsor" An-Li. Geez, we had to show them
certified letters from the bank and my job to prove that we could
survive without my husband trying to collect. Oh well, it's only a
soap after all...

In this case (March 4, 1992), a man "nitpicks" about the credibility of the
show's procedures for arresting a suspect:

OK folks, I know I'm nitpicking here, but this lack of legal procedure
on AMC is driving me nuts. OK, Will buddy gets arrested in NYC.
PV is in Pennsylvania. Does the word extradition mean anything here?
NO, Will buddy is in the PV Cop Cruiser heading right back to the
PVPD 5 minutes later...

Often, when fans find the show unrealistic, they criticize its ideological agendas. In this next post (March 4, 1992), a fan attacks on the
grounds that the story represents teenagers and women inaccurately.
Interestingly, this poster also criticizes the writers for sending a particular
message—"problems cannot be solved with alcohol"—too often:

I don't like the fact that the writers are portraying Haley as a lush. Don't
teens get a bad enough rap without the writers doing it also. Teenagers are
able to handle their problems without drugs and alcohol also. Anyway the
alcoholic story line has been covered twice on this show, once with Tom and
once with Eileen. I think the writers have already made the point that
problems cannot be solved with alcohol. Again they have taken a strong
female character and turned her into a weakling because a man does her
wrong. Enough already give the women on the show their backbones or lets
get Dr. Brothers in there to do some heavy duty therapy. Great story line
all the women in PV in group therapy for the terminally love sick.

Even when the show's flaws are not irritating, r.a.t.s. participants
enthusiastically point out shortcomings in the show's production. In this
post (December 3, 1992), a long-time poster refers to a scene in which a
character was trapped in a crypt and had an unfortunate run-in with a
skeleton. The poster jokes about the disappearance of another character,
Bobby, who, years earlier, went upstairs to get his skis and was never seen
or mentioned on the show again. She goes on to call attention to a "lack of
thoroughness by the prop department:"

When that skeleton fell out onto Erica, my first thought was "HEY — it's
Bobby!". Of course, we all know Bobby is safely ensconced in the Martin
attic. My next thought was that it was probably an illicit Marick
mistress from days gone by who had also been locked in the mausoleum by a

crazy housekeeper/mother-in-law. Alas, it looks like some sort of caretaker
judging by the cloak and ring of keys bigger than any keys a baby ever
teethed on.
Did you notice, however, that the caretaker was wearing a cloak, but had
nothing on underneath it? Lack of thoroughness by the prop department.
It also stayed remarkably intact once it fell, considering there are no
longer any muscles or ligaments to hold it together.

Even though these fans are highly critical, they do not become less involved as result. In fact, r.a.t.s. fans enhance their pleasure in many ways by discussing their criticisms. Venting their frustrations publically and hearing the agreement that ensues creates a community united partly by their opposition to the show, especially its writers. The other participants become allies with whom one can get through the show's sometimes serious flaws. R.a.t.s. participants build solidarity out of their common aggravations. This can be seen in some of the wording in the earlier posts: "OK folks . . ." and "Of course, we all know . . ." As a result, the community becomes more valuable.

Criticism also enhances the value of the community because it leads to socioemotional discussion. When fans criticize credibility by telling of their own experiences and criticize messages by telling how they think the world is, they are negotiating with one another how close relationships work and how they think they ought to work. Again, the soap is transformed into material with which to talk publically about personal concerns. Like speculation, criticism also involves the pleasure of using and displaying genre competence. Finally, and perhaps most importantly, criticism is usually performed as much as shared, as the posts are filled with evaluative markers, clever turns of phrase, creative new ideas, and the like. By using the show's flaws as material with which to entertain each other, the community becomes more than amusing enough to hold the participants' attention through the show's lows.

Reworking

One of the most creative ways in which criticism is handled is through reworking the show, posing what could or should have happened in place of what did (Hobson, 1989, 1990; Jenkins, 1992). Jenkins (1992) argues that fans of many shows find openings for their own elaboration in the text's rough spots. Although soaps, as we have seen, are designed to encourage speculation, their rough spots offer fans additional space for their own creative input, a space that goes beyond that intended by the shows' producers and writers. As Jenkins puts it, fans do not do "textual disintegration" but "home improvements" (p. 52). Hobson (1989, 1990), for instance, comments that fan criticism often comes packaged with suggestions for improvement, suggestions that are created by the fan.

This is illustrated next. The person who complained about the skeleton in a cloak (December 3, 1992) finishes her post by elaborating on her earlier thought of an "illicit Marick mistress," reworking the show's events to support an alternative scenario more imaginative than the one the writers' chose:

> Hmmmm -- the lack of anything on under the cloak kind of goes back to the illicit Marick mistress theory doesn't it? I think they missed a golden opportunity here. Wouldn't it have been a scream (so to speak) if the skeleton had been wearing a tattered ballgown like the one Erica wore for her dinner with "The Count". A note arranging a tryst, clutched in the bony fingers, would have confirmed Erica's suspicion that history was about to repeat itself.

This reworking is performative in many ways. The teller creates an entirely new scenario using the characters, props, setting, and history of the original scene. She peppers the presentation of her scenario with apt word choices ("wouldn't it have been a scream") and dramatic phrasing ("clutched in the bony fingers"). In a sense, this reworking is a show of its own.

In these two cases (August 28, 1992; August 31, 1992), fans respond to their criticism of show events by proposing less fanciful alternative scenarios based on what they would have done themselves:
Scene:

> Erica is sitting in the waiting room, distraught over her mother being admitted into the hopital awaiting surgery and...
> RUTH comes over and starts yelling at Erica about Charlie. I mean really hounds her, totally unjustfied, telling Erica she should be ashamed of herself for going out and leaving her poor mother home alone.
>
> Furiously, she tried to explain the situation to her when Nick comes along and stops the confrontation.

Come, come now. What a B$TCH! If this were me I would logde a complaint with the hospital about Ruth's attitude!!! Who does she think she is pulling this in a hospital when people (when she knows Erica's upset) are upset trying to deal with family crisis?? Poor Erica... Soaps usually don't make me mad, but this was ridiculous!! If I were Erica, I would have slapped her.

>Okay, now a nitpick. Yesterday during the fight scene, you saw a bunch of
>people around the perimeter of the room. Now, if I was in the room I would've
>vacated as soon as possible. I wouldn't wait around to get hit. The way
>they were flying around you think that they'd of hurt someone else. Okay,
>IOAS, IOAS, IOAS.
>

> Actually, if it were friends of mine fighting, I would have gone in a lot
> earlier than Charlie did to stop the fight. I am also sick and tired
> of having only men in the fight scene. IMHO, Brooke should have stepped
> in and helped out.

In the quoted material in this last post, the fan uses the phrase "IOAS," a r.a.t.s. acronym for "it's only a soap." IOAS functions somewhat like a mantra in the group, reminding them all that the show is not worth getting truly upset over. As these reworkings show, one way IOAS is put into practice is by transforming frustrations into creative alternatives. Other reworkings are not stimulated by criticism so much as a desire to present one's own rendition of possible events. Much like criticisms, reworkings enhance the posters' pleasure by flexing their genre competence and performative muscles while they enhance readers' pleasure through their creativity, wit, and interpretive insight.

DISCUSSION

The four practices discussed—informing, speculating, criticizing, and reworking—offer insight into why discussion is so important for soap opera fans. Such discussion increases the meanings, and hence the pleasures, participants can find in the dramas. Soap talk can provide meanings that negate those suggested by the soap or compensate for the show when it is weak (as in the case of criticisms and reworking). Soap talk also enables people to show off for one another their competence in making sense of the genre and their performative skill, and to engage in the social pleasures of performing and garnering praise and admiration. Soap talk also provides fans with the opportunity to negotiate and debate private socioemotional issues.

The analysis also has broader implications for the study of fan communities, suggesting ways in which fan interaction appropriates the media around which they form, supplementing them, personalizing them, altering them, and using them as a springboard for creativity and social exploration. Each of these appropriations takes form in particular genres of practice, genres that arise in response both to the show and the group's social concerns. The question of what practices are crucial to a particular fan group's social interaction is thus an important one for understanding the purposes met in fans' relationships to texts and to one another. Furthermore, it is an empirical question that cannot be adequately answered through survey, interview, or text-analytic methods, though each of those approaches can offer insights. The nuanced practices of fan interaction reside in the ordinary interaction fans have about shows, therefore it calls for detailed observational approaches.

Discussion is a way to provide one another with interpretive resources to which fans may not have access on their own. The information about the shows' history, current events, and production is one such group of resources. Another important interpretive resource is the expert fans who, through their retellings, speculations, criticisms, and reworkings, offer instructive models of how to read soap operas. Interpretive resources also come from fans' experiences, and the pooling of information about the real world further broadens the store of accessible knowledge one has with which to elaborate the meanings of the shows. Other fan communities may carve out other kinds of resources with which to enhance their media's meaning. The ways in which those resources take shape and the practices through which they are distributed are areas ripe for analysis in other groups.

Discussion also provides its own entertainment. As we have seen, the discourse on r.a.t.s. is loaded with expressive and humorous performances. This mitigates the irritation and boredom fans feel when they are not enjoying the show but want to remain engaged with it. We see this with criticism, in which attacks are accompanied by wit, expressions of camaraderie, and suggestions of better alternative scenarios. When the show is not disappointing, the entertaining quality of r.a.t.s. posts offers all its participants additional fun. Those fans who are particularly entertaining are establishing group-specific identities through their performances. By entertaining one another, in short, fans compensate for and enhance the show, establish personalities, and gain recognition. These phenomena too are likely to appear in different ways in other fan communities.

Finally, fan discussions of soaps open private realms for public discussion. Soaps offer safe terrain on which people can discuss their own and vicarious experiences with a broader range of people, comparing, refining, and negotiating understandings of their socioemotional environment. At times, r.a.t.s. participants go on tangents, moving from the soap opera to their own lives, beyond what is relevant to the show. The soap, in other words, is the pretext for discussion of many things other than the soap, including emotion, relationships, and selves. This suggests that a broad account of fandom needs to consider the spectrum of topics raised in conjunction with the object of fandom. The opportunity to discuss particular topics is a motivation for becoming and remaining a fan of a particular medium.

I close by speaking specifically about computer-mediated fan communities. Both the Internet and the commercial networks are growing at extraordinary rates, encompassing ever-increasing amounts of people. There are already hundreds, if not thousands, of fan groups organized through these networks. The expansion of the net offers more and more fans the ability to participate in fan groups, even when they have no other fans in their face-to-face social circles. Besides unprecedented access to fan culture, the net makes it possible for fan groups to attain unprecedented size. It also allows those on the production end to read and talk with their audience. Several celebrities are online; ABC has installed computers in the studios of each of its soap operas; America Online hosts many synchronous celebrity-fan interaction events daily. Producers of many shows read the groups which discuss them (Grimes, 1992). In the case of the (now-defunct) television show *Parker Lewis Can't Lose*, writers even named characters after personalities in the Parker Lewis discussion group. As these groups become larger and more prevalent, they are increasingly likely to influence the phenomena around which they form as well as the social lives of their members.

REFERENCES

Allen, R. C. (1983). On reading soaps: A semiotic primer. In E. A. Kaplan (Ed.), *Regarding television* (pp. 97-108) Los Angeles: American Film Institute.

Allen, R. C. (1985). *Speaking of soap operas*. Chapel Hill: University of North Carolina.

Ang, I. (1985). *Watching Dallas: Soap opera and the melodramatic imagination*. New York: Routledge.

Babrow, A. S. (1987). Student motives for watching soap operas. *Journal of Broadcasting and Electronic Media, 31*, 309-321.

Babrow, A. S. (1989). An expectancy-value analysis of the student soap opera audience. *Communication Research, 16*, 155-178.

Bourdieu, P. (1977). *Outline of a theory of practice.* Cambridge: Cambridge University Press.

Brown, M. E. (1990). Motley moments: Soap opera, carnival, gossip and the power of the utterance. In M. E. Brown (Ed.), *Television and women's culture* (pp. 183-200). Newbury Park, CA: Sage.

Brown, M. E. (1994). *Soap opera and women's talk: The pleasure of resistance.* Newbury Park, CA: Sage.

Brunsdon, C. (1983). Notes on a soap opera. In E.A. Kaplan (Ed.), *Regarding television* (pp. 76-83). Frederick, MD: University Publications of America.

Cantor, M. G., & Pingree, S. (1983). *The soap opera.* Beverly Hills: Sage.

Compesi, R. J. (1980). Gratifications of daytime TV serial viewers. *Journalism Quarterly, 57*, 155-158.

Fiske, J. (1992). The cultural economy of fandom. In L. Lewis (Ed.), *The adoring audience: Fan culture and popular media* (pp. 30-49). London: Routledge.

Geraghty, C. (1991). *Women and soap opera.* Cambridge: Polity.

Grimes, W. (1992, December 1). Computer networks foster cultural chatting for modern times. *The New York Times*, p. B1.

Hobson, D. (1982). *Crossroads: The drama of soap opera.* London: Methuen.

Hobson, D. (1989). Soap operas at work. In E. Seiter, H. Borchers, G. Kreutzner, & E. Warth (Eds.), *Remote control: Television, audiences, and cultural power* (pp. 150-167). New York: Routledge.

Hobson, D. (1990). Women audiences and the workplace. In M. E. Brown (Ed.), *Television and women's culture* (pp. 71-74). Newbury Park, CA: Sage.

Jenkins, H. (1992). *Textual poachers: Television fans and participatory cultures.* London: Routledge.

Kielwasser, A. P., & Wolf, M. A. (1989). The appeal of soap opera: An analysis of process and quality in dramatic serial gratifications. *Journal of Popular Culture, 23*(2), 111-134.

Lemish, D. (1985). Soap opera viewing in college: A naturalistic inquiry. *Journal of Broadcasting & Electronic Media, 29*(3), 275-293.

Liebes, T., & Katz, E. (1989). On the critical abilities of television viewers. In E. Seiter, H. Borchers, G. Kreutzner, & E. Warth (Eds.), *Remote control: Television, audiences, and cultural power* (pp. 204-222). New York: Routledge.

Livingstone, S. M. (1989). Interpretive viewers and structured programs: The implicit representation of soap opera characters. *Communication Research, 16*, 25-57.

Perse, E., & Rubin, R. (1989). Attribution in social and parasocial relationships. *Communication Research, 16*, 59-77.

Reid, B. (1993, August 6). Usenet readership report for July, 1993. *news.lists,* Usenet.

Reid, B. (no date). Monthly Usenet readership report. *news.lists,* Usenet.

Rubin, A. M. (1985). Uses of daytime television soap operas by college students. *Journal of Broadcasting & Electronic Media, 29*(3), 241-258.

Seiter, E., Borchers, H., Kreutzner, G., & Warth E. (1989). "Don't treat us like we're so stupid and naive": Towards an ethnography of soap opera viewers. In E. Seiter, H. Borchers, G. Kreutzner, & E. Warth (Eds.), *Remote control: Television, audiences, and cultural power,* (pp. 223-247). New York: Routledge.

Whetmore, E. J., & Kielwasser, A. P. (1983). The soap opera audience speaks: A preliminary report. *Journal of American Culture, 6*(3), 110-116.

Williams, C. T. (1992). "It's time for my story:" Oral culture in a technological era—Towards a methodology for soap opera audiences. In S. Frentz (Ed.), *Staying tuned: Contemporary soap opera criticism* (pp. 69-88). Bowling Green, OH: Bowling Green State University Popular Press.

▶8

Uncertain Utopia: Science Fiction Media Fandom & Computer Mediated Communication*

Andrea MacDonald
University of Pennsylvania

> "According to my mom, I'm such a big shot that she's threatening to have her uterus bronzed."—Steven Speilberg
>
> I don't know who's weirder, Steven's [Speilberg] mom for saying that, or him for repeating that in public . . . —an email post by Alex

Both computer-mediated communication (CMC) and media fandom have recently become "hot" topics in the academy—for very similar reasons. Computer-mediated communication, that is, the type of communication that occurs across computer networks, offers the promise of more democ-

*Parts of this chapter have previously been published as "They're Virtually Fans," *Antenna: The Newsletter of the Mercurians Special Interest Group, 5*. I would like to thank Larry Gross, Henry Jenkins, and Roberta Pearson for their thoughtful comments on various stages of this project; and Pamela Inglesby for reading and editing drafts of this chapter. Further, my deep appreciation goes to the women who participated in this project and for their willing support, comments, and help.

ratic communication, while fans provide an example of the active audience. Democratic communication, according to theorists, is possible within computer-mediated spaces due to participants' broader access and greater anonymity (presumably including an absence of bodily signifiers such as race or gender) than in traditional media. Those who have studied media fandom closely have found an interpretative community that "rereads and rewrites" (Jenkins, 1991, p. 170) fictive texts, thus demonstrating that audience members are not the passive dupes of the mass media industries. Each area offers the prospect of resisting dominant norms. Studying how a fan group moves to computer-mediated spaces allows for a concentrated look at the potentialities and problems of both CMC and media fandom.[1]

From a theoretical standpoint, studying media fandom within computer-mediated spaces provides a unique opportunity to explore how CMC may change our popular culture and our pleasure time activities and gain insights into how a particular group integrates the possibilities of CMC.[2] For example, answers to such questions as: do computer-mediated spaces replicate face-to-face hierarchies; or how, when, and where are fans allowed to speak, might be found. This chapter addresses these issues by drawing on examples from my experiences with computer-mediated science fiction media fandom. I have spent over four years (Fall 1990 to present) watching *Quantum Leap* fans interact via USENET and email lists.[3] The first email list was initially set up to talk about the popular network television show, *Quantum Leap.* This electronic mailing list has an interesting history that demonstrates how women's conversation in computer-mediated spaces is shoved to the side of mainstream or public CMC, contrary to the expectations of some CMC theorists.

---

[1]One such potential problem is the replication of hierarchies. Fan theorists, for the most part, contend that science fiction media fandom lacks hierarchies of social power. In my observations this is clearly not the case, and I discuss fan hierarchies later in this chapter. Another hierarchy problem stems from theories about CMC conflating the democratizing possibilities of CMC with hierarchicaless communication domains. "Who controls access?", "How can I get access?", and "When am I allowed to speak?" are just a few questions that when asked, clearly undermine the position that CMC lacks hierarchies.

[2]I use pleasure here instead of leisure to emphasize that leisure time activities are supposed to provide pleasure. I also use pleasure here as a provocation to the reader. Studies of CMC usually emphasize the functional or practical aspects—not the pleasurable—and thus I hope to pique the reader by stressing the connection between pleasure and CMC.

[3]Many of these women are well known in fan circles so to protect their anonymity I use the pseudonyms they have chosen themselves.

My narrow focus on women media fans results from my earlier investigations of media fandom and CMC.[4] In my studies of CMC, I have found a milieu that does contain the probability of anonymity and thus an uninhibited form of communication but more often than not replicates many of the hierarchical formations that exist in noncomputer-mediated communication. Presumably, the lack of physical demarkers allows a user to be measured on the basis of their quality of communication, not automatically discounted due to race, gender, or class; yet, on the other hand, users who do not conform to "nettiquete"[5] end up flamed[6] or spammed.[7] This paradoxical communication environment demonstrates how social relations are renegotiated when a new technology is introduced. Marvin (1988) notes,

> New media intrude on these negotiations by providing new platforms on which old groups confront one another. . . . Old practices are then painfully revised, and group habits are reformed. New practices do not so much flow directly from technologies that inspire them as they are improvised out of old practices that no longer work in new settings. Efforts are launched to restore social equilibrium, and these efforts have significant social risks. In the end, it is less in new media practices, which come later and point toward a resolution of these conflicts (or, more likely, a temporary truce), than in the uncertainty of emerging and contested practices of communication that the struggle of groups to define and locate themselves is most easily observed. (p. 5)

In terms of CMC users, the technology provides a new medium through which new communication formulations can percolate. But as computing norms emerge, old social practices merge with new creating a different but not radically new discursive space. Users of CMC, at times, experience uninhibited communication; at other times, they are locked into hierarchical social practices.

I concentrate primarily on the Internet although there are commercial networks (i.e., CompuServe, Genie, America Online) that have very popular science fiction forums or topic groups. The Internet has cur-

---

[4]Some of my results appear in MacDonald (1992).

[5]*Nettiquete* refers to the conventions that are considered good manners in computer-mediated communication, for example, staying on topic, or judiciously quoting previous messages to give context.

[6]*Flaming* is "an acrimonious dispute, especially when conducted on a public electronic forum such as USENET" (Raymond, 1993, p. 182).

[7]A term originated by multiuser dimension users (see footnote 12), "to crash a program by over running a fixed-size buffer with excessively large input data" (Raymond, 1993, p. 389). In practice what occurs is overflowing the offender's email box with garbage messages.

rently achieved notoriety in the popular press and is perceived by the government as being the backbone of the Infobahn. Further, the commercial
networks have started to provide access to the Internet as part of their services, so the Internet is the one "area" that is accessible by commercial
and not-for-profit network services (including universities, military organizations, and the commercial organizations that are a part of the Internet
but are not in the business of providing Internet access).

In the following sections I first briefly describe the television show,
Quantum Leap, whose fandom is one of the focal points of this chapter.
Then I attempt to define what a fan is and begin tracing fan hierarchies and
how they are replicated within computer-mediated spaces. Next, I briefly
foray into how science fiction media fandom and CMC have formed a
symbiotic relationship. I then define two areas of fan computer-mediated
communication: electronic mail and USENET. Finally, I delve into my case
study on *Quantum Leap* media fandom explicating the contradictory communication arena that comprises computer-mediated communication.

AN ANTHOLOGY BY ANY OTHER NAME

Quantum Leap aired from March 1989 to May 1993 for a total of 95
episodes (Kilgour, et al., 1993). The show was created by Donald
Bellisario, who also created *Magnum P.I.*, and was distributed by
Universal Studios. The basic story line concerns a physicist named Sam
Beckett, played by Scott Bakula, who was in the process of creating a time
travel machine. Prior to the government cutting off funding for the project,
Sam jumped into the time machine and disappeared but the time machine
did not quite work. Instead of sending Sam back in time, it sent his
essence back to occupy the body of another person (a different one each
episode) and his body remained behind in the present. His best friend,
Rear Admiral Albert "Al" Calavicci, played by Dean Stockwell, kept contact with Sam through his brain waves and appeared to Sam in the form of
a hologram. Each episode featured Sam figuring out what he had to do to
right some wrong; Sam then leapt on to the next encounter in time.
Supposedly, a higher being was at the root of all this.

Donald Bellisario, in answering a fan's question about how the
idea of the show was developed, said,

> I really can't, other than to say that I wanted to do a show that was an
> anthology, and an anthology is a very nasty word to a network or a
> studio because they never or rarely are successful. And I wanted to
> find a way to do an anthology that could be successful, where we
> could each week tell a different story. And I felt the way to do that was

to have two people that the audience would come to love and be able to follow week to week and know them and therefore we could tell a different story every week. And it just kinda comes. You don't know where it comes from. (Smith, 1990)

Quantum Leap was Bellisario's way of getting around the network's perception that anthologies cannot work. By having Sam travel in time, the show has a new set and new characters every week. Sam's leaps are constrained within his life time,[8] approximately from the early 1950s to when Sam "leapt" back in time in 1995. Bellisario claims that this constraint on Sam's leaping lends believability to the show:

No. No. No. I did not want to go back beyond his own lifetime, because once you start to have him popping into the Civil War, and on a ship with Christopher Columbus, and all that kind of stuff, it loses—this is really gonna sound weird—it loses credibility! . . . I could buy when he leaps into 1953, 'cause I was there. I can't buy back beyond that. (Smith, 1990)

Perhaps Bellisario also worried that the expense of a time travel show, with elaborate period sets, would scare the networks off.

A FAN IS NOT A COOLING DEVICE

The mainstream media and academy define fans along a continuum, ranging from "social deviant" to "aficionado" (Jenson, 1992). They are either zealots of mass culture or magically creative individuals reworking mainstream meanings into new resistant forms. So, what is a fan? For the most part fans are people who attend to media texts, icons, stars, or sports teams in greater than usual detail. Not all fandom is star-driven but stars do play a role in fan's construction of the "fictive universe," a term that describes the rules, history, characters, and so forth of a particular text. Fans use intertextual cues, such as previous story lines and their understandings of the world, to help construct the meaning of their favorite text. An intertextual clue may be related to a star, such as using Dean Stockwell's pro-conservation stance to understand his character, Al, on the television show *Quantum Leap;*[9] or to the rules of a particular fictive universe, for example, *Star Trek's* "Prime Directive."

---

[8]This "rule" was subsequently broken during the fourth (1991-92) and fifth (1992-93) seasons with the shows, "A Leap for Lisa" and "The Leap Between the States."

[9]In several episodes, Al has mini-lectures on conservation topics such as recycling. Fans of Al and Dean have gone so far as to pay for his star on the Hollywood Walk of Fame by earning the money through recycling.

Fans are people who attend to a text more closely than other types of audience members. Texts provide a focal point through which fans can identify to which community they belong. They might even adopt ideals, beliefs, and values (or ideology depending on how you look at it) that they feel the text valorizes. For example, Bacon-Smith (1992) notes how *Trek* fans incorporate the concept of "IDIC: infinite diversity in infinite combinations" (p. 6) (the need for tolerance when dealing with people of different sexuality, race, or gender) into their lives Some fans choose to congregate and share their interests either by talking, writing, painting, or singing about them. Others are "lurkers," either unable or unwilling to actively participate in a community of fans. Some are fans of a star, some are fans of a fictive universe, some are both simultaneously; the type of affiliation depends on the text in question. This instability stems from the fan in question.

The fans I discuss in this chapter are women fans of the television show *Quantum Leap*. Their meeting point, an electronic mailing list, arose out of their interest in *Quantum Leap* and its stars, Scott Bakula and Dean Stockwell. They are by no means a group of orgiastic fans unable to differentiate reality from fantasy. They are capable of critical distance from the show and the actors. They criticize, ogle, share information, and discuss their interests in the show and the actors. These women are not mere vessels of mainstream popular culture; they take that popular culture and use it as the starting point for their community of and for women.

Fan Hierarchies

Fandom, just like the legitimate culture Bourdieu (1984) describes, is hierarchized. Yet, delineating fandom along a hierarchy of any kind is a problematic act because fandom views itself as being antithetical to "mundane" social norms. Part and parcel of fans' social construction of fandom are notions of equality, tolerance, and community. Fans do not explicitly recognize hierarchies, and academics also hesitate to recognize hierarchies in fandom. Jenkins (1991, 1992), although never specifically denying the existence of hierarchies within fandom, does not address them and implies that they do not exist by focusing on the grassroots production of fan culture. Bacon-Smith (1992), although firmly denying the existence of fan hierarchies, notes that fans divide into groups. She calls them "circles" and contends they are more like mini-communes. Yet, she notes that fans are categorized by level of knowledge regarding the fictional universe of a television show (personal communication, Fall 1993). Based on my observations, however, hierarchies can be identified.

Hierarchies exist along multiple dimensions. These dimensions may be broken down by knowledge, level of fandom, access to "inside" knowledge, leaders, and control of venue, and can be defined in the following ways:

Hierarchy of Knowledge. A fan's position within a specific fan community, such as *Star Trek,* is determined by the amount of knowledge that person has about the fictional universe.

Hierarchy of Fandom Level, or Quality. Separates fans by amount of fan participation—those who attend conventions and other organized events versus those who do not. A quality distinction occurs between fans who attend for-fan -by-fan conventions versus fans who attend industry-sponsored conventions. The quality distinction is vexed by *Quantum Leap* convention availability. The only conventions available for *Quantum Leap* fans (at the time of the study) were industry conventions sponsored by Universal Studios and organized by Creation Con. Unlike other commercial cons, attending these conventions serves as a badge of honor, whereas in other fandoms attending an industry convention would not be regarded as highly.

Hierarchy of Access. Some fans have direct access to actors, producers of the show, production personnel, and in some rare cases actual shootings of episodes. For example, this cross-post[10] from Genie about Scott Bakula's appearance on *Murphy Brown:*

> All,
> Yes, MB [the filming of an episode of the show *Murphy Brown*] was great! As [name deleted] mentioned, Murphy was throwing darts at Peter's pic and every second one would bounce off. Everyone, including the actor's were cracking up, especially after they stopped filming so Candice[sic] could practice. Gotall [sic] three, and then proceded [sic] to film again, and again, the second one bounced off! It will be interesting to see what pic of Scott they used, something we all have, or something taken especially for the show. Yes, we can't give away any secrets as you guys will just crack up when you see how this ep. [episode] which airs . . . oops! When does it air? Did they say Oct 25? I think so. Anyway, I have to go to softball, will tell the rest of the story when I get back. Need to tell you about what happend [sic] after the taping. Wish me luck all, be back later!

The posting of such a report of an episode filming is generally followed by expressions of mock (perhaps even real) jealousy on the part of other members of the mailing list.

---

[10]Cross-posting is the act of taking material from one forum and placing it onto another or simultaneously posting to multiple venues.

Hierarchy of Leaders. Each fandom is broken down into smaller groups. These divisions can occur along geographic, fan interest, or friendship lines. A natural dynamic of these smaller groups is that some people are viewed as "leaders" of the group and others are not. As small groups join up with larger groups, such as when a regional fan club attends a convention, there is an implicit recognition of pecking order among the leaders by the followers.

Hierarchy of Venue. Control of venue describes the power role that a fan holds when she shares her home for fan events or helps organize a convention. In electronically mediated spaces, venues are email discussion lists, Multi-User Dimensions,[11] and Inter Relay Chat lines. These areas are controlled by the owner of the email list, the creator of the MUD, or the initiator of the chat area.[12]

Fans may occupy multiple positions simultaneously, and thus fans' positions within fandom are determined by their position within all possible hierarchies. For example, within *Quantum Leap* fandom, a single fan, Alex, runs several electronic mail lists and had direct access to the producer, actors, and set. She helped Universal Studios and Creation Con[13] organize two *Quantum Leap* Conventions. She has also been active in organizing many fan activities centered around *Quantum Leap* fandom such as recycling drives to earn the money for Dean Stockwell's star on the Walk of Fame and write-in campaigns to keep the show on the air. Alex holds multiple positions within the different hierarchies outlined earlier. She is a leader, a controller of venue, has direct access, and is considered the ultimate source, save the show's own personnel, for interpreting the fictive universe. Her centrality to *Quantum Leap* fandom rests on her maintaining multiple positions.

Hierarchy is important on many levels. For example, outsiders to fan discourse (such as journalists and academics) will usually be directed either by fans or by production people to fans who have achieved a cer-

---

[11]MUDs or multiuser dungeons are online real-time virtual reality environments. Users interact with each other either as characters or themselves, depending on the MUD environment. MUD environments usually have themes and are designed with virtual locations that represent that theme. For example, a MUD set in the Middle Ages will have castles and cottages (Raymond, 1993).

[12]Email discussion lists are at the mercy of the owners (as well as other electronic areas), and frequently it is the owners' construction of the fictive universe that is maintained.

[13]A for profit science fiction convention promotions company.

tain level of recognition or authority. The community's determination of who is an authority coincides with the authority's position within various fan hierarchies. Only authorities are able to speak uncontested to outsiders such as journalists. In *Quantum Leap* fandom, Alex has become the voice of *Quantum Leap* fans to journalists from *TV Guide* and *USA Today*, to production people at Bellisarius Productions (the creators of *Quantum Leap*), and even to network executives.

Alex's position as an authority on *Quantum Leap* fandom has several effects. As the sole voice of *Quantum Leap* fandom to the outside world, she has eclipsed the multiplicity of voices that exist within the fandom. Her interpretations regarding the meta-text of *Quantum Leap* have the weight of biblical interpretations; her control of venue, which to this date has been benign, has encapsulated within it the ability to determine who is and is not worthy of participation.

I have gone to great lengths tracing fan hierarchies because these hierarchies also exist within computer-mediated spaces. Theorists of CMC, caught up in the democratic possibilities of CMC, have done little study of the practices within CMC. Fan hierarchies are moving to the new information technologies with minor structural changes. Cherished members of electronic mailing communities frequently are the ones with the most knowledge regarding the canon of the fictive universe. CMC users who also attend conventions, fan club meetings, and industry sponsored events are expected to add to the electronic conversation snippets of their experiences, for they are more of a fan than those who just express their fandom by participating in computer-mediated exchanges. Electronic leaders may be leaders in the face-to-face world, but sometimes they are not, for a new criterion has entered the pecking order—technological competence and access. Those who have easiest access to, or technical expertise in, computer-mediated spaces are the ones whose voices are heard most often, who control venue, or use their computer skills to gain more knowledge regarding the fictive universe. In the next section I define and discuss CMC further and describe how fans use CMC.

FLUID SPACE–A TOPOGRAPHY

Technology and science fiction seem to go hand in hand. Not only are science fiction fictive texts intrinsically linked to technology, many specific practices of science fiction media fandom rest on technology. As one example, Jenkins (1992) notes that fans' "mastery over the narrative" (p. 73) can be attributed to the flexibility of viewing that a VCR allows. Fans' ability to reinterpret or negotiate televisual texts is only possible now that video technology allows for "fans' liminal movement between a relationship of intense proximity and one of more ironic distance . . ." (p. 73).

Fans view this reliance on technology with trepidation. Penley (1991) points out the uneasy alliance between technology and media fans. Use of advanced technology allows the fans to produce many kinds of fan paraphernalia, but being too professional removes a fan cultural product from the world of for-fan-by-fan camaraderie, changing it to something that is mass marketed, largely for profit, and thus regarded with suspicion.[14]

Yet, computers connected to networks now supplement or are supplanting the ways fans gain access to fan community knowledge. Fan status, according to Bacon-Smith, rests on a fan's demonstrated knowledge of a text and her or his fan activities. Another problem with the new technologies is cost: to participate in the electronic exchanges of cyberspace one needs a computer account. Not everyone has access to "free"[15] accounts on the Internet. Instead, users must subscribe to commercial companies such as CompuServe or Genie.

Obsolescence or reconfiguration of fan practices within computer-mediated spaces also requires consideration. CMC allows fans to quickly access each other with a few strokes of a key. Information pertinent to specific fan groups, such as upcoming story-lines, can be distributed almost instantaneously. This January 28, 1991 post is a good example:

> Well, before the shit hit the fan, I got the following info on upcoming episodes, straight from the Home Office in Universal City, CA—
> Some of these ep titles are only working titles, and may be changed before airing. Eventually. :-([At the time *Quantum Leap* was on hiatus]
> IN THE CAN:
> "Piano Man" (lounge lizard, buy [sic], hey, Scott gets to sing!)
> "Future Boy" (50's actor) (written by Tommy Thompson)
> "Private Dancer" (Chippendale dancer) (writer: Paul Brown)
> "8 1/2 Months" (pregnant teenager) (!)
> "Glitter Rock" (glam-rock musician)
> CURRENTLY SHOOTING:
> "Love For Sale" (brothel owner—male) (directed by Chris Ruppenthal)
> _____
> That's all the news I have for now.
> Remember, the more letters of complaint you write to NBC, the better our chances of seeing these! DON'T DELAY! WRITE TODAY! This week is absolutely critical!

---

[14]Commercial dealers of fan memorabilia have been accused of republishing fanzines in a slicker format without paying the original creators and contributors.

[15]Free is a relative term here. Ultimately, the provider of the account is paying for the account via node connection charges, account maintenance, and equipment costs.

Also, television shows that might otherwise be ignored are pointed out as being worthy of interest more quickly. Small fan groups can more easily maintain their identity for they no longer need a large enough group to support the cost of publishing zines. All they have to do is publish and distribute the zine electronically.

The same technology, however, enables social practices and hierarchies to change. For example, the construction of the meta-text of the fictive universe changes. Jenkins defines the *meta-text* as "the mental construct which fans construct surrounding the series text which includes not only information explicitly offered in the program narratives but also extra-textual information (interviews with stars, producers, etc.; novelizations; writer's guides) and inferences by fan critics" (email, 9/23/92). The power relations of whose voice is incorporated into the construction of the meta-text no longer rests solely on who is the most informed on a particular show as it now includes computer competence. Fans with computer expertise are the ones who set up and control electronic mailing lists, upload files, and create messages that are more likely to be attended to for very simple reasons, such as good spelling made possible by the use of spell checkers or the ability to quote previous messages successfully.[16] Fan relations are still hierarchized but proficiency with a computer has been added as a criterion.

Yet, technological competence is problematic for fans. At what point does a fan cultural product become too professional? How is CMC changing fandom? A fan can be a virtual fan, not having to risk ridicule in her everyday world for the frivolity of her hobby. Whether this movement from face-to-face to cybered practices is boon, bane, or both remains to be seen. My case study of a small group of women *Quantum Leap* fans explores these questions.

The USENET posts I refer to are drawn from early 1990 to February 1991. The email messages I report are drawn from September 1993 and February, March, and April 1994. The mailing list membership remained stable at 24 women but it was not the same women throughout the sample period (some individuals joined or dropped from the list). These months are a small subsection of a larger database that has over 3,000 messages from 169 days between June 1993 to July 1994. The mean number of messages per day is 17.91, but this number does not accurately portray the periodicity of message posting on the list. Some days more messages are posted than others; sometimes because the topic is some-

---

[16]The measurement of successful message quoting rests on how aware the message creator is of the norms of the particular online community. Online services such as CompuServe that have threaded interfaces obviate the need for quoting. Further, with services that cost the user (reader) money, users resent messages that are made overly long by quoting because each extra word takes longer to download and thus costs more money.

thing everyone has an opinion on, other times just because the women on the list are talkative. The highest number of messages on any given day was 75. The data reveal that more messages are posted during the week than on weekends. This corresponds to how most of the women gain access to electronic mail—through work.

The messages can be broken down into a variety of categories but these categories are by no means exhaustive or exclusive of each other. Any given email message can belong to multiple categories simultaneously. The categories appear to fall into the following domains:

requests for support/advise;

sharing of stories sometimes in response to requests for support/advise, sometimes not;

offering of support/advise;

teasers—giving just enough information so everyone asks for more; for example, Abby signed off one day with "Abby (who, after this morning, thinks that men can sometimes do completely *wonder* [sic] things without being asked";

related (*Quantum Leap,* and other fandoms); for example, the quote with which I started this paper;

blowing off steam regarding bosses, husbands, and so on;

alerting each other to upcoming events, articles, interviews, and so on that have to do with anyone's specific fan interest; for example, "a number of your fellow fans (incl. me, of course) are holding a QL (*Quantum Leap*) convention in Pasadena on February 19-20, 1994. . . . So, e-mail me with your programming suggestions.";

solidarity, for example, Jennifer's response to a member of the list talking about abuse: "I think there's one thing I can clearly state—you don't have to worry about John ever hurting you—because if he does he won't live long [enough] to tell about it. We will ALL go after him." (all caps in email exchanges is the equivalent of shouting in face-to-face exchanges.)

Quantum Leap Fans' CMC

Electronic mail (email) is an asynchronous or "time shifted" (Raymond, 1993) form of communication. This means that, unlike face-to-face conversations, communication among users of email does not have to occur at the same time and in the same place. Unlike a phone call, the ability to time shift allows people to communicate without coordination of schedules.Further, email allows communication between geographically dispersed individuals without concerns for time zones (e.g., between the U.S. and Japan). However, unlike other forms of asynchronous communication, like regular mail, email can be delivered immediately. It is quicker than regular mail and can allow users to talk to each other with minimal delays. In fact, users of email can have something akin to real-time conversation if both users are online simultaneously.[17]

Fans use email to alert each other to impending events, discuss the fictive text, share gossip, and create an elite community. Email can privatize fan knowledge by limiting who has access to information. Almost all fandoms have email mailing lists that require membership for access, although new members can join fairly easily. Many email lists have a monitor who operates the email list and decides on advertising strategies, topic content, and membership. To my knowledge, monitors refuse access only to people who have demonstrated they can not follow basic email etiquette, or who have harassed members of the email list.

Email lists provide a way for fans to break traditional mainstream hierarchies. One email list that revels in the physical attributes of a particular actor does not refuse access based on gender/sexual preference of the email writers, but rather on their degree of lust for the actor, as in one post that states in part: "Okay, who almost fell off the couch when he walked off the elevator in those jeans???? :-P...". (The funny symbol at the end of the message [:-P] is an emoticon showing a face with the tongue hanging out, drooling.) Now all of the subscribers to a list, which can be world-wide in scope, recognize as knowledgeable fans who otherwise would only be leaders in their own local fan community. Fans can gain notoriety more quickly over computer networks than via the traditional fan methods of demonstrating knowledge or connections at conventions or other fan gatherings.

Fans also use email to organize. When television networks threaten a show with cancellation, email quickly alerts the fan community so that members can take appropriate action, including sending a deluge of mail to the television network in support of the show and collecting fan demographics to "prove" that the show appeals to a desirable audience.[18] Even after a show has been canceled, the fans use CMC to promote related projects.

---

[17]Unlike "real-time" computer-mediated communication, such as IRC, some time delay still exists. This is due to users' writing of the messages and inherent time delays in the actual software and network communications. For example, some electronic post offices use "packet" protocols (i.e., send/receive in groups—akin to bulk mail); others only query the forwarding electronic post office's node every hour.

[18]It is interesting how producers are starting to recognize the power of computer networks. During NBC's last attempt to cancel *Quantum Leap,* Donald Bellasario went directly to the computer networks to garner support for the show.

Both Don Bellisario and Deborah Pratt confirm that "Quantum Leap" is over as a weekly series, and say it's time to move on. No letters to NBC, please, or to any other networks. It's over.

The news isn't all bad, however:

Time to start lobbying Universal for "Quantum Leap: The Movie" (it will probably take a few years, but we can start nudging now!).

The days of mimeographed "calls to action" have been displaced by the raging bitstream.

Email also serves to "place" fans at an event. Although the advent of inexpensive video technology allows more fans to vicariously participate in conventions and special screenings, copying and shipping the videos takes time. Accessing transcripts or reports of events through email quickly and at minimal cost augments the exchange of video data. The following is an example of a transcript from the special screening at UCLA on November 26, 1990.

"QUANTUM LEAP" PROGRAM, UCLA, 11/26/90
Transcribed by Sally Smith
audience laughs
% audience applauds

(The host introduces Deborah Pratt, Michael Zinberg, and Don Bellisario. She is halfway through Dean's [Stockwell] introduction when Scott [Bakula] strolls out on stage. The audience laughs, and Dean drags Scott back offstage. She finishes Dean's intro and he comes out. Then she reads Scott's intro, but he's nowhere to be seen, finally entering on the opposite side of the stage as the others, laughing at having fooled everyone.)

. . .

Q[uestion] (male): I read an article, I think it was in the *Times*, with Mr. Bakula, and he was saying in the article that he'd like to play a character with AIDS. Number one, is there anything like that coming; and number two, is there anything that's off limits, that you won't touch?

SB: Well, the off-limits line, I think you should direct to Don or Deborah or Michael. I think there's an episode out there about AIDS. I don't know what it is exactly, and I don't know if they have something in the works, but I don't think that a show like ours needs to be bound by too many of the normal things you can or cannot do. And I think so far that we live up to that, so hopefully. . . . It's unfortunate that there is even an AIDS show to do. But I think we might be able to do a different one than the other shows and shed some different light on it. Don can answer the rest of it. Or Deborah.

DB: Yeah, it's a tough one. We do not have an AIDS show in the works, although I don't feel that there's anything off limits for "Quantum Leap" at all. We have been working on a show where Sam leaps in as a gay (audience goes "Woo . . . "). That has _not_ worked out to date. It's been written by . . . we've had a gay writer working on it. I'm not happy with the script. # There are a lot of reasons. . . . It's a tough subject. Because I want to present it in a balanced light. I want to be able to represent all views. I hate _any_ kind of bigotry, be it against gays, blacks, minorities of any kind, in its form. It just—sucks, and life's too short. # % But we have some pitches coming in.

Fans now know what happened at an event long before they see the video, although the video still has the value of "placing" the viewer at the event.

Fans use USENET for purposes similar to email. Through USENET postings fans learn of anonymous FTP[19] sites, convention postings, announcements of special screenings, show cancellations, and most importantly, the shared interests of other fans. But USENET does not have the same degree of privacy and control as email, thus limiting the amount of self-revelation fans will post. Nor can users create elite groups because membership is not required.[20]

The original members of the *Quantum Leap* electronic mailing list met via their communiqués on *Quantum Leap* in an USENET area called rec.arts.tv. On the Internet, media fan communication occurs primarily on USENET.[21] USENET in many ways is like a bulletin board system divided first into theme areas such as computers, science, business, or alternative, or in the nomenclature of the "net," comp., sci., biz., or alt. Each theme area is then divided into newsgroups that range from computers to movie reviews, with many dedicated to media/literary fandom. For example, in the newsgroup rec.arts.tv, discussion of many U.S. television shows occurs, or in the news group rec.arts.sf.tv, science fiction media fans talk about their favorite science fiction television shows. Each newsgroup is further subdivided into articles, or in the lingo of USENET, "posts."

---

[19]Anonymous file transfer, based on FTP (file transfer protocol), allows computer users access to information stored on machines that are geographically remote. Anonymity permits users to access data even without an account on that particular machine. These sites offer a myriad of information files, comprised of software applications, text documents, graphics, and utilities.

[20]Additionally, the interactions and discussions that do occur within these limits have largely replaced the Amateur Publishing Associations (APA; round robin mimeographed or xeroxed newsletters). Many APA leaders contend that bulletin board systems have made APAs obsolete.

[21]USENET has many newsgroups dedicated to media/literary fandom. *Star Trek* is the leader with six separate topic areas out of the 20 non-"alt" groups covering Science Fiction. Twenty topic divisions might not sound like very many, but each *Star Trek* area can have over 400 postings a day.

Not all newsgroups are carried by all USENET subscription sites. Alt groups with topics ranging from alt.fandom.dave.barry (for fans of Dave Barry) to alt.sex.fetish (discussions on sexual fetishes) are considered by System Administrators and many USENET users as so frivolous that many System Administrators will not carry them. At the time of this study there were 23 science fiction-related alt groups and 22 non-alt groups. Of the non-alt groups, 7 are dedicated to the television show *Star Trek*. According to the USENET readership report for July 1994, the total number of newsgroups (both alt and non-alt) is 3121. Although the ratio of science fiction-related newsgroups to other newsgroups is only 1.44%, the average number of readers of science fiction groups, 31,564, was greater than the average readership of all groups, 27,200, indicating that this is a very popular topic area among USENET users.

Posts onto rec.arts.tv included such topics as relationships between characters and further discussion of issues with which the TV show dealt. One fan, Alex, moved to the forefront of postings, becoming one of the *official* interpreters of the *Quantum Leap* fictive universe (in part due to her close connection with the production company). Alex not only elucidated various aspects of the show, for example, the "string theory" which explains how the lead character, Sam, could leap around in time, but also posted long detailed accounts of her backstage visits to *Quantum Leap* filming sessions.

As both male and female *Quantum Leap* fans posted more and more frequently to rec.arts.tv, other posters to rec.arts.tv. called for the *Quantum Leap* fans to be moved to their own newsgroup. Had they done so, the *Quantum Leap* fans would have been forced into an alt group, for there were not enough of them to warrant a regular newsgroup. Unlike the fans of alt.tv.twinpeaks who embraced the move to "alt" status as confirmation of their select group status,[22] the *Quantum Leap* fans did not want to be moved to an alt group because not all netnews sites receive the alt newsgroups. In the long run many of the *Quantum Leap* postings, especially those of the women fans, were forced off rec.arts.tv via peer pressure for being what one fan called "too silly."[23]

---

[22]Recently (June 1994) *Quantum Leap* fans managed to gain enough support to start the news group, rec.arts.tv.ql, thus avoiding the precarious status of an "alt" group.

[23]This is not a surprising occurrence in light of common responses to women's contributions to discussion groups. Ebben and Kramarae cite a study on a "friendly composition and rhetoric discussion group in which feminism enjoyed considerable influence" in which it was discovered that only 30% of its messages were posted by women. Further, the messages posted by women "were not responded to as often as the men's . . ." (in Taylor, Kramarae, & Ebben, 1993, p. 17). In fact, they report this rate of response: men to men 33.4%; women to men 21.3%; and women to women 11.2% (in Taylor, Kramarae, & Ebben, 1993, p. 17).

Alex, borrowing time on her husband's work computer account, decided to "pay back" those who wanted *Quantum Leap* postings kept to a minimum by forming her own electronic mailing lists called ql announcements and, for more frivolous mail, ql:frivolous. These lists were comprised of an "elite" group of approximately 35 people whom Alex personally invited to join. What made the lists "elite" was fan activity access. Prior to the creation of the email lists, Alex would post generally to rec.arts.tv any invitations to private screenings or special events organized by Bellisarius Productions, the creators of *Quantum Leap,* as well as her behind-the-scenes stories and the press releases she received from Bellisarius Productions. Once the email lists came into being, she would only post her special "insider" info to the email lists.

Since its creation the *Quantum Leap* mailing list itself has evolved through many generations (see Figure 8.1). The first offshoot from ql:frivolous, qllc (a.k.a. Quantum Leap Ladies Club or Quantum Leap Lust Club, depending on whom you talk to), came about due to teasing from men on the ql:frivolous electronic mailing list. They did not like the women talking

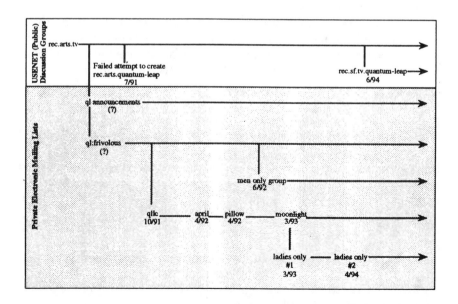

Figure 8.1. Time line of *Quantum Leap*-related public posting areas and private mailing lists

about Scott Bakula's cute butt, or the long discussions of the characters' relationships. The frequent anecdotes and stories that the women drew from their own lives also annoyed many of the male members of the email list.

The membership of qllc was comprised of presumably heterosexual women and one homosexual male.[24] The qllc list has changed names and host machines many times since its inception—once as an April Fools joke (and called april), but the other times to protect the list's existence. Changing the list's name frequently prevents outsiders from having knowledge of the list. The progeny of qllc from which I am drawing my examples is currently composed of all women (24 at last count). As the list became more and more intimate even the lone male was finally excluded due to his suspected "leaking" of posts to the ql:frivolous list and, although he has access to other offspring of qllc (now called moonlight), he apparently is unaware that he is excluded from the final domain of these women (i.e., ladies only #2).[25] I am taking the time to trace the genealogy of this electronic mailing list to give an idea of how women's participation in computer-mediated spaces is subordinated. This subordination is Fairclough's idea in action: "[that] power in discourse has to do with powerful participants controlling and constraining the contributions of nonpowerful participants." (1989, p. 6). Even an email list such as ql:frivolous, created in response to accusations of being off topic and too silly, could not tolerate women's talk.

The women-only list still changes name and host frequently to maintain its hidden-ness. Further, new members only gain access to the list once they have been nominated and vouched for by an existing member as having the requisite knowledge of Quantum Leap. Keeping outsiders or even the ql:frivolous list unaware of the women-only list is incredibly important to its members. Recently, one of the members accidentally sent a post to ql:frivolous that included address information about the women-only list. Within 26 minutes the mailing list had a new name. This constant need to hide the list may seem perplexing when one remembers that nonmembers cannot invade the list with unwanted posts, nor can nonmembers read posts.[26] However, this practice is not perplexing if one assumes that the constant name changes and new membership protocols exemplify the need

---

[24]Women members of qllc did not explicitly list their sexuality like the homosexual male, whose sexual preference for men was a requisite for gaining entrance to the list. The inclusion of the homosexual male demonstrates an aspect of fan ideology that Bacon-Smith refers to as "IDIC" or Infinite Diversity in Infinite Combinations. The women felt they could not possibly discriminate on the basis of sex, only on the basis of sexual preference.

[25]This is a pseudonym for the mailing list.

[26]Unless a member of the list allows an outsider access to their email account.

for these women to police the boundaries of this communication in order to maintain a "safe" space. Safe spaces "frequently . . . provide a climate and situation in which women can focus on their experiences and achievements without pressure to conform to the expectations or dictates of patriarchal authority and without fear of male censure" (Welsch, 1994, p. 65).

Creation of a safe space is key to the continued survival of this women-only list, especially now that the show for which it originally was created is off the air;[27] more so, when one considers the topics that are covered in the conversations that occur there.[28] In the women-only list, going "off-topic" is allowed. Strewn among the discussions of the Olympics skaters, Steven Speilberg's latest effort, and the actors' relative attractiveness, are discussions on what I consider essentially (and I use the term essentially advisedly here)[29] women's topics. Breast cancer, spousal abuse, mother-in-laws, pregnancy, giving birth, and death have all been talked about within the confines of this list.

DISCUSSION

The telecommunications industry is a business viewed primarily as an economic player. But telecommunications gives certain people access to means of influencing certain other people's thoughts and perceptions, and that process—who has it and who doesn't have it—is intimately connected with political power (Rheingold 1993, p. 278)

Computer networking changes the workings of fandom and fan expression, the difference in communication networks reconfiguring fan authority and hierarchies and deaccenting gender and sexual orientation.[30] Through computer networks, fans easily share their conceptualization of fictional universes, encouraging a more uniform understanding of the fictive universe. Computers have also affected what kinds of goods are available to fans as well as how fans interact with them. Customizing the

---

[27]Therefore, there are no new episodes to add to the topics discussed.

[28]Note that I have shifted how I am referring to electronic mail: It has now become a place, a space, and an environment in which one can have a conversation.

[29]I hesitate in using the term essential because I worry about the connection that can be made to what I am saying about women's topics and idea that there is a "natural social community grounded in biology and reproductive characteristics rather than in intellect or temperament or derivation or societal experience" (Kramarae & Treichler, 1985, p. 142).

[30]Part of this is due to the actual activity of fandom—fans pride themselves on their tolerance.

computer interface creates a further extension of an individual's fandom. Now fans can customize their computers to speak in the voice of their favorite star, or quote their favorite author. Digitized artwork enables fans to create start-up screens or posters featuring their favorite persons or objects. Most impressively, fans need no longer commit themselves to fandom physically—just virtually. Virtual fandom broadens participation, allowing those too shy to admit to their fandom to "lurk" in the background of a computer network, no one the wiser; but unlike shy, non-networked fans, a computer-networked fan is an informed fan.

Counter to the wonders of cybered fandom are prosaic considerations such as access. Science Fiction media fandom is predominately a White, middle-class phenomenon. Given the expense of computers and computing time, the group of fans I am talking about narrows considerably. Access is often poached from accounts that do not directly cost the user, for example, student accounts or work accounts. Some users do not have the necessary connections for a "free"[31] account on the Internet and perforce subscribe to user-paid service companies such as CompuServe, Genie, or Prodigy. These provide similar services as the Internet: electronic mail, file retrieval, and bulletin board or discussion areas. Some computer services provide Internet electronic mail access, allowing their subscribers access to other fans who are not subscribers (there is usually an extra charge for this service).

Thus, CMC users on the whole are an elite group: They are either academics or work for companies with connections to the Internet (primarily military and science organizations, though this is rapidly changing with the shift toward privatizing the Internet), or have the necessary finances to purchase computing equipment and pay for online time charges. In a recent demographic study on CompuServe, most users had incomes in excess of $60,000 (with an average household income of $93,000).

Further, CMC technologies have not just enhanced fandom. Fan practices are changing in relationship to the new technologies. Hierarchies of access, knowledge, and so on that exist in face-to-face fandom are changing and becoming broader. The ability to reread a text and synthesize with many minds now easily exist, while at the same time authors of the fictive universe are better able to gatekeep meaning making. Several commercial networks boast that they have Science Fiction authors and television writers using their services and participating in group discussions. So, as fans discuss fictive universes in public discussion areas, authors are able to jump in and correct fan interpretations.

---

[31]Free is a relative term here. Ultimately the provider of the account is paying for the account via node connection charges, account maintenance, and equipment costs.

Cyberspace is a contested frontier—a space of "can be," one of many possibilities—but we are now seeing trends in computer-mediated spaces. For example, CMC can allow for multiple voices, yet in my observations of *Quantum Leap* fandom, there are interpretation leaders. Computer mediated spaces could be nonhierarchical, but cultural conversational norms that denigrate women's talk appear to be winning out in cyberspace—the female *Quantum Leap* fans have been forced to the fringe private realm. Yet this fringe existence has given these women a support group, and the technology permits them to maintain their borders. CMC is neither a utopia nor a dystopia, but a way of communicating that is vexed, fraught with many of our old ways of negotiating social spaces.

REFERENCES

Bacon-Smith, C. (1992). *Enterprising women: Television fandom and the creation of popular myth.* Philadelphia: University of Pennsylvania Press.

Bourdieu, P. (1984). *Distinction: A social critique of the judgment of taste.* Cambridge: Harvard University Press.

Ebben, M., & Kramarae, C. (1993). Women and information technologies: Creating a cyberspace of our wwn. In H.J. Taylor, C. Kramarae, & M. Ebben (Eds.), *Women, information technology, and scholarship* (pp. 15- 27). Urbana: Center for Advanced Study, University of Illinois.

Fairclough, N. (1989). *Language and power.* London: Longman.

Jenkins, H. (1991). "Star Trek" rerun, reread, rewritten. In C. Penley, E. Lyon, L. Spigel, & J. Bergstrom (Eds.), *Close encounters: Film, feminism, and science fiction* (pp. 170-203). Minneapolis: University of Minneapolis Press.

Jenkins, H. (1992). *Textual poachers: Television fans & participatory culture.* New York: Routledge.

Jenson, J. (1992). Fandom as pathology: The consequences of characterization. In L. A. Lewis (Ed.), *The adoring audience: Fan culture and popular media* (pp. 9-29). London: Routledge.

Kilgour, A., Buc, Q., Brown, D., Sailer, V., Smith S., & Urlings, A. (1993). *The Quantum Leap episode guide.* Version 4.6. Available electronically via anonymous ftp from ftp.cisco.com in /ql-archive.

Kramarae, C., & Treichler, P.A. (1985). *A feminist dictionary.* Boston: Pandora Press.

MacDonald, A. (1992). They're virtually fans. *Antenna: The Newsletter of the Mercurians Special Interest Group, 5*(1), pp. 5-6.

Marvin, C. (1988). *When old technologies were new: Thinking about electric communication in the late nineteenth century.* New York: Oxford University Press.

Penley, C. (1991). Brownian motion: Women, tactics, and technology. In
    C. Penley & A. Ross (Eds.), *Technoculture* (pp. 135-162).
    Minneapolis: University of Minnesota Press.
Raymond, E. S. (1993). *The new hacker's dictionary.* Cambridge: The MIT
    Press.
Rheingold, H. (1993). *The virtual community: Homesteading on the elec-
    tronic frontier.* Reading, MA: Addison-Wesley Publishing Company.
Smith, S. (1990). *"Quantum Leap" program.* Museum of Broadcasting
    Festival, Los Angeles County Museum of Art.
Welsch, J. R. (1994). Bakhtin, language, and women's documentary film-
    making. In D. Carson, L. Dittmar, & J. R. Welsch (Eds.), *Multiple
    voices in feminist film criticism* (pp. 162-175). Minneapolis:
    University of Minnesota Press.

▶9

Male Pair-Bonds and Female Desire in Fan Slash Writing*

Mirna Cicioni
La Trobe University, Australia

Representations of male pair-bonding—a constant feature of many genres of action films and television series—have often been criticized as adolescent and mysogynist (Fiske, 1987; Haskell, 1974; Mellen 1977). Yet it can be argued that they have a complex appeal for some women, who read them within a specifically female perspective and reconstruct them to give form to some of their own needs and desires. The following discussion is based on a documented instance of women's active reconstruction of representations of male pair-bonds, namely, "slash" fan writing.

*I would like to thank Valerie Burley for her assistance with several English-language drafts of this chapter, and Jill Carr, Ruth Collerson, Sue Jenkins, Joanne Keating, Louise Keene, and all the women who introduced me to "slash" and discussed it at length with me. Special thanks are due to Henry Jenkins for his constructive suggestions on the first draft, and to Trish Darbyfeld, who has contributed invaluable ideas, comments, and perspectives on fandom.

The authors of slash fiction are almost entirely female and prevail-ingly heterosexual. However, the focus of slash production, and the only relationship represented as a fully satisfying one between equals, is appar-ently a homosexual bond in which women are excluded or marginalized. This apparent contradiction is discussed in early analyses of K/S fiction[1] such as Russ (1985a, 1985b), Lamb and Veith (1986), and Penley (1991); they conclude that slash texts are not discourses about homosexuality, but rather fantasies that articulate women's desires concerning relationships in which men are involved.

Drawing on these writers' discussions, I argue that slash writing also reflects some of the ambiguities that characterize the position of women with respect to heterosexuality. My examination focuses on two particular instances of slash texts based on two British television series: *The Professionals* (57 one-hour episodes produced by London Weekend Television and first aired between 1978 and 1983) and *Inspector Morse* (28 two-hour episodes produced by Zenith/Central TV, based on charac-ters created by the British writer Colin Dexter, and first aired between 1987 and 1993). Although the volume of fan output is much greater for *The Professionals* than for *Inspector Morse*, I decided to discuss both because, despite the profound differences between the two series, there are strong similarities in the fans' recontextualizations. Other relevant shared elements are that, through formulaic structures and styles, both these slash subgenres articulate complex ideas about women's desires, and that the interaction between readers, in the form of comments pub-lished in fanzines and letterzines, contributes to the constant redefinition and interrogation of the desires expressed in the texts.

My own position is at the same time that of a slash fan and that of a not-very-heterosexual feminist academic. From this position, which is partly inside and partly outside slash fandom, I investigate why the notion of a romantic and sexual involvement between two men appeals to writers and readers who are often firmly committed to heterosexuality and its con-comitant institutions, such as marriage. My approach to slash texts is con-cerned with what the texts reveal about the desires of their writers and implied readers rather than with their literary merit; I also deliberately avoid value judgements of all kinds as irrelevant to the question of "what some women want".

After a brief examination of the way the two series and their main characters are recontextualized in slash fiction, I look at several subgenres and features of slash ("first-time" stories; "virtual marriage" stories; "hurt/comfort" and nurturance; sex scenes) in order to ascertain what female desires find expression and fulfillment there. My argument is that

---

[1]Slash production based on *Star Trek* and representing an emotional and sexual bond between Captain Kirk and his first officer Mr. Spock.

slash writing is at the same time an eroticization of same-sex nurturance, the expression of a desire for a relationship that satisfies all the basic needs of the people involved, and an unspoken reflection of the writers' tensions about heterosexual relations. I have based this mainly on an examination of approximately 350 *Professionals* stories (also known as "hatstands"[2]) and approximately 20 *Inspector Morse* stories of varying lengths. Other helpful insights have been supplied by fans and writers in personal correspondence, informal conversations, and discussions in letterzines. Additional useful perspectives are provided by feminist analyses of the structures, language, and themes of romance fiction, which has many aspects in common with slash writing. An interpretation of slash writing would not be possible without taking psychoanalytic discussions of fantasy into account because, as the feminist critic Alison Light states in her examination of romance fiction, psychoanalysis "takes the question of pleasure seriously, . . . as the explorations and productions of desires which may be in excess of the socially possible or acceptable" (1984, p. 9).

GENRE RECONCEPTUALIZATION: THE SERIES AND THEIR FANS

The Professionals revolves around the activities of a special squad known as CI5 (the initials stand for "Criminal Intelligence"). Its brief is to prevent and stop all kinds of criminal activities—nothing is outside its jurisdiction—"by any means necessary," legal or otherwise. Not only is CI5 only nominally bound by the law and answerable to higher authorities, but most of the villains—with the exception of a few white supremacists, bent police officers, or corrupt Cabinet ministers—also tend to be stereotypes of "enemies of the State" such as the KGB, the IRA, anarchists, left-wing terrorists, and international drug traffickers. Part and parcel of the ideology of the series are the values embodied by its characters. The unit's agents are almost exclusively men and commanded by a stern father figure, the tough but fair Controller. They do not appear to have many close family or personal ties or many outside interests, and are seldom shown in activities not connected with their jobs (stakeouts, car chases, shootouts, and hand-to-hand fights with the villains). Conflicts are inevitably solved through violence, with the predictable justification that the enemies are violent people and "fire must be fought with fire." Feelings and emotions are generally understated and always secondary to the action.

---

[2]The term "hatstands" is used by fans exclusively with reference to *Professionals* slash stories. Its origin is the British idiom "bent as a hatstand," used to refer to male homosexuals.

The two leading CI5 agents are the partners Bodie and Doyle, two men in their early 30s whose previous histories make them the ideal team to combat the aforementioned enemies of the state: Bodie is an ex-mercenary and SAS sergeant; Doyle is a former police detective with Drug Squad experience. The fact that the two men complement each other is emphasized by contrasts in their past experiences, physical appearance (Bodie taller, stockier, and usually neatly dressed; Doyle lean, curly-haired, and frequently scruffy), and dispositions (Bodie arrogant and at times violent, but generous and giving; Doyle sensitive and rational, but volatile and given to feelings of guilt and self-doubt).

Throughout the series a homoerotic subtext—an implicit emphasis on the closeness between Bodie and Doyle as the main emotional focus of the series—is clearly visible. Both men are single and constructed as actively heterosexual, enjoying casual liaisons with women ("birds") and occasionally becoming emotionally involved with them. However, all heterosexual relations end at the close of each episode, with the women dying, becoming disillusioned with their lovers' death-dealing profession, or simply fading out of the scene. In some episodes, furthermore, emotional involvement by either Bodie or Doyle triggers off resentment in the other man, who sees the bond threatened by the new relationship. In addition, not only do the partners trust each other completely and save each other's lives regularly—time-honored conventions of male pair-bonds in action adventures—but they exchange tender and intense gazes; touch each other often and at times in ways that are subtly, but clearly, sexual; and tease each other verbally with a good deal of sexual innuendo for the sole benefit of each other.[3]

Unlike Bodie and Doyle, Detective Chief Inspector Morse and Detective Sergeant Lewis are divided by rank, age, education, and class. Inspector Morse is in his 50s, comes from the affluent South, and was educated at Oxford, where the series is set. Sergeant Lewis is in his late 30s, has not lost the accent of working-class Newcastle where he was born, did not go to university, and "wishes he had time to read books." Neither man is conventionally good-looking, although both could be called attractive.

The ideology of the series is considerably less clear-cut than that of *The Professionals* and reflects the changing social values of the 1990s. The villains are often upper-class or upper middle-class (university lecturers, industrialists, media figures), and their wrongdoings are constructed more as violating trust or using people as means to an end than as endangering public order. Their retribution is arrest and imprisonment far more

---

[3]Evidence that a homoerotic subtext could be read in the series by people other than fans is provided by a scene in a British spoof, *The Bullshitters*, in which the two characters based on Bodie and Doyle clinch passionately and declare mutual love after rolling into a gravel pit.

often than death; Morse and Lewis never carry guns and seldom engage in physical struggles with lawbreakers, and Morse is shown as actually being afraid of blood, corpses, and heights.

Like Bodie and Doyle, Morse and Lewis complement each other in many ways that become evident as the series develops. The cumulative construction of Morse is that of a highly intelligent and sensitive man, with considerable skills, expertise, and intuition, who is, however, short-tempered, inhibited in personal and social encounters, lonely, and inclined to seek comfort or relaxation in drink. These characteristics are counterbalanced by Lewis's easy-going, open nature, and by his strong loyalty to Morse and emotional protectiveness of him. Like Bodie and Doyle, Morse and Lewis are constructed as heterosexual in both Dexter's books and the television series: Lewis is married with two children, Morse is a bachelor who tends to develop rather one-sided attractions for women he meets in the course of his investigations. The relationship between the two men has, rather than an obvious homoerotic subtext, clear elements of emotional closeness and trust demonstrated through unspoken dependence on each other in times of crisis instead of through dramatic shootout or rescue scenes. Lewis is the person to whom Morse feels closest and in whom he confides, and Lewis's relationship with Morse is represented as more demanding and more involving than his family life.

Both series quickly gained popularity throughout the English-speaking world, and *The Professionals* also had a considerable following in Germany. Fans began to write narratives based on *The Professionals* at the beginning of the 1980s, while the series was still being shown in the United Kingdom. The very first ones were "hatstands," written by a small group of friends for their own enjoyment, and photocopied and circulated among their acquaintances. Subsequently "general" (a shorthand term for "not containing any slash elements") stories began to be written and published in several small zines circulated by a British fan press (Blue Jay Press). Once the series began to be shown in the United States and Australia, the number of fan writers increased, with slash stories outnumbering "general" stories by about seven to one. *Professionals* slash fandom has continued uninterruptedly for nearly 15 years among women from several countries and with various levels of education, and by 1993 it had produced almost 3,000 stories and novels (ranging in length from one to over 300 pages), 45 fanzines, and 5 letterzines.[4]

---

[4]My most recent source of information, a database list published in the United States in early 1992 and entitled *The LIST of PROFESSIONALS stories*, or *the Ultimate "Hatstand" List* , gives 2,024 titles of stories, 32 titles of novels, 49 titles of fanzines, and 5 titles of letterzines. My estimate of the 1992-93 production is extremely conservative.

Inspector Morse fandom started in early 1991 and is much less extensive than that of *The Professionals*: It seems to be restricted to educated women over 30, living prevailingly in Great Britain, with smaller groups in the United States and Australia, and its output appears to be limited. It is exclusively slash, and by the end of 1993 it had produced one letterzine and about 20 stories, none longer than 40 pages.

The fans' discussions of the two series in the letterzines[5] provide initial indications on the way the episodes and the characters are reconceptualized. Comments focus almost exclusively on personal themes (the relationship between the two main characters, the way each of them is constructed cumulatively in the subsequent episodes, and the interaction between each man and other characters) and pay little attention to other elements such as ideology or politics. This emphasis on "the personal," common to fans' readings of many action series, has been interpreted by Jenkins (1992) in the framework of recent feminist literary theories about gender-specific reading: He shows that a focus on relationships rather than action or politics is a subversive reading strategy, an appropriation of male-oriented genres to express women's specific desires.

A comparison of the views that fans of *The Professionals* and *Inspector Morse* have of the relationships between the two central pair-bonds shows clear, if subtle, differences in focus. Some women in both fandoms reject the notion of more than a close friendship between the two pairs of partners as inconsistent with the way they are characterized in the series; most, however, extrapolate the signs of intimacy and closeness present in some episodes and explicitly state that they could be read and reconstructed as part of the wider context of a deep emotional/sexual involvement.[6] However, B/D fans tend to focus more on the homoerotic subtext of the series, whereas M/L fans tend to concentrate more on the emotional closeness between the two characters:

---

[5] *The Professionals* letterzines to which I have been able to gain access are *The Hatstand Express* (produced first in Australia and subsequently in the United States between 1984 and 1989), *Short Circuit* (produced in the United States between 1990 and 1992, and in Australia since late 1992), and *Be Gentle With Us* (produced in Northern Ireland between 1991 and 1994). An *Inspector Morse* letterzine (*Oxford Blue/Newcastle Brown*) ran in Britain between early 1991 and late 1992. *Inspector Morse* was also discussed extensively in another British slash letterzine, *Late for Breakfast.*

[6] Although some stories and contributions to letterzines are signed, most are anonymous or written under pseudonyms for fear of reprisals from television producers, negative reactions by family members, co-workers, and employees; and possible prosecution under obscenity laws, particularly in Britain. In this article I respect the fans' wish to anonymity by mentioning only the titles of the stories quoted and the names of the letterzines.

In "The Ojuka Situation"—after Doyle's famous line about "you priapismic monster", when Bodie rang shortly afterwards to come up, notice he didn't say, "it's THE priapismic monster", but rather, "it's YOUR priapismic monster"! Little things like that I always notice. Later, at the hotel, when the desk girl asked them if they'd "mind sharing", the look that passed between them was priceless. Smug, and amused. (*The Hatstand Express* #12)

The final sequence [of the episode "Dead on Time"] said so much. Lewis, still worried about Morse, goes looking for him. When he eventually finds him Morse does not seem that surprised that Lewis had sat outside his house all night. Maybe it confirmed what he hoped was true—that Lewis had become the close friend he had always wanted, that he hoped he was. How far that friendship would go, well, I know we would like to see! . . . [Lewis's respect for Morse] is more important than anything else—his wife, even his job which he puts on the line by destroying evidence. (*Oxford Blue/Newcastle Brown* #7)

This genre reconceptualization becomes central in the fans' own production: The meanings constructed by the two series are appropriated in order for notions of masculinity to be reconstructed and for women's desires to be at the same time expressed and displaced.

FANTASY SCENARIOS AND WOMEN'S DESIRES: (1) THE "FIRST-TIME" STORY

In their seminal essay "Fantasy and the Origins of Sexuality," Laplanche and Pontalis (1964/1968) argue that the primary function of fantasy is "to be a setting for desire" (p. 27), with a number of recurrent scenarios that give fantasies coherence and continuity. In her analysis of the representation of fantasy in films, Cowie (1984) develops this notion, arguing that the main pleasure experienced by viewers is in the setting rather than in the consummation. This is apparent in one of the main features of slash writing, namely, the displacement strategy already noted in the fans' discussions. Although the main emphasis of the two series is on action (hunts for villains and violent confrontations in one case, discovery of clues and motives in the other), with the relationship between the two main characters an important but subsidiary element, the stories reverse this by making the relationship between the two men central and any action subsidiary to it. Many stories have some connection with one or more episodes of the series, but focus on the interaction between Bodie and Doyle or between Morse and Lewis in situations in which their preoccupation is with each other rather than with their colleagues and opponents. Slash texts are often set in off-duty times (evenings, weekends, days off, holidays). Even the stories in which villains do appear and are foiled contain comparatively little action, with the plot emphasizing instead the different ways each partner reacts to complicated or dangerous circumstances and to the other.

Additional evidence for the argument that the main pleasure of fantasy lies in its setting rather than its plot is provided by the fact that slash stories are constructed around a limited number of scenarios, which are easily identifiable and classifiable (see Jenkins, 1992). The most frequent is that of the "first-time" story, namely, the first sexual encounter between the two partners.[7] Jenkins (1992) connects this scenario to Sedgwick's (1985) theoretical notion of the "homosocial continuum," with "homosocial" defined as "a social bond between persons of the same sex," and "continuum" as the area of experience between homosocial and homosexual relations (pp. 1-2). He shows that the narrative formula of "first-time" stories is based on a series of movements from the initial comradeship toward a reconfirmation of the bond through sexual intimacy. Russ (1985b) and Lamb and Veith (1986) have connected the fascination with "first times" to women's socialization and desires: They have argued that, in representing the move from friendship to deeper intimacy, women—socialized not to initiate sexual relationships—express at the same time a sexualization of their conditioning and their own needs. That these analyses are complementary is clearly shown by some recurring features of the "first-time" formula.

The first feature is the fact that in many stories the sexual encounter is represented as the very first homosexual one for at least one of the two men. In *Professionals* stories, the inexperienced partner is usually Doyle: Bodie is often constructed as having had some loveless homosexual experiences among sex-starved mercenaries in the African jungle. In *Inspector Morse* stories, the never-married Morse is usually (re)constructed as being interested in men more than women, and the hitherto completely (or almost completely) heterosexual Lewis as discovering, and acting on, his love and desire for his superior officer. In fact, whereas in B/D hatstands the decision to initiate a sexual relationship is fairly evenly distributed between Bodie and Doyle, in M/L texts the initiative is nearly always attributed to Lewis. This may be because writers want to avoid depicting anything that might be construed as sexual harassment by a superior officer, but also—and in my opinion more probably—because the older, inhibited man's delighted realization that he is the object of another person's desire compensates for the frequent endings in the television series which foreground Morse's loneliness and unfulfilled emotional

---

[7]Of the texts I have examined, over half of those based on *The Professionals* and nearly two-thirds of those based on *Inspector Morse* are "first-time" stories.

needs after he has solved a case. Penley (1992), in her analysis of K/S stories based on Laplanche and Pontalis's psychoanalytical model, argues
that the stories in which either or both partners had previously been exclusively heterosexual allow women a greater range of identification: "In the
fantasy one can *be* Kirk or Spock (a possible phallic identification) and
also still *have* (as sexual objects) either or both of them, since, as heterosexuals, they are not *un*available to women" (p. 488; emphasis in original). Shifting, rather than fixed, identification—an important feature of
Laplanche and Pontalis's model—becomes the core of a number of perspectives for fans, who at different times may choose to identify with the
more "realistic" or the more "idealistic" partner (respectively, Bodie and
Lewis, and Doyle and Morse), and with the more open or the more
reserved partner.

A second significant feature of "first-time" stories is connected
both with shifting identification and the fact that an important characteristic of one of the partners is his introverted, withdrawn disposition. "First-
time" stories focus on the processes through which these men learn to
admit their emotional needs to themselves and their partners, overcoming
their fears of rejection and discovering dependence and intimacy as
sources of strength. The significance is salient in view of the fact that most
of the authors of the texts are heterosexual women: What is central is,
rather than the exploration of homosexuality, the representation of men
discovering their own capacity for openness and tenderness.

A third—and in my opinion the most important—feature of "first-
time" stories is the fact that sex is always intimately linked to the pre-exist-
ing partnership. The sexual relation either starts off as a lighthearted casual
romp and then triggers the realization that the partner is needed as more
than a close friend and backer, or develops as the consequence of
increased intimacy through a crisis, which makes it possible for both to
acknowledge the depth of their mutual dependency. This obviously
reflects the writers' and readers' desire—conditioned as it may be—for sex
as a part of a relationship already established on a basis of friendship and
full mutual acceptance. Many texts, in fact, make explicit references to
each partner acknowledging and accepting the other's physical and emotional shortcomings: Bodie's thickening waistline, Doyle's broken cheek-
bone, Morse's unfitness, Bodie's arrogance, Doyle's guilt feelings, Morse's
short temper and tendency to drink, and Lewis's intellectual naiveté.

> "No," [Bodie] agreed mildly, "you never have liked admitting that
> that self-sufficient image is just so much crap. You're forgetting, sun-
> shine, this isn't exactly some wild fling on my part. I've worked with
> you for over five years, day in, day out. I know exactly what I'm get-
> ting." He drew an impatient breath. "You stupid sod, d'you think I'd
> want you any different?" ("Beggar's Banquet")

> "I know you're kind," offered Lewis by way of an apology, "and
> compassionate, and sensitive, and . . . " At Morse's grimace he broke
> off, then continued with, "Obstinate, rash and downright argumenta-
> tive when the mood takes you." ("At the End of a Bloody Day")

In fact, I would argue that in "first-time" stories entering into a sexual relationship can be read primarily as a metaphor for the making of a priority
commitment: Once affection and trust have found a physical expression,
each of the partners becomes the most important person in the other's life,
and the relationship takes priority over any previous involvements, particularly heterosexual ones.[8] This is especially evident in the Morse/Lewis
stories, in which the priority commitment between the two men must be
reconciled with Lewis being married. In some recontextualizations by the
writers, the relationship between Morse and Lewis initially coexists with
the marriage and creates conflicts within it; more often it develops after a
rift has become apparent between Lewis and his wife, and it always
becomes an exclusive, monogamous commitment for both men after the
final breakdown of the marriage. Thus, in the fantasy settings the institution of heterosexuality is defeated by a stronger, more satisfying form of
pair-bonding. This can be interpreted as an implicit oppositional strategy
to the prevailing (heterosexist) construction of social relations, in which
heterosexual love and commitment almost automatically take priority over
"mere" same-sex bonds. The tensions about heterosexuality as an institution are examined in more detail later in the chapter.

THE EROTICIZATION OF NURTURANCE

Another recurrent feature of slash texts, both "first-time" stories and stories
in which there already is a sexual bond between the partners, is intimacy
growing through one partner providing physical and/or emotional comfort
to the other who is sick, wounded, or troubled. This is such a frequent formula that it has come to be identified by a shorthand label of its own, h/c
(hurt/comfort). Hurt/comfort has already been discussed by Russ (1985b),
Lamb and Veith (1986) and Jenkins (1992), all of whom point out that the
"hurt" suffered by one partner is clearly the pretext for the "comfort" pro-

---

[8]In the explicit words of one of the best British slash writers, "Who cares about
C15 and international terrorism? We all know that what the fans are really dying to
see is B and D share sandwiches/exchange backchat in the car/save each other's
lives. Slash just takes this further, and personally I find it essential that B and D
mean more to each other than anyone else ever could, therefore they have to be
lovers so that there is absolutely no possibility that any perky women can come
along and get between them" (Be Gentle With Us #9).

vided by the other. It must be stressed, however, that hurt/comfort is the extreme instance of a process of eroticization of nurturance, which is possibly the most fascinating feature of slash. In a great many stories the discovery of mutual love occurs as one partner recognizes and satisfies a basic need of the other—physical (warmth, food, care during illness) or emotional (reassurance)—and, more or less explicitly, "mothers" him. Recurrent settings of B/D stories are enclosed, but cold environments (unheated rooms, tents, cars in night stakeouts), where one of the partners seeks warmth and the other provides it, with the warmth moving from the physical dimension to the metaphorical one of closeness and tenderness:

> "Feet're warm again now," Doyle said sleepily, just as Bodie was on the point of dropping off again, and feeling strangely comfortable with Doyle's skinny frame pressing against him, warming him. ("A Very Different Kind of Hotwater Bottle")

The gratification of the desire for food, like that of the desire for warmth, comes to represent protectiveness by one partner toward the other, often expressed in the form of orders combining affection and authority:

> "Another cup?"
> "Yeah, thanks."
> [Bodie] poured it, piled chicken and chips on two plates, plonked one in front of Doyle, and sat beside him.
> "Get outside of that, sunshine. It'll do you the world of good."
> "You'll make someone a wonderful mother," Doyle said, acid in his voice, but his initial picking at the food did not last more than a few mouthfuls. His hunger had only been dulled by exhaustion, and once started, he cleared his plate but for the bones. ("Of Tethered Goats and Tigers").

> "This is nice, Robbie. You spoil me."
> "Thought you might need a proper breakfast—especially after last night."
> "Any regrets?"
> "None. Eat up, it's getting cold." (story fragment in *Oxford Blue/Newcastle Brown* #5)

Although not specifically sexual in themselves, warmth and food are eroticized because they give a physical dimension to the closeness of the bond between the partners and lead to, or become a part of, an intimacy that also has a sexual component. The shifting identification mentioned earlier probably also applies to this scenario, with writers and readers choosing to identify with the character who nurtures, or with the character who is being nurtured, or with both.

Inspector Morse's pleasure in being looked after is particularly interesting in view of the character's age: Writers and readers explore and identify with the need for nurturance even in people who are no longer young, and who have apparently reached self-sufficiency with maturity. In fact, the need to maintain a competent, cool façade—part of the basic construct of all heroes of action series—is regularly recontextualized in slash texts, becomes an important part of the expressions of nurturance, and is in turn eroticized: One partner encourages the other to admit and explore the fears and insecurities that lie beneath the façade, and the ensuing emotional closeness enables both men to acknowledge the depth of their bond and extend it to the physical dimension. In one of the longer M/L stories, Lewis encourages Morse to express his repressed feelings for him by forcefully pointing out that they are both adults, responsible for their actions:

> "I do know . . . that I've never had the destruction of anyone else's career on my conscience."
> "You let *me* worry about *my* career," Lewis told him, aggressively.
> "Oh, for God's sake, Lewis . . . "
> "My name's Robert Paul," Lewis told him suddenly, sharply. "I don't care which."
> Those world-weary blue eyes stared sadly across the room at him from beneath shaggy white eyebrows. In the silence Lewis held the gaze confidently, chin lifted, returning with interest the concern in Morse's expression. ("Oak and Mistletoe")

In a *Professionals* story set during one of the episodes of the series, on the eve of a deadly confrontation with dangerous enemies, Bodie's attempt to jolt Doyle out of his gloomy forebodings about the following day is both assertively protective and strongly eroticized:

> "No," [Bodie] said fiercely, gripping the green-clad shoulders, shaking him. "No way. You cut this out, d'you hear me? You've got to stop it now, Ray, before it goes too far. You're not gonna die tomorrow. I won't let you. We're not going to die," he said with emphasis; and waited, staring frowning into his partner's strangely beautiful face. Then:
> "Someone is," said Doyle bleakly. "So why should we be the lucky ones?"
> Bodie had no answer for that. No words.
> Doyle watched with unflickering eyes as Bodie leant towards him, his own eyes steady; but he was a little unsure, hesitant as he touched his lips to Doyle's forehead. When Doyle didn't flinch, he drew in a deep shuddering breath as a flood of strangeness and longing ripped through him, and his suddenly hungry mouth sought out and found Ray Doyle's. ("Between the Lines")

FANTASY SCENARIOS AND WOMEN'S DESIRES: (2) VIRTUAL MARRIAGE

The texts that focus on the progress of the relationship between the two partners beyond the first sexual encounter show that it extends to cover almost all aspects of their lives and becomes fusional, with each partner fulfilling most of the other's physical and emotional needs. In many stories the bond develops into a virtual marriage: The partners make an explicit commitment to each other, promise to forsake all others of either gender, and decide to live together.

> Doyle gave [Bodie] an uncomplicated smile. "Would you marry me?"
>
> "In a heartbeat." Bodie helped himself to another kiss. "But we can't. Not legal, remember?"
>
> With one hand flattened against Bodie's chest, Doyle said confidently, "We can. In here. Much more important than on a piece of paper. . . . You won't ever leave me?"
>
> "Have to beat me away, you silly sod."
>
> . . . "And you won't ever want anyone else?"
>
> . . . "What d'you think? No, I won't."
>
> . . . "Then I, Raymond Doyle," he whispered formally, "am yours. And only yours. Forever, Bodie."
>
> . . . "Then I, William Bodie. . . . " He faltered, knowing that once said, these words would bind him for the rest of his life. It surprised him that they came so easily. "Will be yours for as long as you want me." ("And Memories Die")

In the longer established, and therefore more varied, B/D output, there are some sequences of stories which—with varying degrees of sentimentality—map the progress of Bodie and Doyle's intimacy over the years and explore various conflicts and problems that arise within it. A humorous sequence of 26 short pieces by a British author, known under its overall title "The Party Spirit," describes their interaction "between the lines" of the sequence of episodes in the television series: The relationship moves from a semi-drunken sexual romp supposed to take place just before the first episode, through increasingly more tender and meaningful encounters after some of the incidents represented in the series, and ending after the last episode with Bodie and Doyle declaring their relationship to the Controller, agreeing to resign from CI5, and deciding to live together and work as partners in a private security firm. In the "Emma" series (14 stories by an American author, set between 1975 and 1990), Bodie and Doyle start off by having casual sex, then live together nonmonogamously, and finally, 15 years after their first encounter, formalize their bond by making a public commitment to each other and to monogamy. In the "Rainy

Days" series (14 stories by an Australian author, set between 1980 and 1991), the two men decide to be monogamous from the start and show their commitment through presents, celebrations of anniversaries, and trips to romantic places. In these last two series Bodie and Doyle are provided with what the author of the "Emma" series calls "an extended family":[9] estranged parents who decide to heal previous rifts, surrogate children in the form of nieces and nephews, or even children one or the other partner had while still in his teens, who reappear as young adults and form stable relationships with both men. Similarly, in the more limited M/L output, two of the longest stories have the relationship between Morse and Lewis progress over several months from mutual respect to mutual attraction, gradual overcoming of the differences between them, acknowledgement of love, Lewis parting from his wife, and finally commitment to a life together; middle-aged, childless Morse also gradually establishes a satisfying, continuing relationship with Lewis's children.

This aspect of slash fiction clearly shows that many women's fantasies express a desire for a lasting monogamous commitment and recognized, even if unofficial, family ties.[10] The stories also, however, subversively suggest that men develop most positively through long-term interpersonal relations rather than professional activities and violent action. Furthermore, they are indicative of the desire for a complete partnership, in which both people maintain their identity and the personal and the public spheres are not separate. The household chores are seen as just as valid a part of life as the confrontations with the villains, and shared just as equally.

> Wash the windows, take out the refuse, and push the Hoover around the flat—fine by me, I said, and only when I'd said it did I realise what I'd agreed to. By that time it was too late to take it back, and I shocked myself again: I didn't want to take it back. I was pleased to do "the roughs" in exchange for home cooking. . . . Damn, if we weren't settling down into marriage, what the hell were we doing? ("Rainy Days")

---

[9]In an interview published in *The Hatstand Express* #16, she stated: "[W]hile a settled, happy family life is unlikely for men in that position, they are human enough to want something that approximates a family. . . . Despite strong feelings that fan writers tend to romanticise B&D (these are not nice guys who just happen to kill people sometimes, these are the next best thing to hired killers), I do think domesticity is possible within certain parameters even for B&D, and I love exploring those parameters."

[10]As one fan puts it, "This is my fantasy world and I make the rules. Therefore Bodie and Doyle . . . are not going to spend their time having sexual encounters with other people, male or female, once they have settled in a sexual relationship with each other. Yes, it's a very idealised view of life, but that's what escapism is all about." (*Late for Breakfast* #13)

THE ROLE OF SEX SCENES: SLASH AS PORNOGRAPHY?

Sex is, of course, an integral part of this complete partnership fantasy—and thus an integral component of slash texts—and is usually portrayed in explicit detail. Heterosexual female desire and writers' and readers' identification are inscribed as long, detailed descriptions of male bodies as objects of desire and of male arousal and orgasm as sources of joy and gratification for both partners.

> [Morse] found the hot, secret place between Lewis's legs, heard Lewis's soft cry of pleasure, felt the rich, wet heat of Lewis's love on his fingers, and let go completely, as he could only with Lewis, his eyes fixed on the blackness outside of the car as he climaxed in luscious, contracting waves of joy. ("Fragile Citadels")

In the literature on slash, the sex scenes have been interpreted either as romantic metaphors or as outright women's pornography. In their discussion of the role played by sex in K/S stories, Lamb and Veith (1986) state that the descriptions of sexual intimacy are mainly metaphors for the intensity of the emotional intimacy. Both Russ (1985) and Penley (1992) take the opposite view. Russ emphasizes "the raw sexual and emotional starvation the writers are expressing so openly" (p. 96), and Penley argues that a focus on slash as romance "slights the pornographic force of these stories" (p. 491). Both strengthen their argument by mentioning that some slash fiction contains sado-masochist sex scenes, which range from playful bondage to detailed rape and torture. They firmly situate slash within the complex debates of the 1980s between radical and libertarian feminists on the politics of pornography.[11] Siding with the libertarian position, they state that sexual fantasies are separate from women's reality (Penley, 1992, p. 491), not literal representations of women's desires (Russ, 1985b, pp. 88-92), and one of the most powerful channels of expression of female subjectivity.

I am entirely convinced by Russ's and Penley's view that slash sex scenes reflect what some heterosexual women find arousing and what they would like to experience in sex with men. The emphasis is on the diffuse pleasure that comes from physical closeness (touching, licking, and exploring each other's bodies) as opposed to direct genital stimulation: The female point of view is evident, for instance, in the central part played by the caressing of pectorals, nipples, and buttocks (see Russ, 1985a). A particularly interesting heterosexual female perspective, if possibly prob-

---

[11]For an overview of these debates, see Berger, Searles, and Cottle (1991). For libertarian feminist perspectives, see Segal and McIntosh (1992).

lematic from a feminist viewpoint, can be seen in the descriptions of anal intercourse: In an implicit (and at times explicit) ranking of sexual acts, penetration is often represented as the ultimate sign of trust and the ultimate surrender of self to the partner.

> Their loving was indeed slow and gentle, but was quite fulfilling for Doyle, sheathed in warm, strong muscle, and judging by Bodie's sighs and the shivering that racked his body as Doyle picked up the pace slightly. They swam leisurely to climax . . .
> "You know," said Bodie, cuddling Doyle, who was still cradled on top of him, although his cock had slipped out, "we've just accomplished the double consummation. Does that mean we're married?"
> ("Sword of Damocles")

However, I would argue against Russ's and Penley's identification of slash with pornography. In the definition of the leading radical feminist Helen Longino (1980), pornography is the representation of "sexual behavior that is degrading or abusive to one or more of the participants *in such a way as to endorse the degradation even if the person has chosen or consented to it*" (p. 43, emphasis in original). Slash sex scenes, far from representing degrading behavior, are usually set in contexts of deep emotional closeness, which, as Russ (1985a) herself points out, are as much part of the fantasy as the sexual activities themselves. Sado-masochist scenes, which would meet Longino's definition, are relatively infrequent: There are none in the *Inspector Morse* texts produced so far, and they occur—mainly as depictions of male rape—in about 10% of *Professionals* texts.[12] These scenes are either extreme instances of hurt/comfort, with the main emphasis on the rape victim being nurtured by his partner, or else they are displaced expressions of women's very real and constant fears of rape and violence. This applies particularly to the few texts which represent one partner being raped by the other. The readers' responses in the letterzine discussions range from acknowledgment that sado-masochism does appeal erotically to some writers and readers ("I like S/M stories, and I'm very much interested in the concept of S/M, of what it means in terms of trust, love and different ways of enjoying one's sexuality," *Be Gentle With Us* #10) to the recognition that rape stories are "a method of writing in safety about something which is . . . in real life, repulsive and frightening" (*Short Circuit* #16).

---

[12]The estimate is provided by a contributor to *Short Circuit* #16.

THE SEXUAL POLITICS OF SLASH

The problematic fact that the ideal relationship in slash texts is one between two men reflects an inescapable tension inherent in them. As Russ (1985b), Lamb and Veith (1986), and Penley (1991) have persuasively shown, slash fiction is basically a fantasy of authentic love which can exist only between equals; specifically, people who are strong and share adventures as well as emotions. The texts emphasize equality also in partnerships—such as the one between Morse and Lewis—in which there are differences in age, rank, and competence: The younger or less experienced man is shown to be equally valuable in human terms because he is constructed as perceptive, open, and affectionate, and thus exerts a humanizing influence on his (usually more morose) partner. The fact that, in women's fantasy scenarios, this egalitarian love is constructed as impossible between men and women reveals a pessimistic unease about the institution of heterosexuality; this is despite the majority of writers and readers of slash texts being committed to heterosexuality in their own lives. Some of this tension emerges in the complex *Professionals* novella "Starlight, Starbright." Bodie and Doyle, while working separately on an undercover assignment, start having dreams about each other; however, the dream partner, although retaining all the original psychological and most physical traits, is female. The dreams function as a catalyst: As each man gradually discloses them to his "real-life" partner, both realize the depth of their bond, seal it with lovemaking, and decide to live together while continuing to work for CI5. The dreamed heterosexual relationships, however, develop differently. The partners also fall in love, nurture each other, and get married, but although the "female" Bodie and Doyle are competent and tough agents, their husbands become unhappy about their staying in their dangerous jobs, and the women end up leaving CI5 and settling into domesticity as soon as they become pregnant. In M/L stories, the elimination of Mrs. Lewis can also be read as a rejection, in the fantasy scenarios, of the sex role division that assigns women to the maintenance of the private sphere and men to activity in the social sphere.

The focus on interpersonal relations also explains why comparatively few stories represent the main characters as explicitly gay-identified and/or concerned with political issues related to homosexuality such as discrimination, the threat of AIDS, and safe sex practices. In 1988 the popular author of the "Emma" series forthrightly stated her belief that an avoidance of gay politics was due to implicit homophobia:

> What bothers me is a vague suspicion that there are a whole lot of other writers who find homosexuality sort of icky. After all, homosexuality is being . . . queer, isn't it? And queers are effeminate and they have nasty diseases from doing gross things, don't they? And our boys would never do things like that, would they? (*The Hatstand Express* #16)

Some *Professionals* narratives written in the late 1980s and early 1990s do reflect a growing awareness of the fact that homosexuality is a political question. They extend both the relevance and the parameters of slash by dealing with specifically gay issues such as safe sex practices and "outing." One recent novel, *Shadows over the Land*—set in the late 1980s—is explicitly political: Doyle is forced to resign from CI5 after being "outed" by the British gutter press, and he becomes a gay activist involved in a number of campaigns. In a 1993 Australian novel, *Sword of Damocles*, Bodie and Doyle confront the possibility of having contracted AIDS during their past sexual experiences: The main theme is the growth of love out of friendship and comfort, but the social and political aspects are the pervasive, if understated, background.

Political perspectives have—so far—not been part of *Inspector Morse* stories, in spite of their having been written in the 1990s. An M/L fan indirectly voices the widely shared feeling that stories in which gay issues are the dominant topic would run the risk of becoming driven by the need to make political statements rather than by the need to express spontaneous desires about relationships:

> [S]orry, but the homosexuality issue doesn't really seem relevant to me. With M/L we're dealing with slash, which is a different thing entirely, i.e. fantasy. What we want to see on the screen and write and read bears very little resemblance to "real" homosexuality. Don't know about you, but I don't want "reality" in my slash. Slash is my escape. (*Oxford Blue/Newcastle Brown* #5)

SLASH AS ROMANCE FICTION

A reading of slash texts as repetitive scenarios of "what some women want" coincides to some extent with the conclusions of recent analyses of heterosexual romance fiction. As the fans themselves acknowledge,[13] these two genres have evident similarities, based on a number of shared features.

The first feature is the narrative formula, which develops from an initial unfulfilled desire, through one or more crises and protracted delays, to a happy ending in which the relationship between the two main characters is stronger and more rewarding for both. As surprising as at first sight it may seem, this formula also applies to "death stories," which generally focus on one of the partners coping with his mate's (usually unexpected

---

[13]In the words of another leading British B/D writer, "Slash is the idealized romance, two against the world, forsaking all others: the ultimate Mills and Boon" (*Short Circuit* #15).

and violent) death. These apparently pessimistic texts are in fact further explorations of the depth of commitment in the relationship: Often one man sacrifices his life to save the other, who continues to love his partner beyond the grave. In "Endgame," a much-admired, powerfully written *Professionals* story, the mood is one of overwhelming bleakness: After Doyle's death, Bodie goes to pieces, realizing that his partner embodied everything that was valuable to him. Yet Bodie's own death, which he relentlessly seeks and finally achieves, is represented not so much as an ending but as a reunion: "He did not see the crowds, nor the rising sweep of the ancient weapon. He looked into [Doyle's] smoky green eyes, and he was laughing as the shining arc of steel sang down."

The "happy ending" formula of both heterosexual romance and slash fits perfectly the description of what has been identified by psychology researchers as a typical female fantasy pattern: a movement from an initial state of physical or emotional "deprivation" through a dramatic turning point to a final outcome of "enhancement" (satisfaction, success, and growth).[14] The cultural competence needed to decode both sorts of texts is also the same. For both slash and romance readers the eventual outcome of "enhancement" is given, and the pleasure lies in the sequence of events leading to it and in the variations on this sequence.

A second shared characteristic is the construction of sex as part of a committed relationship: In both slash and romance, passionate lovemaking between the protagonists usually takes place after each acknowledges the primacy of the other in his or her life.

Another common feature is the nurturance fantasy scenario. Socialized since early childhood to be responsive to others' needs and to ignore their own,[15] many women feel the lack of nurturance in their own lives and in their relationships with men.[16] As May's (1980) analysis of male and female fantasies clearly shows, women structure their fantasies around interpersonal relationships, with aspects of love and caring as central themes. Both heterosexual romances and slash narratives can be defined as fantasies in which the sexual desires women are trained to suppress and the nurturance they are trained to cultivate come together, have a positive outcome, and result in satisfaction.

Radway's (1984) study of women's responses to romance fiction highlights their deeply felt need for representations of men who are at the same time assertive partners and active nurturers. In romances,

---

[14]See May (1980, pp. 17-32).

[15]The extensive literature on women's socialization is summarized in May (1980) and Chodorow (1978, 1989); see also Dinnerstein (1976/1987).

[16]See, among others, Dinnerstein ([1976] (1987), Rich (1977), and Chodorow (1978, 1989).

the final goal of each narrative is the creation of that perfect union
where the ideal male, who is masculine and strong yet nurturant too,
finally recognizes the intrinsic worth of the heroine. . . . [T]he reader,
as a result of her identification with the heroine, feels herself the
object of someone else's attention and solicitude. (Radway, p. 97;
emphasis in original)

In slash texts, women's desire for nurturance is eroticized and displaced
onto masculine bodies. This displaced identification can be traced back
partly to the male-dominated nature of society (and women's alienation
from their own bodies) and partly to the fact that men are the main object
of heterosexual women's erotic interest.

However, Radway (1984) also argues that this yearning for nurturance from someone who is both gentle and strong

seems to mask a covert and unconscious wish to regress to the state of
infancy in order to experience again, but this time completely and
without the slight withholding born of homophobia, that primary love
the infant received at the breast and hands of her mother. (p. 145)

She draws on Chodorow's (1978, 1989) model of the pre-Oedipal mother-
daughter relationship, in which the young girl has all her physical and
emotional needs fulfilled by her mother, whom she must reject as a primary love object in favor of her father in order to become heterosexual.
However, the girl retains the need for the original fusional relationship
even after she becomes an adult and establishes satisfactory, if not so nurturing, relationships with men (Chodorow 1978, 1989).[17] Penley (1992)
argues against too broad an application of this model to women's fantasies, claiming that reducing female identification to a pre-Oedipal position would be limited and would not take into account the multiple subject positions afforded by fantasy. It would undoubtedly be an over-simpli-
fication to read slash texts *exclusively* as pre-Oedipal fantasies of complete
same-sex nurturance. However, it cannot be denied that the central aspect
of slash fantasies is the notion of a same-sex working partnership being
extended to the emotional/sexual sphere, with each partner being relied
on to always be there and never—unlike the dynamics of the
mother/daughter relationship—rejecting the other for someone of the
opposite sex. Chodorow's model cannot be disregarded, but it needs to be
integrated with psychoanalytic fantasy theory and expanded with an
analysis of the fans' ambiguous and contradictory position vis-à-vis the
institution of heterosexuality.

---

[17]Chodorow's model is discussed, from feminist standpoints, in Flax (1990),
Rowley and Grosz (1990), and Whitford (1991).

In this respect the intertextual references to heterosexual romances found in slash texts are particularly significant. The most obvious are the descriptions of Bodie's shady past and tall, dark, and brooding looks which are found in many *Professionals* stories.[18] In a considerable minority of slash texts, intertextuality is evident also in the polarization of the partners into one who is rational and dominant and one who is emotional and submissive. In some B/D narratives, Bodie's protective attitude toward Doyle, occasionally visible in the television series, is reconstructed in the discourse of romance fiction: The references to Bodie's "large capable hands," "arrogant mouth," "powerful thighs," and "forceful" behavior are often paralleled by references to Doyle's "slight frame," "come-hither eyes," tendency to weep, and manipulative disposition—personality traits stereotypically attributed to women. In a few M/L stories, the loneliness and inhibitions attributed to Morse in Dexter's books and in the television series are reconstructed as clinging fragility, and Lewis's working-class directness as assertive, if loving, control:

> [Lewis] kissed Morse again, nothing gentle about this kiss, he thought, almost ashamed of the brutal passion that rose in him, causing him to thrust his tongue roughly down Morse's throat, and eliciting a ragged moan of—no, not complaint: complicity. Morse loved it, loved this powerful handling. Well, he could have more of it, Lewis thought. ("Heat and Flush'd")

This trend has also, however, been criticized in very strong terms in the letterzine discussions as totally inconsistent not only with the original characterizations, but also with the basic notion of slash as a fantasy involving two equal partners:

> The thing I really hate most is this dominant/passive characterization. First of all, neither of these men are weak or ineffectual. And second, even if your particular mindset requires that one member of a couple be male and the other female (no matter what they have between their legs), women are NOT weak and ineffectual either. (*The Hatstand Express* #16)

This polarized heterosexualization of the male pair-bond can be traced back to both the pre-Oedipal nurturance fantasy and the ambivalence of writers (and readers) vis-à-vis heterosexuality. The texts reflect the conflict

---

[18]Bodie is also occasionally compared to some heroes of 19th-century English literature. In one hatstand ("Coldwater Morning") he is explicitly defined as "the poor man's Heathcliff" and in another ("Flu 2"), repeated parallels are drawn between him and Jane Austen's Darcy.

between the desire for protection and the desire for equality, and the tension inherent in the attempt to imagine men who can simultaneously look after a loved person with the affectionate authority of a mother and respect that person's autonomy as an adult. The intertextual references to romance fiction are therefore both tribute and rejection.

CONCLUSION: HOW SUBVERSIVE IS SLASH?

Slash fiction is a complex and constantly evolving genre. Just as there can be no one definitive answer to the question of women's motivations in writing and reading it, there can be no single evaluation of its functions and potential. Jenkins concludes his analysis of slash by stating that, although not all of it is politically conscious, progressive, or feminist, it has considerable progressive potential because it "provide[s] common terms within which a dialogue about the politics of sexuality may be conducted, and create[s] opportunities where the social construction of gender may be explored with greater openness and self-consciousness" (p. 221). This evaluation can be expanded in the light of studies of romance fiction by feminist scholars. Radway (1984) expresses concern at what she sees as an inherent ambiguity of romance reading. On the one hand, it can be interpreted as "an activity of mild protest and longing for reform" (pp. 212-215) with regard to the institutions of heterosexuality and monogamous marriage. On the other hand, from a feminist point of view, romance reading can also be seen as an activity that vicariously supplies women with their needs and thus potentially disarms their impulse to change those institutions. Modleski (1984) argues instead that, although romance texts appear to support patriarchal myths and institutions, "the anxieties and tensions [these institutions] give rise to may be said to provoke the need for the texts in the first place" (p. 113). It is therefore crucial to let the "very omissions and distortions [of the texts] speak, informing us of the contradictions they are meant to conceal and, equally importantly, of the fears that lie behind them" (p. 113).

Slash narratives lend themselves to similar open-ended interpretations. As in romance fiction, their reconstructions of male characters are indicative of a desire for change in the concept of masculinity and in relations involving men. However, the fact that these narratives are scenarios of utopian "ideal partnerships" suggests that they are, rather than a stimulus for change, a safety valve for the stress women experience in their daily lives and in their relationships with men.[19]

---

[19]Further research could usefully prove or disprove this hypothesis, although slash fans would probably be even less prepared to discuss their personal problems than to reveal their identities. A first analysis—problematic for its tendency to overgeneralize—is in Bacon-Smith (1992)

Yet slash has a greater subversive potential than romance fiction. First, although it focuses on men, slash gives voice to some women's desires which are outside the dominant notions of acceptable love relationships. In fact, slash could be convincingly situated within "queer cultural criticism," with the term "queer" used to denote a wide range of non-heterosexual responses to mass culture: "The non-straight work, positions, pleasures, and readings of people who . . . don't share the same 'sexual orientation' as that articulated in the texts they are producing or responding to" (Doty, 1993, p. xviii). Second, slash fiction, although not explicitly about radical sexual politics, reflects tensions that are implicitly political. Although most slash writers have a stake in heterosexuality, many of the texts they produce indicate an awareness that heterosexual relations, however fulfilling, have less potential for equality than same-sex relations. Furthermore, although the majority of slash texts avoid specifically gay issues, most slash fans are opposed to discrimination and homophobia.[20] Finally, slash fans are—unlike the readers of romance fiction—much more than passive consumers. Many move from reading fantasies to writing their own, and most, through their comments on other women's stories and their exchanges in the letterzine discussions, participate in a valuable learning and liberating process: They recognize and verbalize their own—at times problematic and contradictory—needs and desires and begin to analyze the relationship between their sexuality and their subjectivity.

REFERENCES

Bacon-Smith, C. (1992). *Enterprising women: Television fandom and the creation of popular myth.* Philadelphia: University of Pennsylvania Press.

Berger, R. J., Searles, P., & Cottle, C. E. (1991). *Feminism and pornography.* New York: Praeger.

Chodorow, N. (1978). *The reproduction of mothering: Psychoanalysis and the sociology of gender.* Berkeley and Los Angeles: University of California Press.

Chodorow, N. (1989). *Feminism and psychoanalytic theory.* London: Polity Press.

Cowie, E. (1984). Fantasia. *m/f: A Feminist Journal. 9,* 71-105.

Dinnerstein, D. (1987). *The rocking of the cradle and the ruling of the world.* London: The Women's Press. (Original work published 1976 as The Mermaid and the Minotaur.)

---

[20]Some slash fanzines sold at conventions are produced for AIDS-related projects, with part of the sale proceeds going to those projects.

Doty, A. (1993). *Making things perfectly queer: Interpreting mass culture.* Minneapolis: University of Minnesota Press.

Fiske, J. (1987). British cultural studies and television. In R. C. Allen (Ed.), *Channels of discourse. Television and contemporary criticism* (pp. 254-289). London: Methuen.

Flax, J. (1990). *Thinking fragments: Psychoanalysis, feminism, and postmodernism in the contemporary West.* Berkeley: University of California Press.

Haskell, M. (1974). *From reverence to rape: The treatment of women in the movies.* New York: Holt, Rinehart and Winston.

Jenkins, H. (1992). *Textual poachers. Television fans and participatory culture.* New York: Routledge.

Lamb, P. F., & Veith, D. L. (1986). Romantic myth, transcendence, and *Star Trek* zines. In D. Palumbo (Ed.), *Erotic universe—Sexuality and fantastic literature* (pp. 235-255). New York: Greenwood Press.

Laplanche, J., & Pontalis, J-B. (1964). *Fantasme originaire. Fantasme des origines. Origines du fantasme* [Fantasy and the origins of sexuality]. Paris: Hachette. (Reprinted in V. Burgin, J. Donald & C. Kaplan (Eds.), *Formation of fantasy* (pp. 5-34). London and New York: Methuen).

Light, A. (1984). "Returning to Manderley": Romance fiction, female sexuality and class. *Feminist Review, 16,* 7-25.

Longino, H. (1980). Pornography, oppression and freedom: A closer look. In L. Lederer (Ed.), *Take back the night: Women on pornography* (pp. 40-54). New York: Morrow.

May, R. (1980). *Sex and fantasy—Patterns of male and female development.* New York: Norton.

Mellen, J (1977). *Big bad wolves: Masculinity in the American film.* New York: Pantheon Books.

Modleski, T. (1984). *Loving with a vengeance: Mass-produced fantasies for women.* New York and London: Methuen.

Penley, C. (1991). Brownian motion: Women, tactics, and technology. In C. Penley & A. Ross (Eds.), *Technoculture* (pp. 135-161). Minneapolis: University of Minnesota Press.

Penley, C. (1992). Feminism, psychoanalysis and the study of popular culture. In L. Grossberg, C. Nelson & P. Treichler (Eds.), *Cultural studies* (pp. 479-494). New York and London: Routledge.

Radway, J. (1984). *Reading the romance: Women, patriarchy, and popular literature.* Chapel Hill: University of North Carolina Press.

Rich, A. (1977). *Of woman born: Motherhood as experience and institution.* New York: Bantam Books. (Original work published 1976)

Rowley, H., & Grosz, E. (1990). Psychoanalysis and feminism. In S. Gunew (Ed.), *Feminist knowledge, critique and construct* (pp. 175-204). London: Routledge.

Russ, J. (1985a). Another addict raves about K/S. *Nome, 8,* 27-37.
Russ, J. (1985b). Pornography by women for women, with love. In *Magic mommas, trembling sisters, puritans and perverts: Feminist essays* (pp. 79-99). Trumansberg, NY: Crossing.
Sedgwick, E. K. (1985). *Between men: English literature and male homosocial desire.* New York: Columbia University Press.
Segal, L., & McIntosh, M. (Eds). (1992). *Sex exposed: Sexuality and the pornography debate.* London: Virago.
Whitford, M. (1991). *Luce Irigaray: Philosophy in the feminine.* London: Routledge.

▶10

WAR OF THE WORLDS: Richard Chaves, Paul Ironhorse, and the Female Fan Community*

Cinda Gillilan
University of Colorado

Since the mid-1980s, interest in fans and various fan subcultures has increased among media scholars. Academic inquiries address a wide range of fans, including romance readers (Modleski, 1990; Radway, 1984), music groupies (Lewis, 1987, 1990), film buffs (Taylor, 1989; Uricchio & Pearson, 1991), and others. In recent analyses of television fans by Bacon-Smith (1992), Jenkins (1988, 1992), and Penley (1991, 1993), the authors describe the television fan subculture, as well as the products and practices found in this subculture. These foundational texts provide the basis on which more in-depth analyses of the television fan phenomena can be built. This chapter is one such effort.

---

*My heartfelt thanks to Dr. Eileen R. Meehan, University of Arizona, and Ms. Jody Norman, without whose efforts and support this chapter would not have happened.

This work is an interpretative analysis that examines the sources of television fan pleasure and activity in their own words.[1] Through personal interviews, participant observation at fan conventions, and an analysis of fan comments in various publications,[2] I examine the fans' appropriation of the character Paul Ironhorse from the television series *War of the Worlds*. In particular, I survey the reasons for this attraction, as they explain it.

To explore the relationship between the fans and Ironhorse this chapter first describes the series *War of the Worlds* and Ironhorse's role in it. Next, it provides an overview of *War of the Worlds* fandom and discusses how that community operates as a "wild-zone"—a zone of resistance and reinterpretation. Third, it describes how Ironhorse and the actor who played him, Richard Chaves, were incorporated into this "wild-zone" through the fans' construction of both as "feminine heroes."

WAR OF THE WORLDS: THE PROGRAM[3]

Paramount's *War of the Worlds* aired for two seasons (1988-1990) on the Fox network, running from 8 to 9 p.m. in most markets. Following *Star Trek: The Next Generation*, it was the lead-in show for *Friday the 13th.* The series was marketed with an emphasis on horror; *TV Guide* ads proclaimed: "Viewer Alert! . . . Get Your Saturday Night Shivers on Thursday,"

---

[1]I want to thank the fans who were so generous with their time and opinions. And, in keeping with the fans' desires for privacy and anonymity, I have chosen not to identify any of my informants except by a numerical designation. This study is the beginning of a larger ethnography and should not be taken as a qualitative study, although I employ tools of the qualitative approach, including personal and phone interviews, participant observations, and fieldwork undertaken at several fan conventions.

[2]This chapter records and briefly analyzes the concrete responses of a specific television fan subculture. I make no claim that these fans represent the program's reception by non-fan viewers. As Jenkins (1991) explains, fan audiences adopt modes of reception that facilitate their subsequent participation in fan culture. This includes close textual readings of series episodes to tease out character background, narrative inconsistencies, and the identification of topics important to the understanding of character(s) and/or series diegesis. Therefore, the quotes that appear in this chapter were specifically chosen because they are representative of the general feelings and comments in the fandom as a whole.

[3]The broadcast industry is intimately involved in the construction of *War of the Worlds*, its characters, and star personas. However, this chapter does not include an industrial analysis or a political economy of the series, although those influences certainly inform the text. In a more detailed analysis of fan engagement or a more interpretative ethnography, this context would be crucial and I do not want to dismiss it or the ideological framing it provides. The purpose of this particular chapter, though, is to allow the fans to identify their own pleasures in relation to the series.

and "It's a terrifying trio of new shows!" By concentrating the ad campaign on the series' horror elements, Fox marketed *War of the Worlds* primarily as a lead-in to Friday the 13th and targeted a male horror audience, downplaying female viewers from the start. The series' position in the line-up also tapped established science fiction and *Star Trek* fans, many of them already members of television fandom. Whether or not this was intentional on the part of Fox or Paramount, it resulted in the series quickly entering fandom through an established fan audience inclined to embrace it.

The series aired concurrently with the celebration of the 50th anniversary of the 1938 Orson Welles radio broadcast of *War of the Worlds*. Public awareness of the *War of the Worlds* phenomena was high. Metacom released a 50th anniversary audio cassette of the 1938 radio broadcast in bookstores. Grover's Mill, NJ, hosted a celebration marking the anniversary of its role in the Welles program,[4] and the Princeton, NJ-based War of the Worlds, Inc. sold t-shirts, cups, and other merchandise celebrating the long and diverse history of the classic science fiction story. National Public Radio released a re-creation of the original radio broadcast. Prior to the television series debut, a pocket paperback novelization of the pilot appeared in bookstores. And Fox's on-air promotion of the pilot ensured widespread audience awareness of the series.

Rooted in Paramount's 1953 film *War of the Worlds*, the studio's television version of the classic invasion story integrated footage, props, characters, and one actress from the film. The invading aliens of 1953, resurrected 35 years later in the series pilot, set out again to take over the planet. To counter this re-invasion, the government created a special team, the Blackwood Project, comprised of three civilians and their military liaison, Lieutenant Colonel Paul Ironhorse. From the pilot on, Ironhorse was odd-man-out—Indian among whites, soldier among civilians, skeptic among believers. He was pitted against Harrison Blackwood, the Project's civilian head, increasing the possibilities for narrative tension.

Scoring poorly with A.C. Nielsen audiences—ranking near the bottom on a 1 to 15 scale for its first 12 episodes[5]—*War of the Worlds* still ranked third overall among syndicated series during its first season ("Calling it quits," 1990). Despite the ratings, the series rapidly gained a

---

[4]Paramount capitalized on this, filming an episode, "Eye for an Eye," of *War of the Worlds* on location in Grover's Mill.

[5]The *Nielsen Fast Weekly Syndication and Occasional Network Report* listed the following numbers for the first 12 episodes of *War of the Worlds*. The dates are the week ended, and the number following the date is the series ranking (between 1 and 15).

10-16-88 1	10-23-88 6	10-30-88 7	11-06-88 9
11-13-88 10	12-04-88 15	12-18-88 14	01-15-89 10
01-22-89 9	01-29-89 12	02-05-89 13	02-12-89 13

large following in television fandom, and the most popular character among fans was Paul Ironhorse, played by Richard Chaves.[6]

Paramount's printed and electronic presskits described Ironhorse as the series' "action hero," a decidedly Rambo-type character.[7] The electronic presskit also made it clear that the studio did not intend Ironhorse to serve as the point of identification for female viewers—that role fell to Dr. Suzanne McCullough (Lynda Mason Green) or Dr. Harrison Blackwood (Jared Martin), who was described as the series "sensitive, witty, and caring" male lead.

Paramount's emphasis on *War of the Worlds* as the lead-in show for *Friday the 13th* eventually led the studio to turn the series over to a new producer, Frank Mancuso, Jr., after what they perceived as a shaky first season. Mancuso, the producer of *Friday the 13th*, drastically redesigned *War of the Worlds*, replacing the series writers and production staff, and "killing off" the characters of Ironhorse and Norton Drake (the disabled African American computer expert). As a result of these changes, *War of the Worlds* took on a much darker tone that angered the majority of active first season fans. Fan #20 summed up the general sentiment:

> Second season was nothing like the first. It's all doom and gloom, and that's *not* what I'm interested in seeing. I like the characters, and Ironhorse in particular, but also the team as a whole and how they deal with the situations they find themselves in. Second season is garbage! (Fan #20, personal interview, May 26, 1994)

Not only did the fans reject the premise of the second season; they took great pains to rewrite the story line, "resurrecting" Ironhorse and Drake or creating fictional explanations that negated the second season. As of 1995, over 700 pieces of fiction, written by more than 200 authors, ignored the second season altogether; over 150 explained it away; and only 50 remained true to the aired second season diegesis.[8]

---

[6]Philip Akin, who played Norton Drake, commented at a fan convention in New York that Chaves was reputed to receive five to seven bags of fan mail for each bag received by his co-workers.

[7]Indeed, Chaves had already established a track record playing this kind of character in *Predator*. The *War of the Worlds* bible described Ironhorse: "He's what Clint Eastwood would have been had acting not worked out. . . . The Colonel can pilot a plane, handle a helicopter, shoot damn-near every type of gun ever manufactured, use an edged weapon like a gladiator, can live off the land indefinitely, make explosives from simple household products, and recite all the books of the Bible—King James and Catholic. During a crisis like this alien invasion, if someone like Lt. Colonel Paul Ironhorse did not already exist, the country would have had to invent him."

[8]Beginning in 1993 a small revival of popularity surrounding the second season of *War of the Worlds* occurred in fandom. This popularity was the result of fans of Adrian Paul, the actor who took the Ironhorse-like role in the second season, finding *War of the Worlds*. Adrian Paul is currently starring in the fan-popular series *Highlander*. The fan interest is not in *War of the Worlds* for itself, but in Adrian Paul. This is an example of the fans' use of intertextuality.

Following Mancuso's changes, the overnight ratings for the series slumped and Paramount was besieged with mail and calls from irate fans. Ironically, Chaves told attendees at the 1990 Time Con convention that Mancuso explained the departure of Ironhorse as the result of the character being "written into a box," and that Ironhorse was "inaccessible to fans, particularly female fans."[9] Some of these female fans continued to pressure Paramount about the changes until the president of Chaves's fan club asked them to stop because:

> Neither Richard or his agent is sure whether fan-generated write-in/call-in campaigns are helpful or detrimental to his career, so please, if you have any doubts, DON'T DO IT! [sic]. (Wo Ha Li, October, 1989)

By the end of the second season, Paramount cancelled the series. An issue of *Daily Variety* (Lowery, 1989) stated that the studio found the ratings no longer justified the series' high budgets, approximately $600,000 to $700,000 per hour episode.

WAR OF THE WORLDS: THE FANDOM

War of the Worlds fandom is typical of television fandoms. Individual fans form networks and organize "zine" and "letterzine" projects focusing on the show. *Zines* are collections of fan-written fiction based primarily on television series and characters.[10] *Letterzines* are forums for discussions of favorite series, characters, and topics.[11] Both products provide sites for fan interaction, discussion, and participation with a particular series, its characters, and actors. It is an ongoing process and practice: Interaction fuels

---

[9]Time Con was a yearly science fiction convention held in San Jose, CA in early July. Chaves appeared there in 1989, 1990, and 1991. The convention has since been cancelled.

[10]Zines generally run 80 to 200 pages in length and cost from $10.00 to $30.00; editors typically do not profit from zine production. As of June 1995, 81 all-*War of the Worlds* zines have been produced, and more than 80 multimedia zines have included War of the Worlds stories along with stories based on other television series.

[11]As of June 1995 there have been several *War of the Worlds* news/letterzines: *The Blackwood Project* (11 issues), *It Is What It Is* (ongoing), *The Phoenix Mountain Project* (15 issues), *War of the Worlds Surplus* (2 issues), *War of the Worlds Fan Club Newsletter* (10 issues), *The Weird Stuff* (5 issues), and *The Whitewood Bulletin* (1 issue). There are also two news/letterzines specifically for fans of the actor Richard Chaves: *Wo Ha Li* (8 issues) and *The R.C. Dispatch* (ongoing).

the fan network, which thrives and spreads, absorbing new members and losing old ones who move on to involvements in new series.

The production and distribution of fiction, information, art, and other fan-made merchandise, as well as the consumption of these materials, creates an elaborate intertext in which fans operate. Fandom is information-rich: Participants research and dissect aspects of the narrative, the characters, and the performers, and incorporate what they learn into their stories, essays, discussions, presentations, videos, games, art, and so on. Disseminated through the fan network, these materials provide a foundation on which future fan-generated materials are created and judged. As materials circulate, fans create and re-create consensus regarding the meaning and significance of the series and its characters.[12]

War of the Worlds fandom used the letterzine *The Blackwood Project* as its primary site for discussion. From April 1989 to March 1991, 11 issues of the letterzine were published before the editor ceased production due to health problems. In early 1992, a second letterzine, *It Is What It Is*, started with the stated goal of filling the gap created by the loss of *The Blackwood Project*. These letterzines created the locus of *War of the Worlds* fan culture.[13]

FANDOM: WILD ZONE AND WOMEN'S CULTURE

Television fandom in general and *War of the Worlds* fandom in particular are a "wild- zone"—a women-centered cultural space in which reinterpretations of the text can occur—both theoretically and demographically. Members of television fan networks are overwhelmingly female; women control the activity and production. Demographic information collected on the individual women constituting *War of the Worlds* fandom reveals a mixture of class, race, and sexual orientation.[14] This heterogeneity is representative of television fandom as a whole, but a general fan "type" can

---

[12]This exploration includes information and items with tangential connections to the show and characters. In the case of Ironhorse, this includes knowledge about Cherokee and Blackfoot culture, the history of Vietnam and the Special Forces, and Army protocol.

[13]This locus was one of talk and discussion. Popular fiction zines also acted as a locus of fan activity and were often advertised, reviewed, and talked about in the letterzines.

[14]This demographic information emerged out of personal surveys, participant observation at several fan conventions, and extensive, ongoing correspondence with many *War of the Worlds* fans. This project is the beginning of a more detailed ethnography, to be conducted over the next two years. The completed fieldwork focuses on establishing a basic demographic description of television fandom as a whole, and several particular fandoms such as *War of the Worlds*.

be identified: female, white, college-educated, middle-class, heterosexual, between the ages of 25 and 50.[15] Together, these women comprise a network of individuals with a shared culture.

In theoretical terms, feminist media scholars argue that the male-dominated broadcast industry generates texts that support the patriarchal status quo (Kaplan, 1992, Kervin, 1991). Fans embrace this material but resituate the texts in the female-dominated space of the wild- zone. "Women's culture" refers to the dual perspective of living and participating in dominant male culture rather than in an isolated subculture (Showalter, 1977). Relying on commercial products as the basis for its activities, television fandom cannot exist as an isolated subculture.

However, when the dominant patriarchal culture cannot fully contain women's culture, such as occurs in television fandom, wild-zones, or spaces that escape enclosure, are created (Moi, 1985). In the wild-zone, women can take control of cultural products that would otherwise fall outside their influence. They create, consume, and mediate their activities apart from the dominant culture industry.[16] The wild-zone applies to all levels of fan activity—public, such as conventions, and private, such as individual acts of production and consumption. It is a place where activities are controlled by women, for women. The television fandom wild-zone exists both as a place without any permanent or specific physical location, which members enter and leave at will, and as a state of belonging centered in a sense of shared interest and community. The desire to belong to a fannish community motivates individuals to seek out others who share similar interests:

> I'd felt trapped in a WOW black hole . . . save for my roommate, none of my mundane friends could sit through an entire episode. . . . That initial driving need to seek out other fans . . . has been realized. Now all we have to do is find a convention where we can all get together . . . wouldn't that be dangerous? (Fan #1 *The Blackwood Project #2*)

> I can't believe I finally found it! WOW fandom! I'm a happy camper once again. I was starting to think I might be the only one, but I knew that couldn't be. This show has too many wonderful aspects not to have a fandom, and here you are. Now I can finally talk to others who are as nuts about this show, and a particular Cherokee colonel, as I am! (Fan #2, letter to the author)

---

[15]Although the majority of members are middle-class and professional women, working-class women are also included in fandom's ranks. However, they constitute a definite minority and are usually college or self-educated. Racially and ethnically, fans are mixed. A majority are white, but there are African American, Hispanic, Asian, and those with Native American blood. And, although most fans are heterosexual, there are also lesbians and bisexuals in the ranks.

[16]This notion of a female-centered space has also been discussed by Connell in relation to issues of gender and power. Connell's "liberated zones" are social spaces where "counter-sexist practices are sustained" (Connell, 1987, pp. 281-282).

As illustrated in the quotations, fans typically distinguish between their fannish and "mundane"—non-fan related—activities and relationships. In doing so, fans delegate time, effort, and activity to both aspects of their lives. They are active participants in the mass communication process, not passive recipients of industrialized culture. The emphasis in both fan statements is on the desire to "talk" with other fans, sharing thoughts and ideas. Through this activity fans take control over *War of the Worlds*, its characters, and its performers.

IRONHORSE AND CHAVES: INTO THE WILD-ZONE

Through their writings and interpretations in letterzines and their discussions at conventions fans demonstrate a complex understanding of human behavior and industry protocol. This knowledge is augmented through ongoing discussions in fandom, creating a basis for understanding the complex dynamic between the actor Richard Chaves and the character of Ironhorse. Although all television characters are potential candidates for importation into the wild-zone, few are actually chosen. Even fewer actors are reconciled into the female-dominated space.[17] The fact that fans embraced both Chaves and Ironhorse suggests there is something specific about them that allowed this to occur.

Even though Chaves had a vested interest in the series, as well as in building a track record and personal following to enhance his marketability in the industry, he was repeatedly described by fans as "sincere, warm, and a nice person who really cares about the character of Ironhorse and the fans" (Fan #22, personal interview, April 2, 1991). Another stated: "I think Richard Chaves is as neat as Cheese Whiz" (Fan #8, *The Blackwood Project #3*).

Fans do not universally or uncritically evaluate every actor who attends a convention as positively as they did Chaves. Many have "horror" stories concerning arrogant or offensive performers who denigrated them at a convention or in a response to a fan letter, and they worried that Chaves would do the same.

> I thought seeing Richard in person was worth all the effort it took his fans to get to San Jose. I would have hated it if he had turned out to be a real jerk. You know the type—"I'm a star, you're just a fan!" (Fan #6, *The Blackwood Project #3*.)

---

[17]The mechanism behind this choice is one area of inquiry that needs further examination.

But Chaves's willingness to talk to the fans and his appreciation of their support set him apart from many other actors involved in fandom. One fan summed up this sentiment in a letter of comment following the 1989 Time Con convention:

> Special thanks must go to Richard himself because without his gen-erosity and sincerity and just his wonderful openness to all his fans, I never would have met him or talked to him as much as I did . . . no person I have ever known, actor or not, was as genuine as he was. He overwhelmed me with his honesty of feelings for all his fans and their support to him; support which is clearly deserved and which will con-tinue beyond WOW. (Fan #12, *The Blackwood Project #3*)

This praise, although not universal, is representative of the fans' feelings toward Chaves. And, though fans were pleased with Chaves personally, they were critical of how the studio and Mancuso treated him and the character of Ironhorse.

Fans repeatedly tried to affect the decisions made by Paramount.

> I have written to Paramount, and I telephoned Frank Mancuso Jr.'s office once to register my *extreme displeasure* over the fact that Richard Chaves and Philip Akin are to be removed from the program. . . . I have seen nothing to indicate that either Mancuso or Paramount are the least bit interested in the opinion of WOW fans. It is this completely bored, almost contemptuous indifference that infuriates me . . . no matter how much they violate the character or the original concept, they think the viewers will accept it. That may backfire on them . . . (Fan #24, *The Blackwood Project #3*)

Although they were unable to influence the studio's decisions concerning the series, fans did have control over the characters in their fiction, as well as access to Chaves. Off the air for five years, *War of the Worlds* fans con-tinue to support two news/letterzines and several fiction zines, and over 1,400 pieces of fan fiction have been generated—this is in contrast to the 24 one-hour episodes and the two-hour pilot they have to work from.

From 1988 to 1994, Chaves attended 13 conventions with *War of the Worlds*-related panels and guests. Most fans attended at least one, if not many of these conventions.[18] There fans observed and interacted with Chaves, teasing out the "real man" from his public persona or personality

---

[18]The last convention Chaves attended, The Eagle's Summit '94 in Omaha, NE (October 7-9, 1994), was a convention specifically for Chaves and his fans.

created specifically for his television characters. By doing so, fans distinguished between the actor and the character, importing the elements of what they appreciated into the wild-zone. This distinction was clearly stated by one fan:

> Richard isn't Ironhorse, but a lot of Ironhorse's depth and emotional intensity comes from Richard and his talent. Still, I think the Colonel is a lot more balanced emotionally than Richard is. When I write, I try to remain true to the character, not to Richard, even if they are a lot alike. . . . I use a few things from Richard's past and personality when I write Ironhorse, but mostly I use what I see in the episodes and pad that with research. (Fan #24, phone interview with author, May 30, 1994)

Chaves's persona, like that of all actors, is a synthesis of personal self, public persona, and existing commercial intertext. As a "real" person, a member of the "mundane" dominant culture, Chaves required more negotiation by the fans than did his character because Ironhorse was wholly accessible to fans as a fictional construct. Chaves's willing and active participation with the fans cemented the popularity of Ironhorse.[19] Two features Chaves and Ironhorse shared, vulnerability and status as mystic warriors, became a central focus of the fans.[20]

IRONHORSE AND CHAVES: VULNERABILITY

A feminine hero is "other"—a man who exhibits traditionally masculine traits like aggressiveness and competition as well as more feminine traits like nurturing and emotional expressiveness. This psychological androgyny, it is argued, makes the feminine hero more accessible to women readers because their experiences are closer to those of women (Showalter, 1977).

---

[19]Chaves's convention attendance record is unusual and contrasts with the other stars of the series. Philip Akin (Norton Drake) attended four conventions; Jared Martin (Harrison Blackwood) two; and Lynda Mason Green (Suzanne McCullough) attended none.

[20]The series bible describes Ironhorse as "a West Point graduate, Vietnam veteran, Native American, and pragmatist stuck in a group of idealists." Chaves is himself a Vietnam veteran, and part Cherokee. This verisimilitude between the character and the actor was more coincidental than planned. Chaves was not Paramount's original choice to play Ironhorse, but after negotiations fell through with the studio's original choice, he found himself with the part. In the series bible and the pilot novelization, Ironhorse is described as a Blackfoot Indian. Chaves requested this detail be changed to Cherokee, matching his own racial background. Paramount agreed, allowing Chaves to mold the character to fit his own image.

The vulnerability demonstrated by Chaves and the Ironhorse character fit the model of the feminine hero, and, as "other," both were therefore more easily negotiated into the women-centered space of the wild-zone.

Showalter argues that the heroes popular among female readers are those who experience helplessness and dependency. Through these experiences, the feminine hero discovers what it feels like to be a woman, oppressed and marked as "other." The emotional vulnerability Chaves demonstrated in front of fans during his convention appearances was the key to his inscription as a feminine hero. Echoing the sentiments of the majority of fans commenting in *The Blackwood Project*, the following convention attendees articulated Chaves's demonstration of vulnerability with particular clarity:

> What moved me was watching his expression. He was hurting, and then when his voice would catch, and I felt the anger, frustration and sadness well up inside myself. . . . It amazes me that Richard is so open, so vulnerable around his fans. It shows a lot of trust, and today, that's a rare commodity. (Fan #3, Time Con convention report, July 1991)

> Richard Chaves stood before us, looking out at a sea of welcoming faces and said this convention in Northern California was special, and indeed it was. Each of us felt that magic, a spiritual union bonding our hearts together, with a strange mixture of sadness and joy—sadness, because our beloved Lt. Col. Paul Ironhorse was leaving us, joy that we could share Richard Chaves' burden of disappointment, and in doing so, perhaps lighten the darkness a little. . . . He told us about his last day on the set of WOW—as he took off his uniform for the last time, he cried. He broke down as he told us this, and we somehow felt honored that he was sharing such a private and painful experience with us. (Fan #4 *The Blackwood Project #3*, September 1989)

As this commentary suggests, fans gained an emotional intimacy with Chaves at the conventions. Fans read his expression of emotion as genuine, authentic, and something to be valued. His willingness to disclose his feelings publicly was read as authentic vulnerability.[21]

---

[21]However, this did not mean that fans did not criticize Chaves. They also discussed his perceived mistakes, weaknesses, and faults:

> When Richard was doing a *MacGyver* episode he made a stink about how a still picture they had to take was blocked. He refused to wear a helmet for it, and stormed off to his trailer until they gave in and let him to it the way he wanted—which was actually more realistic since he knows what the guys in Vietnam did and didn't do—but it got him labeled as a "trouble-maker" and he hasn't worked much. If he'd just gone along they might have brought him back for another episode. (Fan #15, personal interview, May 30, 1994)

It must be pointed out that the veracity of these comments is not at issue. This fan could be right or wrong in her interpretation of the events described. What is important is this fan's (and others) willingness to acknowledge Chaves as a man who can make mistakes and who can be wrong. For the most part, they do not idolize or embrace uncritically.

Chaves's repeated appearances at conventions helped maintain the integrity of the wild-zone and allowed a continual renegotiation of Chaves's and Ironhorses's place in it. Reports written by fans attending these gatherings appeared in T*he Blackwood Project* and other letterzines. Other reports circulated independently in the fandom. Both expanded the intertextual knowledge of Chaves and Ironhorse among the fans. Stories told by Chaves about his career, work on other shows, and personal background were repeated across conventions or in the convention reports, giving all fans access to the information and providing a sense of connection with the actor. Those who missed one convention picked up the information through video and audio tapes made there, the written reports, and oral accounts.

Chaves also affirmed the fans' uses and interpretations of his character. At a few conventions, he was presented with fan fiction still in the draft stage and made corrections and suggestions.

> With only a page to go on the story, the bar turned the lights out as a subtle reminder that it was time to close. . . . X—(always prepared)[22] pulled out a penlight and Richard continued to read by flashlight until the story was completed. (Fan #6, Dreamwerks convention report, November 1989)[23]

Thus Chaves's willingness to express himself and interact with the fans, as well as his caring and generous actions like the one just described, cemented his popularity in the fan community. Each appearance complicated and enriched the overall intertext, strengthening the connection between actor, character, and fan, and providing the foundation and the bonding necessary to a shared sense of being the "other."

On the whole, fans perceived Chaves as accessible, accommodating, and vulnerable due to his emotional openness. Fan writing cast Ironhorse in a similar light. Textual references from the series made this interpretation easy for the writers, and they focused on the character's vulnerability, which was expressed in several episodes. The following three examples are representative of the comments found throughout *The Blackwood Project.*

> In "Dust to Dust" I see Ironhorse to be discovering his vulnerable side. (Fan #24, *The Blackwood Project #1*)

---

[22]The name was edited by the author to protect the fan's privacy.

[23]At his next appearance Chaves read the then-completed story aloud to the fans in attendance, to great success.

"Among the Philistines" stands out as another of my favorite episodes. The emotions were great, with Ironhorse relating an obviously painful incident from Vietnam. (Fan #14, *The Blackwood Project #1*)

In "Choirs of Angels" . . . despite the vicious accusations hurled against him, Ironhorse showed his loyalty to his friend by staying with him throughout the night. (Fan #17, *The Blackwood Project #1*)

Ironhorse's moments of self-discovery, vulnerability, communication, friendship, nurturance, and loyalty are all traits of a traditional feminine hero. These examples and other textual illustrations were discussed at length in *The Blackwood Project*. But repeatedly singled out for the insights it provided on Ironhorse's character was the episode "Vengeance is Mine," which dealt with the emotional aftermath following Ironhorse's accidental murder of an innocent girl. In this episode, Ironhorse was shown speaking to a psychiatrist, having nightmares, and acting irrationally. Fans explained the episodes' appeal in several ways, but the following comments, focusing on the character's emotional displays, are representative of the general consensus:

"Vengeance is Mine" is a real gut-twister. Ironhorse was just stripped bare and we got to see that he really is a deeply compassionate, sensitive individual. (Fan #33, *It Is What It Is #13*)

Chaves gave a wonderful portrayal of a man in emotional torment. . . . Some favorite moments in the episode: Ironhorse, kneeling over Sarah's body, desperately shouting "Medic!" . . . the nightmare . . . it was very moving. (Fan #17, *The Blackwood Project #2*)

I have to start with "Vengeance is Mine." I LOVED [sic] it! . . . his voice cracking . . . his eyes welling, his anger, angst, torment was palpable and really got to me. . . . The hour was packed with emotional power . . . and opened a floodgate of revelations into Ironhorse's inner self and vulnerability. (Fan #10, *The Blackwood Project #2*)

Fans selected elements of Chaves's convention appearances that fit the persona of Chaves they found most comfortable. In the same way, fans used "Vengeance is Mine" and a variety of moments from other episodes as building blocks for reading Ironhorse as a feminine hero with whom they could identify.

IRONHORSE AND CHAVES: THE MYSTIC WARRIOR/"OTHER"

As mystical warriors, Chaves and Ironhorse were most obviously "other" in relation to their racial backgrounds as Native Americans and their status as

Vietnam veterans. *War of the Worlds* offered fans two possible sites of mysticism—Blackwood, the Anglo-Saxon scientist, and Ironhorse, the Native
American Special Forces colonel. Fans rejected the privileged mysticism of
Blackwood, focusing instead on the more clearly "other" that Ironhorse
represented, and fan fiction, art, and letters of comment focused on it:

> Ironhorse isn't white, he's Cherokee, and even worse, he's an Indian
> in the military, a Vietnam vet to boot. He's also aware of his cultural
> background and practices—witness the ghost dance shirt and his
> speech on the meaning of coyote barks, and traditional rituals. But no
> matter which way he turns, Ironhorse is different. I like that. I can
> identify with that. Harrison's too much like my boss, or my uncle—
> even if he does have some nifty intuitions concerning the aliens. (Fan
> #31, interview with author, April 2, 1991)

The key to this fan's preference lies in the association of mysticism as a
symbol of "other." The series constructed Ironhorse as "other" in several
ways, including his association with the world of Native American spirits
("Dust to Dust"), rituals ("Heal the Leper"), and powers ("The
Resurrection"). Blackwood, on the other hand, was not a member of an
oppressed group; indeed, he occupied a privileged position as a White
male scientist. He was also unconventional and intuitive, a stereotypical
sensitive man of the 1980s.

 Fans realized that Blackwood should be their point of identification but still found Ironhorse more appealing.

> By all rights, I should be crazy about Dr. Blackwood—intelligent,
> eccentric, full of weird humor—that's exactly what I love in a man
> and, don't get me wrong, I think Harrison's terrific, but still there's Lt.
> Col. Paul Ironhorse. . . . I'm attracted to that colonel guy. I mean, mili-
> tary men and I have never gotten along. Granted, being Cherokee is
> an enormous plus, but still there's that gung-ho Rambo side. (Fan #6
> *The Blackwood Project #2*, July 1989)

As this quote demonstrates, Blackwood was coded with many characteristics that should have made him a figure popular with female viewers.
Blackwood's dabbling into the mystical centered on New Age philoso-
phies and activities. He appeared in episodes meditating ("Multitude of
Idols"), using hypnosis ("Thy Kingdom Come"), and doing yoga ("The
Second Seal"). He also exhibited an instinctive understanding of the aliens
in several episodes. He could guess when the aliens were responsible for
unusual activities ("To Heal the Leper"), knew what the aliens were planning before it happened ("Epiphany"), and knew what to do to counter
alien plots ("Eye for an Eye"). These mystical overtones were personal idio-

syncrasies or inheritances from his family, who had fought in the 1953 invasion. Even his abilities to intuit what the aliens were planning echoed that of his surrogate mother, Sylvia van Buren, who was also "tuned in" to the aliens and their activities, but unstable and confined to a mental institution as a result. Blackwood's instability appeared in the narrative of the series as an odd sleeping pattern, his need to meditate, and his bouts with depression. Despite Blackwood's New Age tendencies, fans still found Ironhorse more interesting, more "other." Or, as Fan #6 stated earlier, Ironhorse was someone with whom they could "identify," whereas Blackwood was someone they thought was "terrific."

In contrast to Blackwood's internally based mysticism, Ironhorse's was externalized. Ironhorse tapped the mystical through storytelling ("The Resurrection"), the use of tribal knowledge to interpret ongoing events ("To Heal the Leper"), and an acknowledgement of wrongs committed against Native people and the possible metaphysical consequences ("Dust to Dust").

The episode "Dust to Dust" was particularly popular among fans and used blatant mystic-Indian stereotyping as the Blackwood Project became immersed in the location and destruction of an alien war machine on an Indian reservation.[24] That mission was accomplished with the help of Joseph Lonetree, the tribal shaman, who conjured up a totemic spirit which took the form of a storm-bear who destroyed the warship. This singular invocation of the stereotypical mystic-Indian is in contrast to the series' regular use of Blackwood's intuitions to solve alien-based problems in 12 of 25 first season episodes.

Fans maintained Blackwood's New Age practices and institutions in their writing but did not expand or explore them in any depth. The same cannot be said of Ironhorse. For example, in 12 issues of one popular *War of the Worlds* zine, *Green Floating Weirdness*, only 25 stories focus on Harrison Blackwood, exploring his character, motivations, and mystical associations, whereas over 75 stories do so for Ironhorse, and nearly 30 deal specifically with Ironhorse's metaphysical talents.

The representation of Native Americans in primetime series is traditionally that of "other," even if they are being played by Anglo actors (Berkhofer, 1978; Sollars, 1986; Steadman, 1982). The Native American is forced to "amputate" his or her identity, culture, and tradition in order to merge with white culture; simultaneously, white culture creates images of the Native American that blocks the possibility of assimilation. Native Americans, and Ironhorse as well, can never be white because they are

---

[24]There are brief references to Native American cultural and spiritual aspects over the course of the series, but they add up to only six minutes of on-screen narration.

"other"—mystical instead of pragmatic, oppressed rather than free, and natural in contrast to civilized (Takaki, 1990).

> What snagged me was Ironhorse . . . how neat, a character who respects Indian traditions! And best of all, the show does have respect for the medicine, and metaphysics in general. (Fan #10 *The Blackwood Project #2*, July 1989)

> It seemed so typical of Ironhorse, and so significant that—torn between two worlds—he would sensibly go to an Anglo "shaman" and yet cling to the Indian amulet for comfort. (Fan #23, *The Blackwood Project #2*)

The fans saw Ironhorse as negotiating both the White and the Indian world, much like they themselves negotiated the fan and mundane worlds (or the wild-zone and the dominant culture). He also struggled to survive and negotiate a war whose U.S. casualties for the most part did not come from Blackwood's privileged class.[25] The representation of the Vietnam veteran Ironhorse as both victim and warrior was also central to the fans' construction of him as "other."

> It was so nice to see a character like Ironhorse, someone who was both a decorated vet and a compassionate man. He isn't crazy, or mean, or arrogant. Ironhorse is compassionate, understanding, and oh-so human. His experiences were terrible, but they made him a better human being. (Fan #28, *It Is What It Is #3*)

Ironhorse's "terrible" experiences, mentioned briefly in a few episodes,[26] connected the fans with him through the vulnerability it generated in the character. These experiences also set him apart from Blackwood and the other characters, adding another layer of "otherness."

This was reinforced by the fact that Chaves was also a Vietnam veteran, who served in-country for 11 months during 1971-72. However, Chaves's association with Vietnam extended beyond his actual time in service. Fans were aware of his work co-writing and acting in the award-winning off-Broadway play *Tracers*, which marked Chaves's break into the industry. At several of the conventions, he performed readings from the play. His work in other Vietnam-based projects, like the play *Vietnam Trilogy*, the film *Cease Fire*, or the made-for-TV movie *To Heal a Nation*, were well known to fans, who read and/or viewed these projects.

---

[25]For example, the episodes "Multitude of Idols" and "To Heal the Leper."

[26]These episodes included "Multitude of Idols," "Thy Kingdom Come," and "To Heal the Leper."

Thus, *War of the Worlds* provided an excellent example of a privileged, sensitive male character loaded with mysticism who should have appealed to the fans, but Blackwood was not embraced. Fans responded to the oppressed "otherness" of Ironhorse. Ironhorse had a "tradition" they could respect, whereas Blackwood remained an extension of the dominant culture. Ironhorse, Chaves, and their classification as outsiders—Native Americans and Vietnam veterans—marked them as "other," making them accessible to the wild-zone.

CONCLUSION

As this chapter suggests, the *War of the Worlds* fans' attraction to Ironhorse, Chaves, and the series is complex. By appropriating Chaves's persona and Ironhorse's character into the wild-zone, fans began a process of rereading and rewriting both persona and character from a position somewhat outside the constraints of industrialized culture. Their decisions suggest that there is something about Ironhorse and Chaves that makes them more capable of serving as the icon through which the fans can work out their cultural concerns and aspirations. Given the predominance of women in television fandom, the "feminine" traits of mysticism, otherness, and vulnerability so tied to Chaves and Ironhorse made them both easily appropriated to the wild-zone. Here fans created a large body of cultural materials suited to their own interests, social position, and cultural capital.

The television fan community and the activities occurring there create unique relations of pleasure and entertainment intertwined with the relations of cultural production and empowerment. Fans actively participate, and they care deeply about that participation. Further, they do not have to sacrifice their pleasures because they control the wild-zone. Paramount gave fans a place to start with *War of the Worlds*, Paul Ironhorse, and Richard Chaves, but it was the fans who took control in the end.

Although no quote can completely speak for itself, I give the final word in this chapter to the fans. This quote comes from the editor's introduction to *Bring 'em Back Alive #1*, a zine dedicated to fiction that "fixed" the changes imposed by Paramount and Mancuso in the second season.[27]

---

[27]Clearly, more work needs to be done to examine how viewers interact with popular entertainment and to trace how this relationship impacts and empowers their daily lives. Women are "other." The character of Ironhorse and the persona of Chaves are also "other." Fan activity, then, is the elaboration of "other" by "other." What this activity means for the women who do it remains to be explored, as does the question concerning why particular series, characters, and actors are imported into the wild-zone and others are not. I hope that future scholarship will examine these questions and provide the answers.

To enjoy, we must participate, if not physically, then emotionally. To participate, we have to care, and that is where we run into a bit of trouble. For we, gentle reader, came to care. Who can deny that the major attraction of *War of the Worlds* is that the characters became real to us? Who would argue that the joy of the series came because we grew to love the characters. . . . We ached for their losses, celebrated their triumphs, and, finally, grieved over their deaths. . . . But here we claim advantage over the pains and disillusionment of the "real" world . . . a tiny dose of imagination is sufficient to free us from all constraints and limitations of mundane existence . . . reality becomes supremely malleable—moldable into our own image. . . . This zine is dedicated to all those contributors and readers who hold to the insane idea that life is more than eating, sleeping, and earning a living, and that TV is where you start from, not where you end up.

REFERENCES

Bacon-Smith, C. (1992). *Enterprising women: Television fandom and the creation of popular myth*. Philadelphia: University of Pennsylvania Press.

Berkhofer, R. J. (1978). *The white man's Indian: Images of the American Indian from Columbus to the present*. New York: Knoff.

Calling it quits. (1990, February 26). *Broadcasting, 118*(9), p. 35.

Connell, R.W. (1987). *Gender and power*. Stanford: Stanford University Press.

Jenkins, H. (1988). Star Trek rerun, reread, rewritten: Fan writing as textual poaching. *Critical Studies in Mass Communication, 5*(2), 85-107.

Jenkins, H. (1991). "It's not a fairy tale anymore": Gender, genre, beauty and the beast. *Journal of Film and Video, 43*(1-2), 90-110.

Jenkins, H. (1992). *Textual poachers: Television, fans, and participatory culture*. New York: Routledge.

Kaplan, E. A. (1992). Feminist criticism and television. In R. Allen (Ed.), *Channels of discourse, reassembled* (pp. 247-283). Chapel Hill: University of North Carolina Press.

Kervin, D. (1991). Gender ideology in television commercials. In L. Vande Berg & L. Wenner (Eds.), *Television criticisms* (pp. 235-253). New York: Longman.

Lewis, L.A. (1987). Consumer girl culture: How music videos appeals to women. *OneTwoThreeFour: A Rock 'N' Role Quarterly, 5*, 5-15.

Lewis, L. A. (1990). *Gender, politics and MTV: Voicing the difference*. Philadelphia: Temple University Press.

Lowery, B. (1989, June 29). Mancuso's hometown films take shot at "war." *Daily Variety.*

Modleski, T. (1979). The search for tomorrow in today's soap operas. *Film Quarterly, 33*(1), 12-21.

Modleski, T. (1990). *Loving with a vengeance: Mass-produced fantasies for women* (2nd ed.). New York: Routledge.

Moi, T. (1985). *Sexual/textual politics.* New York: Routledge.

Penley, C. (1991). Brownian motion: Women, tactics and technology. In C. Penley & A. Ross (Eds.), *Technoculture* (pp. 135-162). Minneapolis: University of Minnesota Press.

Penley, C. (1992). Feminism, psychoanalysis, and the study of popular culture. In L. Grossberg, C. Nelson, & P. Treichler (Eds.), *Cultural studies* (pp. 479-493). New York: Routledge.

Radway, J. (1984). *Reading the romance.* Chapel Hill: University of North Carolina Press.

Showalter, E. (1977). *A literature of their own.* Princeton: Princeton University Press.

Sollors, W. (1986). *Beyond ethnicity: Consent and descent in American culture.* New York: Oxford University Press.

Stedman, R. W. (1982). *Shadows of the Indian: Stereotypes in American culture.* Norman: University of Oklahoma Press.

Takaki, R. (1990). *Iron cages: Race and culture in 19th century America.* New York: Oxford University Press.

Taylor, H. (1989). *Scarlett's women: Gone With the Wind and its female fans.* New Brunswick, NJ: Rutgers University Press.

Uricchio, W., & R. E. Pearson (Eds.). (1991). *The many lives of Batman: Critical approaches to a superhero and his media.* New York: Routledge, Chapman and Hall.

▶11

Secrets, Closets, and Corridors Through Time: Negotiating Sexuality and Gender Through *Dark Shadows* Fan Culture*

Harry M. Benshoff
University of California-Santa Cruz

From 1966 until 1971, ABC-TV aired a daily 30-minute soap opera entitled *Dark Shadows*. The serial was unique in its subject matter for rather than focusing on "real-life" issues such as unwed motherhood or careerism, *Dark Shadows* showcased a panoply of fantastic characters including vampires, werewolves, warlocks, and witches. Of course, even within this supernatural netherworld, many common soap opera narratives (the evil woman, alcoholism, jealousy, tangled love affairs) were pressed into service. And it was clearly a *family* romance first and foremost: *Dark Shadows* tells the story of the monstrous Collins family and its various

*The author would like to thank the many *Dark Shadows* fans who contributed their time, energy, and insights to this project. Addresses for several of the major *Dark Shadows* fanzines can be found listed among the references.

tribulations. However, most of the show's central storylines were cribbed from famous gothic novels or else focused on supernatural elements such as time travel and parallel universes. Thus, from the outset, *Dark Shadows* must be understood as something of a postmodern hybrid, a TV show perhaps best described as a gothic soap opera.

Dark Shadows also differed from other soap operas of its day in terms of its reception, for the show was pitched to children as well as to housewives. Because it aired at a later hour in the programming day (3:30 or 4:00), many children could run home from school in order to watch it.[1] Ostensibly these youngsters were attracted to the show's monstrous nature rather than its traditional soap opera storylines. The show's producers capitalized on this appeal and heavily marketed *Dark Shadows* to a youth audience with records, comic books, games, novels, and two feature films, *House of Dark Shadows* (1970) and *Night of Dark Shadows* (1971). The appeal of its gothic characters and their ability to transcend "reality" and evolve over time has kept *Dark Shadows* alive in the minds of its fans for over 20 years. Fan clubs for the show started during the initial run of the serial and continued to grow in strength throughout the following decades: over 1,700 people attended the 1993 national convention in New York City. For the last 25 years, fans have been successful in bringing *Dark Shadows* back to television via syndicated re-runs (frequently on public television stations) and home video releases (from MPI Video). The fans were also instrumental in producer Dan Curtis's decision to remake *Dark Shadows* as a prime-time television series, which aired on NBC-TV during Spring 1991 (Pierson, 1992).

Like *Star Trek* and other science fiction fandoms, *Dark Shadows* currently exists as an ever-increasing multitude of texts, produced both "legitimately" by the film and television industry and by the fans themselves. Besides attending conventions and lobbying television producers, many *Dark Shadows* fans are active in writing and publishing fanzines, or other artifacts such as amateur theatricals and video tapes. These activities are neither officially sanctioned by the show's producers nor created for (anyone's) profit. In many cases they represent the active reappropriation of a copyrighted media text by its consumers; often such fannish artifacts re-read and rewrite the original text in surprising ways. Cultural critics such as Jenkins (1992) or Penley (1992) champion their potential for subverting the ideological status quo. Conversely, other critics such as Modleski (1982) argue that although women (or any other subaltern group) may be able to commandeer a patriarchal capitalist media text and rewrite it to their own ends (no matter how far afield from the text's original inten-

---

[1]Some sources speculate that teenagers made up approximately 90% of the original *Dark Shadows* audience (Javna, 1985).

tions), such a process must still necessarily entrap spectators within the engines of patriarchal capitalist representation.

Such criticism always seems to come back to a simplistic dichotomy: "Is this a good thing for women, gays, African Americans, and so on, or is it a bad thing?" The answer to the question as it is asked is complex and probably "both." A more useful and productive reformulation of the question might be: Where within the dominant system of representation can we find potential sites of rupture? What might these sites be like and how do they differ from one another? These are questions that cultural studies in general and the model of cultural hegemony has sought to investigate. Fannish activity is interesting not because it is necessarily subversive nor automatically coopted, but because the practice of subcultural reappropriation dramatizes the active counter-hegemonic negotiation of very serious political issues such as the fair and equal treatment of all human beings. Reappropriative fans represent not the "other" of "normal" media audiences, but rather the advance guard of adapting culture to media self-awareness in the postmodern world state. To some extent, we are all fans. How we read and rewrite popular culture today will determine the course of the culture of tomorrow. Genre fandoms create a material record of textual and generic evolution, mapping the ways in which a text's or genre's social meanings and signifying practices ebb and flow.

Like the varied artifacts they produce, *Dark Shadows* fans come in all shapes and sizes, ages, races, classes, genders, and sexualities. This chapter rests on data collected over several years of personal interaction with the fans and their artifacts. Surveys, interviews (both formal and informal), correspondence, and active participation/observation within the fan culture have been the ethnographic tools employed; material artifacts from the last 20 years or so have also been randomly collected and assessed. Unlike the predominantly female science fiction fandoms discussed by Penley (1991, 1992) and Bacon-Smith (1992), *Dark Shadows* fandom is comprised of approximately equal numbers of men and women. Most were children or teenagers during the show's initial run (1966-1971); nostalgic memories of childhood are often intermingled with their appreciation of the show. The developmental stages of childhood and adolescent identity formation may thus be another factor in why these individuals have continued to be attracted to this gothic text. And although the overall appeal of *Dark Shadows* (as well as its fandom) is clearly multifaceted, this chapter examines why the gothic genre in general holds a special appeal for many of its consumers, and how *Dark Shadows* fandom itself differs from science fiction fandoms in regard to matters of sexuality and gender.

THE GOTHIC

Unlike the larger and more well-known science fiction fandoms, *Dark Shadows* fandom exhibits a more focused relation to its text and to the gothic genre. Theorists from Freud (1919/1955) to Todorov (1975) have noted that the power of the fantastic (or the uncanny, or the gothic) lies in its ability to evoke uncertainty and call into question the very nature of "reality" and its subsequent social constructs. Science fiction, fantasy, and gothic horror all share this power to construct alternative realities, although science fiction and fantasy are more prone than horror to construct pleasant utopic visions. The classical form of gothic horror has frequently been called reactionary because of its punishing and violent recapitulation to patriarchal norms and its insistence on female victimization; yet it is precisely the genre's queerly sexualized villains and monsters that have become it's most recognizable icons. These sexual outlaws, mad scientists, and monsters might be understood as a queer force that disrupts the heterosexual status quo. As the genre has evolved, the textual arbiters of normality (the vampire hunters, the traditional heterosexualized hero and heroine) have become a less necessary part of the formula. Today's gothic horror novels (cf., *Interview with The Vampire*) are more often about the monsters' struggle with their own identity crises than any attempt to vanquish them in the name of some traditional moral order.

Gothic horror has also been traditionally considered a form of "low" or disreputable popular culture, not only because of its subject matter, but because it often eschews sophisticated plotting and intricate philosophical arguments in favor of a visceral "gut reaction"—the production of fear or shock in the spectator. In his work on the 19th-century sensation novel, Miller (1988) has noted that "the genre offers us one of the first instances of modern literature to address itself primarily to the sympathetic nervous system, where it grounds its characteristic adrenalin effects: accelerated heart rate and respiration, increased blood pressure, the pallor resulting from vasoconstriction, and so on" (p. 146). Although I do not wish to blindly conflate the sensation novel with the gothic novel or the classical Hollywood horror film, the effects that each seeks to produce on the body of the spectator are nearly identical. Williams (1991) has also pointed out that the horror film is a "body genre" analogous to pornography, low comedy, and the weepie, in that its primary source of pleasure is to be found in the spectators' bodily response. This argument, in which "sensation is felt to occupy a *natural* site entirely outside meaning" (p. 147; emphasis added) has been used by some poststructuralists to privilege the body as being outside the symbolic order and the sign systems of patriarchal hegemony. That claim is problematic: The body may be understood as the locus of a "natural" sign system, that although more immediate and "real" to the subject, is nevertheless still dependent on the symbolic order for its meanings. Thus, although bodily sensation is not in itself a counter-hegemonic site of meaning production, it does afford a context that may allow potentially subversive aspects to arise and to be spoken. As Miller puts it, the complex interactions between bodily "sensations and their narrative thematization allows the sensation novel to 'say' certain things for which our culture—at least at its popular levels—has yet to develop another language" (p. 148).

This notion that the gothic may be speaking ideas impossible to contextualize in any other way within the discourse of the dominant popular culture is central to understanding the genre.[2] Miller argues that the text of terror actively "feminizes" its reader, even when the reader being addressed within the text is supposedly male. If we accept that "nervousness remains a signifier of femininity" and that "the [sensation] novel makes nervousness a metonymy for reading," then the reader is situated by the text to "identify with nerve-racked figures" and to experience the "thrill" of the traditionally feminine (p. 151). Thus, the male reader or viewer of gothic texts may undergo a form of writerly cross-dressing during the experience of the text.

> The drama in which the novel writes its reader turns on the disjunction between his allegedly masculine gender and his effectively feminine gender identification (as a creature of "nerves"): with the result that his experience of sensation must include his panic at having the experience at all, of being in the position to have it. (p. 163)

Although this model barters on an essentialist notion of the feminine (to be frightened = femininity), it does provide a hypothesis for the gothic's subversive appeal to men: to enjoy the gothic is to participate in the inversion of traditional gender roles.

Where this model places the female reader is far less potentially disruptive to cultural norms. It apparently places her "back where she belongs," in the world of the "feminine" as defined by the patriarchal hegemony. The stereotyped hysterical woman, which the genre must invariably first construct within its narratives before it can use her to metonymically construct the reader, is always ready to scream, faint, or fly away into flights of fancy. She is regularly incarcerated within an asylum, perhaps an apt metaphor for the position of the female reader trapped

---

[2]Clover (1992) champions the modern horror film for the same reasons: Although gratuitously violent and frequently misogynist, slasher films and their ilk demonstrate on a manifest level the "psychosexual wilderness" of otherwise repressed and latent cultural dynamics. See also the work of Wood (1986) and Britton (1979) for expressly psychosexual readings of modern horror films.

within the world of the gothic. And despite the fact that the hysteric's "delusions" often prove to be "true" within the diegesis, she is usually situated by novel's end firmly within "the norm of the Victorian household" (Miller, 1991, p. 159). Such texts ultimately work toward "the dissolution of sensation in the achievement of decided meaning. . . . In short, the novel needs to realize the normative requirements of the heterosexual menage whose happy picture concludes it" (p. 165). This formulaic conclusion, which, "of course, marks the most banal moment in the text" is a staple of the classic gothic narrative form in both literature and film (p. 165).

Despite its last minute recapitulation of dominant ideological norms, the gothic text does not really celebrate said norms, but rather the lure of the deviant, which has been given full metaphoric reign throughout the course of the work. Indeed, the modern gothic often eschews the genre's traditional narrative closure, allowing its increasingly sympathetic monster to live on past the final reel. And if the male reader is able to be feminized by the text as Miller argues, what of the female reader? As Clover (1992) notes about recent slasher films, "Because horror operates in an allegorical or expressionist . . . mode, whereby characters are understood to concretize essences," films such as these display "obviously" and "spectacularly" the blurring of traditional sex roles (p. 231). These processes (of the blurring of traditionally gendered reader responses) and the representation of a monster's queer sexual desire within the genre's texts themselves may be among the genre's chief appeals to women and homosexuals, who rarely find themselves represented in adequate ways within popular culture narratives.

THE GOTHIC SOAP OPERA

How might these concerns play out when looking at a serialized television show or soap opera, a narrative form that is itself frequently gendered as feminine? First, we can see that a serial such as *Dark Shadows* constructs much of its narrative pleasure around the audience's identification with the supernatural and monstrous characters, both male and female, instead of with their eventual realignment with patriarchal norms. Serialized narrative is under no imperative to provide a happy heterosexualized ending to its tale. "Soap operas continually insist on the insignificance of the individual life" (Modleski, 1982, p. 91). In so doing, they may force the spectator into a state of multiple character identification and subject positions. Modleski has demonstrated how soap operas work to ultimately situate women within the home, how they construct a distracted viewer, acclimate her to housework, and "invest exquisite pleasure in the central condition of a woman's life: waiting . . ." (p. 88). Thus, she persuasively argues, the female viewer of the soap opera (gothic or otherwise) may be trapped within the formal construction of the text.

However, there is a subversive potential to be found in the serial's construction of the spectator as a sight of multiple subjectivity. The formal construction of a text such as *Dark Shadows* calls attention to the complex nature of identification and subject construction in a multitude of ways. First, the show employed a stock company/repertory approach to characterization: most of the continuing actors on the show played several roles. In different time periods, each actor doubled for his or her ancestors or parallel time selves; many played several different characters even within the same time frame. Furthermore, each actor/character "sign" is shown to be unstable: parts of each character bleed into others performed by the same actor. This blurring of actor and character also takes place during the voice-over narration that opens each episode. Are these voices those of the characters or the actors? This odd amalgamation of character and actor in one narrational voice, along with the gothic genre's obsession with doubles, mirrors, doppelgangers, haunted portraits, spiritual possessions, and secret selves, foregrounds a deeply decentered subjectivity.

As might be expected from the aforementioned list, this formal structure is also played out within the show's multiple storylines. Characters' identities frequently undergo some sort of transformation. When one is bitten by a vampire, one undergoes a marked personality change. Other characters, having become the object of a magical spell or curse, behave as if they were possessed by other personalities. One remarkable narrative thread from the episodes set in 1897 focuses on the spirit of Count Andreas Petofi (currently inhabiting the body of the child David Collins) avenging himself on the denizens of Collinwood by means of a transformational kiss that causes each individual subject to reveal his or her "true" hidden self. Thus, the master of Collinwood becomes its butler, and Charity Trask, the upright and uptight daughter of the hypocritical minister, finds herself possessed by the spirit of Pansy Faye, a free-wheeling songstress and hard-drinking burlesque performer.

Elsewhere I have argued that much of the narrative content of *Dark Shadows* actively critiques patriarchal structures such as the Christian family (Benshoff, 1991). The one unregenerate and truly unsympathetic villain on the show is a two-faced minister, the Reverend Mr. Trask. (Indeed, the show was frequently criticized during its initial run by right-wing fundamentalist groups for its focus on witchcraft, as well as for its characterization of Trask.) Collinwood itself is figured primarily as a matriarchy and the men who live there are often absent or dissolute. There are traditionally naive gothic heroines within the text, but there are also strong professional women who more forcefully drive the narrative instead of being acted on by it.[3] Many of the sexist codes of classical Hollywood representation are also inverted within the text: men become spectacularized sex objects far more frequently than women. And, as many of its fans and creators have discerned, there is even the occasional hint of the homoerotic lurking in the shadows of Collinwood.

MATTERS OF SEX AND SEXUALITY IN THE FANDOM

As might be suspected, most of the *Dark Shadows* fan-produced artifacts are quite different from those produced in science fiction fandoms. One of the major differences is the seeming reticence to focus on an explicitly sexualized reappropriation of the original text. Perhaps this is due to the nature of the two fandoms' generic conventions. Whereas the science fiction genre more frequently partakes of a utopian future vision that encompasses all sorts of imaginable and queer possibilities, gothic horror is more historically earthbound and determined by much more programmatic formal characteristics. Matters of sex and sexuality exist within the gothic in a metaphoric secret closet, that is to say on a more latent or metaphoric level, filtered through the acts of vampiric seduction and/or the creation of monsters. Whereas sophisticated readers may understand the gothic as about little else but sex, many of its consumers value it precisely for its manifest denial of sexual content. As one *Dark Shadows* viewer from the late 1960s remarked, she liked the show because it was "not like all the other ones during the day, with all the sex, abortions, and illegal pregnancies . . ." (quoted in Barthel, 1967). Conversely, other fans were well aware of the genre's sexual implications and reportedly sent nude photographs of themselves to vampire star Jonathan Frid (Barnabas Collins). If one situates the gothic form within the larger Western Christian or American Puritan tradition of sexual repression, it is not hard to imagine the psychic mechanisms at work within the minds of the gothic's naive readers. By displacing the topics of sex, gender, and sexuality onto monstrous signifiers, the gothic invites its readers to experience the thrill of the sexually deviant within the safe or "innocent" zone of a fictional, make-believe generic construct.

Analysis of the short stories written by fans and printed in fanzines reveals an interest in certain recurring themes derived from the original

---

[3]When the show began its run, it was always introduced by the character of Victoria Winters, the new governess at Collinwood. Her voice-overs privileged her perceptions and acted as a locus of spectator identification; she did in effect "write" the narrative. Later, her voice-overs were replaced by those of different cast members as described earlier.

text(s): vampirism, time travel, romance, and love as a force capable of transcending time and history. Barnabas Collins (or vampirism) figures prominently in most of these stories. The majority of the stories are serious in tone and written by women; conversely, most of the stories with a comedic edge seem to be written by men. As would be expected from the latent/manifest quality of the genre, when sex and sexuality appear in these fictions it is usually dramatized within monstrous signifiers. The following excerpt is from a first person story, entitled "To Serve Her" (the vampiric Angelique):

> She stroked my head as she held it and I knew that her mind was further entering mine. I could feel her inside me becoming part of me more and more. It was terrifying and yet I was uncontrollably excited by it and even satiated in a primal, emotional way. . . . Once more I held onto her as I licked the running blood up her body and buried my face between her breasts. She in turn coiled her arms around me and began stroking my back with her hands while making low groaning sounds. I sucked her blood ravenously. (Haycock, 1991, pp. 138-139)

In an interesting blur of gender, in this story it is the man who is penetrated by a female vampire. Other stories soften the vampire's animalistic magnetism into romantic longing. Generally speaking, the stories by women seem to be less sexually explicit than those by men, although one novella by two women entitled *Are Old Acquaintances Best Forgotten?* is self-described as "an adult fanzine [that] will not be knowingly sold to anyone under twenty-one years of age" (Raymond & Van Houten, 1991). It too contains many of the requisite thematic elements: time travel and a focus on Barnabas and his newest reincarnated love. However, the novella seems hardly more "adult" than the earlier story excerpt.

As is typical of many *Dark Shadows* fans, the authors of *Are Old Acquaintances Best Forgotten?* seem almost apologetic about their work, reluctant to offend:

> adult writing is often a matter of opinion, and what is "fluff" to one person is "smut" to another. I don't know how you'd classify the sexual situations in my 'zine. I tried to be as tasteful as possible. The 'zine was read by three high school students, (without my knowledge until it was too late) who thought that the scenes were no worse than things they had seen on afternoon soap operas. On the other hand, I had a friend tell me it was "filthy". (personal communication)

Again we can observe how the sexual components of the gothic are mitigated or otherwise negotiated; some *Dark Shadows* fans remain unaware of these aspects whereas others seem remarkably sophisticated in matters

of sex and sexuality. It seems that fandoms centered on different media
texts cater to specific tastes; some are more adult in nature, others remaining resolutely "PG-13." For example, the fandom surrounding the recent
television version of *Beauty and the Beast* has given rise to a great deal of
explicit erotic fanzine activity, but there seems to be less overtly "X-rated"
material produced in *Dark Shadows* fandom.

Slashzines based on *Dark Shadows* characters are rare; most *Dark
Shadows* fans have never even heard of them. "Slashzines" are fan-produced fictions that posit a homosexual relationship between the two male
leads on a particular television show: In the case of *Star Trek*, K/S
slashzines depict a love affair between Kirk and Spock, oftentimes complete with graphic drawings and descriptions of sexual acts. Penley (1991,
1992), in her ground-breaking research on the subject, has reported that
these stories were initially produced mostly by and for heterosexual female
fans, arguing that they reconfigure heterosexual romance through a homosexual matrix. (More recently other fans and theorists have begun to question the degree of homosexual expression this positioning might be mask-
ing.) As Penley has argued, slash relationships are seemingly dependent on
the equality of their participants, making use of a homosexual premise to
reconfigure or reimagine a heterosexual union between two "truly equal"
partners, neatly side-stepping the culturally encoded "inequality" inherent
in male/female relationships. Interestingly, most of the homosocial male-
male pairs that *Dark Shadows* constructs are not based on equality but
bounded by rigid power hierarchies: between men and boys (Quentin and
Jameson, for example); between master and servant (Barnabas and Ben,
Barnabas and Willie); or Count Petofi and his foppish pretty-boy assistant
(Aristede). This fact is consistent with male relationships within the gothic
genre itself and may be another reason for the lack of slash fiction as it has
been identified and defined in science fiction fandoms. Also, because *Dark
Shadows* was a daily soap opera and not overtly pitched at adult male
spectators, the original text may have had less need to construct the kind of
intensely bonded homosocial relationships that characterized evening television shows such as *Starsky and Hutch* or *Miami Vice*, the other type of
media text that is most readily slashed. Nevertheless, even without the
practice of slash writing, *Dark Shadows* and its fandom exhibit an interesting relationship to the gay and lesbian community and its politics.

HOMOSEXUAL HORRORS

Wood (1986) and Sedgwick (1985) (among others) have discussed how
homosexuality is one of the sexual discourses that the gothic speaks in its
repressed and displaced ways. Jenkins (1992) has noted the same about

fandoms in general: They often serve as "a vehicle for marginalized sub-cultural groups (women, the young, gays, and so on) to pry open a space for their cultural concerns within dominant representations . . ." (p. 174). Thus, it is not surprising that *Dark Shadows* fandom is tied to the gay community in many suggestive ways.[4] I first became aware of this fact when I discovered "The *Dark Shadows* Fan Club of Southern California" listed in the 1991 edition of the *Los Angeles Gay and Lesbian Community* Yellow Pages under the classification "Lesbian & Gay Community Resources, Organizations, & Survival Services." At the very least, *Dark Shadows* is a signifier well known within gay culture, to the extent that it can be freely referenced, as in the following passage from the gay literary magazine *Christopher Street*:

> Before him was Todd, who had two interesting features that initially captivated me. One, a chin cleft you could park a Vespa in; two, a tattoo on his left pec, a red and black depiction of a grinning demon poking a trident at his nipple as if it were some hellish *hors d'oeuvre*. He also belonged to the *Dark Shadows* fan club. (Taylor, 1993, p. 36)

Dark Shadows and its fans have also been the focus of various articles and essays within the gay press. One such piece that appeared in the *New York Native* noted the appeal of *Dark Shadows* for gay men and lesbians, but also pointed out "inside jokes, like naming the two bars the characters frequented the Blue Whale and the Eagle, after the Fire Island and Manhattan gay bars" (Helbing, 1989, p. 25).

In general, *Dark Shadows* fans tend to be interested in gothic matters such as secrecy and troubled romantic entanglements; gay and lesbian *Dark Shadows* fans (who comprise far more than the expected 10% of the fandom) often read these signifiers in explicitly homosexual terms. Thus, Barnabas Collins's vampirism becomes an apt metaphor for homosexuality. Barnabas is plagued by his unnatural appetites and much of his characterization comes from his reluctance, but concomitant burning need, to indulge himself. Also, the perceived need to hide this very important facet of the self from one's friends and families is amply dramatized within the text. The revelation of Barnabas's vampirism in the episodes set in 1795 destroys his family and drives his mother to suicide. Ultimately, Barnabas's father chains him in a coffin in order to protect the family honor. The terri-

---

[4]"Deviant" sexualities are frequently conflated with the gothic as well as its fans. Consider the following piece of information attributed to Bela Lugosi's widow, Hope Lugosi. In an interview printed in the *National Enquirer* the year following her husband's death, she took the opportunity to question the propriety and implicit sexuality of her late husband's fans, noting that they were "all boys—no girls. They wear makeup and hang around funeral parlors" (reported in Skal, 1993, p. 254).

ble secret must be repressed—both within the text and within American society, a fact that the show makes clear by constructing Barnabas's father, Joshua, as an old-fashioned Biblical patriarch and veteran of the American Revolutionary War; in other words, the very voice of the founding principles of American Puritan morality.

As many gay fans have pointed out, Barnabas Collins even had his own "fag hag," Dr. Julia Hoffman.[5] Julia first arrives at Collinwood to investigate the vampire but eventually falls in love with Barnabas and subsequently attempts to cure him. Her unrequited love for Barnabas can also be read as an aspect of the homosexual experience. One fan notes: "Gays know what she must be going through every time she looks at Barnabas with those 'I love you' eyes, and he simply ignores her." Among gay men and others with similar sensibilities, however, Dr. Julia Hoffman is central to another aspect of the show's appeal—that of camp. To put it as politely as possible, the actress who played Dr. Hoffman (Grayson Hall) was something of an expressionistic player. (Actually, most of the actors had "unique" performance styles.) Grayson Hall's over-melodramatized style of performance, coupled with her mannish manner (the role was originally written for a male actor), make "Grayson Hall as Julia Hoffman" ripe for much camp reappropriation, including the impersonation of her by gay male *Dark Shadows* fans in assorted skits and videos. Her gender-bending appeal is often cited in fan fiction, but more frequently than not she is recouped to traditional constructs of sexuality and gender. For example: Dr. Hoffman's "voice was softly husky, deeper than most women's, but not at all masculine. . . . She was a lady, in the proper sense of the word" (Sutherland, 1991, p. 105). Nonetheless, most of her fans are well-aware of a significant intertextual tidbit: namely, that she was nominated for a supporting actress Oscar in 1964 as the neurotic lesbian school teacher in the film version of Tennessee Williams's *Night of the Iguana*.

Camp, of course, has been linked with what some theorists have called the "gay sensibility" and its counter-hegemonic politics. Camp has a special affinity with low cultural forms such as melodrama, the musical, and the gothic. Babuscio (1977) has pointed out that "[t]he horror genre, in particular, is susceptible to a camp interpretation" (p. 43), and Sontag even goes so far as to suggest that "the origins of Camp taste are to be found [in] Gothic novels" (1966/1983, p. 109). Not only does camp con-

---

[5]I use the term "fag hag" with caution because it has often been used to denigrate gay men, straight women, and the friendships between them. Nonetheless, the term is a common one among many gay men. This is perhaps reflective of their own misogyny and internalized homophobia; however, I tend to use the term in a reappropriative sense, much as I might use the word "queer," hurling the negative connotations embedded in the term back at the heterocentrist society which continues to demonize homosexual love and even friendships.

flate high and low and foreground the processes of textual reception, it also celebrates the "convertibility of 'man' and 'woman,' 'person' and 'thing'" (p. 109). Perhaps most importantly, "the Camp sensibility is one that is alive to a double sense in which some things can be taken" (p. 110). In other words, the spectator constructed by a camp text is at least dual, if not multiple. In the case of *Dark Shadows* and its fandom, the pleasures of the text may therefore lie within the complex interplay of character, actor, diegesis, and extradiegetic elements, queering both the production and the reception of the various texts. Amesley (1989), in her work on *Star Trek,* observes that its fans are able to respond to the diegetic world of *Star Trek* while simultaneously engaging in a meta-critical discourse regarding the show's stars, production values, plot mechanisms, and so on. *Dark Shadows* fans also seem to engage in this sort of "double viewing." One fan summed up both appeals in this well-worded response: *Dark Shadows* is an "excellent combination of campy soap opera and classic gothic horror." Likewise: "Now I appreciate the show's campiness and (strangely at the same time) the emotional depth and pathos of some of its characters and stories." Thus, it appears that even individual subjects may simultaneously relate to the show in seemingly contradictory ways: first constructed as the heroine, next constructed as the gothic hero, now constructed (via camp) as an affectionately acerbic critic totally outside the text. The multiple subject positions afforded by "normal" soap operas and classical gothic horror texts are thus developed and extenuated by the form, content, and reception of *Dark Shadows,* making the show and its fandom a welcoming space for women and men seeking respite from the usual hetero/sexist hegemony.

THE HISTORICAL CONSTRUCTION OF GENDER

The changing nature of traditional gender roles, which was also a staple of the original *Dark Shadows* text, is another thematic element that some fans continue to investigate through their writing. Whereas science fiction fans have an unlimited future space in which to imagine some vision of gender equality, *Dark Shadows* fans find themselves confined within the historical epochs of recent American history, yet still manage to address the issues in complex ways. One such story, entitled "The Challenge of Her Destiny," deals with reincarnation and the ability of love to transcend time. It negotiates many issues surrounding sexuality, gender roles, and historical progress. Primarily, the story is a dialogue set in Heaven in 1839 between the spirit of Julia Hoffman and the angel Gabriel. Julia's spirit is concerned with being reincarnated so that she may return to Earth with her soulmate, who has been reincarnated as the vampire, Barnabas Collins. Gabriel hits on a plan to send Julia back to Earth in the 20th century where she might train to be a doctor and thus cure Barnabas of his "blood disease."

> "I . . . I see," she said, slowly. "But . . . there are no doctors who are women. Are you suggesting that I change my—" "No dear lady, I am not," he chuckled, amused. "I must tell you that the time is coming when there will be many changes on Earth. Women will begin to do things that they have never been allowed to do before . . ." (Sutherland, 1991, p. 110)

The possibility of transsexuality and/or homosexuality is herein raised but dismissed with an amused chuckle. More interesting is the postulation of history as a model of progressive change: Julia must wait until the 20th century to be reincarnated as a doctor because the idea is unthinkable in 1839.

However, Gabriel acknowledges the sexism inherent in even the 20th-century medical institution:

> "You will have to make up your mind to be a doctor, in a time when it is not quite yet very widely accepted. There will be scorn, ridicule, and opposition, from friends and family as well as teachers and co-workers. They will tell you that it is a woman's place to be a nurse, not a doctor. They will say that a woman cannot handle being a doctor." (Sutherland, 1991, p. 110)

Gabriel tells Julia that she may have to "become cold, and hard . . . a bossy unpleasant woman" (p. 110) just to get through the ordeal of medical training. He warns her that this might have an adverse effect on Barnabas: "A strong, argumentative woman would bring much of his fear to the surface, and excite his anger" (p. 110). Interestingly, in another example of the blurring of essentialist gender roles, Barnabas is somewhat "feminized" (i.e., given traditional signifiers of femininity) in this particular story: following his portrayal on the show, he is a creature of whims and moods, natural cycles, with a tendency toward "over-romanticizing everything." Julia acknowledges his weaknesses, especially those inherent in his fixation on nubile young ingenues, but she insists on being strong for both of them.[6]

Ultimately, Julia accepts "The Challenge of Her Destiny" and the story ends with a coda set in 1942 in which the teen-aged Julia tells her

---

[6]As is typical of much fanzine writing, the author told me her story was written specifically to address perceived discrepancies in the original text—in this case how and why it was that Julia seemed to be such a hardened character when she first came on the show. Both Barnabas and Julia "mellowed out" considerably during the run of the show.

family that she wants to become a doctor. Thus, this story does address the nature of sexism within society and posits a historical cure for it: in time, things will get better. Yet, somewhat problematically perhaps, the only reason offered by the author for Julia's future interest in medicine is her "superhuman love" for Barnabas: She wants to study medicine in order to cure him and facilitate a happy ending through idealized romantic coupling. Like Radway's (1994) romance aficionados, readers of "The Challenge of Her Destiny" may find issues of history, gender, and sexuality being addressed, but ultimately they may be more or less trapped within the fortress of patriarchal ideology via its use of romantic love as tool for once again subjugating women to men.

An interesting comparison can be made between "The Challenge of Her Destiny" and *A Doctor Remembers*, a 20 minute faux-documentary made in 1985 by Tom Soderberg and Owen Robertson. In it, Dr. Julia Hoffman (played by Soderberg) reminisces about her/his years spent at Collinwood. *A Doctor Remembers* works in ways similar to a drag cabaret act for those in the know. The tape is full of witty (inter)textual references. Julia mentions that she is up for a part in Aaron Spelling's newest TV show "Dark Mansions," and an alleged photo of her father "Judge Herman Hoffman" reveals *Dark Shadows* cast member Louis Edmonds as he was then appearing on another soap opera (*All My Children*). Julia also tells us that Vicky has run off with a millionaire who supposedly murdered his wife.[7] Soderberg-as-Hoffman satirizes many of the show's more outlandish credibility gaps in a dead-pan style of delivery. Standing in the woods between Collinwood and the Old House, Julia remembers how she used to go from "one house to the other, one house to the other, one house to the other . . . at the end of a busy night I'd go to bed quite dizzy." Julia also discusses her ability to wear so many different hats: "You see, besides being an M.D., blood specialist, biologist, and family historian, I'm also a licensed psychologist." Ultimately, Julia confesses to the camera and comes to "realize and confront the truth, that yes, I had a love-jones" (for Barnabas).

Within its campy diegesis, *A Doctor Remembers* raises many of the same issues as did the short story, "The Challenge of Her Destiny." Both productions focus on Julia, her difficulty in overcoming patriarchal oppression in becoming a professional woman, and her unrequited love

---

[7] Actress Alexandra Moltke, who played governess Vicky Winters, was the alleged "other woman" in the Claus von Bulow trial. This fact is common knowledge among *Dark Shadows* fans; some even have collected footage of "Vicky" at the von Bulow trial, recorded from television's *A Current Affair* show. *A Doctor Remembers* plays on this fact as well as the *Dark Shadows* diegesis when it reports that "Vicky was never very good at trials." (Vicky had been on trial for witchcraft in the 1795 flashback sequence.)

for Barnabas. The two works are interesting to compare because *A Doctor Remembers* ostensibly represents a (gay?) male point of view, whereas the story, "The Challenge of Her Destiny," is written by a (straight?) female. Whereas the written story posits a transcendent love affair between Barnabas and Julia as the necessary force behind her choice of medical career, the video Julia becomes a doctor simply because she wants to be one, not because she has any prescient plan to save Barnabas from the curse of vampirism. Thus, on the level of narrative, the video version of Julia Hoffman appears to be less in line with the patriarchal project. On the other hand, a feminist argument against the male drag of *A Doctor Remembers* might also be invoked: Here we see men performing as women in order (a) to allegedly make fun of them, and (b) to show them the proper way to be "independent" (as in Sydney Pollack's film *Tootsie* [1982]). There *is* an element of cruelty in Soderberg's satire of Grayson Hall, yet at the same time the tape is dedicated "In Loving Memory of Grayson." Like many points of popular cultural negotiation, the artifacts themselves are frequently overdetermined and contradictory.

There is another important difference between the taped (male) Julia and the written (female) Julia. Although both Julias are resigned to Barnabas's preference for young ingenues, the written Julia continues to fight for her man against all odds, even against Heaven and Earth. The taped Julia is less overtly romantic. Indeed, the overall camp tone of *A Doctor Remembers* quite effectively deflates the overweening romanticism of "The Challenge of Her Destiny." The taped Julia finds nonromantic relationships to be equally meaningful: "I was always there for [Barnabas], even after Vicky left, and he found other Josette substitutes. But I really didn't mind. He could be so kind and gentle sometimes, and we were always the best of friends." Ultimately, the video Julia rejects the false promises of heterosexual romance as promulgated by the patriarchy in favor of more egalitarian relationships based on friendship and trust. The tape concludes with the lines: "Memory and old friends . . . . I can't think of a better prescription." The sentiment echoes those of the fans, many of whom also find memory and friendship to be among the most pleasurable aspects of both *Dark Shadows* and *Dark Shadows* fan culture.

CONCLUSION: "THE SECRET ROOM"

Dark Shadows fandom negotiates issues of sexuality and gender in ways more different from than similar to science fiction fandoms. Science fiction fans and their self-produced artifacts can often find a possible future space for queer peoples and their concerns. For *Dark Shadows* fans and the artifacts they produce, both sexuality and gender are encoded within the generic tropes of gothic horror: gender issues are often dealt with as part of a past-historical, time-traveling continuum, whereas sexuality is invariably relegated to the realm of monstrous signifiers. Although this queer = monster idea might be understood as a blatantly reactionary trope, some *Dark Shadows* fans have been able to reappropriate this and other gothic conventions in order to de-repress the homosexuality inherent in the genre. They also use camp and a model of historical progress to challenge both traditional notions of gender and the nature of heterosexual romance. However, there is still the indelible linkage of queer sexuality with monstrosity, which, although possible within science fiction tropes, is much more likely to be a trope of gothic horror than science fiction, and one that will most likely continue to oppress gay and lesbian people until it has been sufficiently explored and deconstructed within the popular sphere. Such fannish artifacts may be contributing to that process.

In recent years, specifically gay and lesbian fan groups from both generic camps have been formed. Within *Dark Shadows* fandom, a fanzine calling itself "The Secret Room" has been announced (though not published as of this date), and Henry Jenkins has reported on the activities of a group of gay and lesbian science fiction fans who call themselves the Gaylaxians. A comparison between the two groups indicates the differing ways in which each generic set influences the groups' agendas and modes of representation. The Gaylaxians are considerably more outspoken in their activities and goals, chanting "2, 4, 6, 8, how do you know Kirk is straight?" during gay pride marches, while continually lobbying producers for visible gay and lesbian characters within the *Star Trek* universe (Tulloch & Jenkins, 1995, p. 237). Conversely, "The Secret Room"'s goals are couched in careful negotiation. In the words of its founder: "I would like it [the fanzine] to contain some gay-oriented art work on *Dark Shadows*, as long as it's not too 'hot,' and some gay-oriented fiction involving *Dark Shadows* characters." His caution echoes that of other gothic (straight) fanziners mentioned earlier, who are also worried that their "too sexualized" reappropriations might offend other fans. The founder of "The Secret Room" continues:

> I'm not trying to form a splinter group and thus divide *Dark Shadows* fandom in anyway. . . . I'm not trying to be a militant leader out to form a group for disruptive purposes, or to "out" members of the group, other fans, or the stars themselves. I also plan to use a disclaimer in the fanzine that will explain that all art work and fiction do not in any way indicated (sic) a stars (sic) sexual preference, nor is it meant to imply such, insult them, etc. (personal communication)

"The Secret Room" thus draws quite heavily on the metaphor of the closet and is very clear about its intentions not to make any open challenges to the status quo, even though (as I would argue) its very existence contributes to the changing nature of *Dark Shadows* fandom.

Of course, *Dark Shadows* is no longer in production, but I would be surprised to see a campaign waged for visible gay and lesbian characters within the gothic world of *Dark Shadows*, where, in accordance with generic imperatives, the monster queer is more likely to remain in his or her closet, secure in the secret pleasures of metaphor and the mask. This connotative shadow realm has long been the preserve of gay and lesbian characters within mainstream representation, and authors such as Miller (1991) and Doty (1993) have argued persuasively that this connotative realm is but another form of the closet's oppressive function. However, one would be wrong to conclude from these statements that all gay and lesbian *Dark Shadows* fans are more or less closeted; in fact, at the 1992 Halloween *Dark Shadows* Convention in Los Angeles, literal signifiers of gay and lesbian political power (including red AIDS ribbons, "Lesbian and Gay Men for Clinton" buttons, and "Censorship is UnAmerican" tee-shirts) were out in abundance. These gay and lesbian fans may connect with the gothic trope of the monster queer within their preferred textual systems, even as in real life they may be more politically active than their generic tastes would otherwise suggest.

One might compare these two approaches to gay and lesbian visibility within media fandoms to the debate going on in the gay community at large concerning how best to secure civil rights. This argument is frequently reduced to the debate in the homosexual community between the words gay and queer: Should we be conciliatory and try to fit in, as suggested by Marshall Kirk (1989) in his book *After the Ball*, or should we be actively confrontational, as Larry Kramer and groups like Queer Nation have advocated? Again, I like to think that the answer to this question is complex and probably "both." Like the similar yet differing social stances implied by the words gay and queer, science fiction and gothic horror represent two different ideological viewpoints, perhaps equally valid ways of interpreting "reality" and its potentialities. The science fiction fan can more often envision a utopian potential for equal rights, whereas the gothic horror fan views the world in more paranoid, violent terms, where the retribution for being queer is sometimes quite literally a stake in the heart. In that respect, the monster queer remains a more truly counter-hegemonic figure, a sexual outlaw who cannot be incorporated into the changing hegemonic sphere, whereas the presence of gay and lesbian Star Fleet officers (should they in fact appear) could more easily be read as less-than-optimal tokens, co-opted figures devoid of an acutely queer political agenda. Whether working within the dominant system as gay Republicans or queer Star Fleet officers, or outside the system as radical AIDS activists or lesbian vampires, the struggle to change society's views about homosexuality must be fought on all fronts, in nice soothing ways and in dramatically visible ways. Each of these positions is defined against the dominant ideology and exerts its own particular force on the hegemonic membrane. Fannish activity, as it rewrites many of these same topical issues through favorite media texts, might thus be understood as nothing less than a microcosmic model of how society transforms itself.

REFERENCES

Amesley, C. (1989). How to watch *Star Trek*. *Cultural Studies, 3*(3), 323-339.

Babuscio, J. (1977). Camp and the gay sensibility. In R. Dyer (Ed.), *Gays and film* (pp. 40-57). London: British Film Institute.

Bacon-Smith, C. (1992). *Enterprising women: Television fandom and the creation of popular myth*. Philadelphia: University of Pennsylvania Press.

Barthel, J. (1967, July 30). Out in detergent land: A hard day's fright. *The New York Times*.

Benshoff, H.M. (1991). *Dark Shadows: Narrative structure and ideological effect*. Unpublished manuscript.

Britton, A. (Ed.). (1979). *The American nightmare: Essays on the horror film*. Toronto: Festivals of Festivals.

Clover, C. (1992). *Men, women, and chainsaws: Gender in the modern horror film*. Princeton, NJ: Princeton University Press.

Doty, A. (1993). *Making things perfectly queer: Interpreting mass culture*. Minneapolis: University of Minnesota Press.

Freud, S. (1955). The uncanny. In J. Strachey (Ed. and Trans.), *The standard edition of the complete psychological works of Sigmund Freud* (Vol. 17, pp. 219-252). London: The Hogarth Press. (Original work published 1919)

Haycock, R. (1991). To serve her. In K. Resch (Ed.), *The world of Dark Shadows* (pp. 137-140). 57/58.

Helbing, T. (1989, October 9) Weekend of the living dead. *New York Native*, 25.

Javna, J. (1985). *Cult TV*. New York: St. Martin's Press.

Jenkins, H. (1992). *Textual poachers: Television fans and participatory culture*. New York: Routledge.

Kirk, M. (1989). *After the ball: How America will conquer its hatred and fear of homosexuals in the 90s*. New York: Doubleday.

Miller, D.A.. (1988). *The novel and the police*. Los Angeles: University of Los Angeles Press.

Miller, D.A.. (1991). Anal rope. In D. Fuss (Ed.), *inside/out: Lesbian theories, gay theories*. New York: Routledge.

Modleski, T. (1982). *Loving with a vengeance*. Hamden, CT: Archon Books.

Penley, C. (1991). Brownian motion: Women, tactics, and technology. In C. Penley & A. Ross (Eds.), *Techno-Culture* (pp. 135-161). Minneapolis: University of Minnesota Press.

Penley, C. (1992). Feminism, psychoanalysis, and the study of popular culture. In L. Grossberg, C. Nelson, & P. Treichler (Eds.), *Cultural studies* (pp. 479-500). New York: Routledge.

Pierson, J. (1992). *Dark Shadows resurrected*. Los Angeles: Pomegranate Press.

Radway, J. (1984). *Reading the romance: Women, patriarchy, and popular culture*. Chapel Hill: University of North Carolina Press.

Raymond, K. J., & Van Houten, C.. (1991). *Are old acquaintances best forgotten?* Woonsocket, RI: Amateur Efforts.

Sedgwick, E. K (1985). *Between men: English literature and male homosocial desire*. New York: Columbia University Press.

Skal, D. J. (1993). *The monster show: A cultural history of horror*. New York: Norton.

Sontag, S. (1983). Notes on camp. *A Susan Sontag Reader* (pp. 105-120). New York: Vintage Books. (Original work published 1966)

Sutherland, M. (1991). The challenge of her destiny. In K. Resch (Ed.), *The world of Dark Shadows* (pp. 103-114). 59/60.

Taylor, J. (1993, August). Why I need therapy. *Christopher Street, 104*, 34-37.

Todorov, T. (1975). *The fantastic: A structural approach to a literary genre*. New York: Cornell University Press.

Tulloch, J., & Jenkins, H. (1995). *Science fiction audiences: Watching Doctor Who and Star Trek*. New York: Routledge.

Williams, L. (1991). Film bodies: Gender, genre, and excess. *Film Quarterly, 44*(4), 2-13.

Wood, R. (1986). *Hollywood: From Vietnam to Reagan*. New York: Columbia University Press.

▶ 12

Is There a Text in This Audience? Science Fiction and Interpretive Schism

Thomas R. Lindlof
University of Kentucky
Kelly Coyle
Debra Grodin
University of Washington

Recently the field of communication has reappraised the notion of *audience* as a way to describe what people do with media. This development is partly a response to changes in the media themselves: The emergence of new technologies has disrupted the coherence of audience behavior in both time and space. However, traditional conceptions of audience have been challenged on theoretical grounds as well. The image of audience that has most influenced popular and scientific imaginations is of a social membership that publicly comes together to be addressed directly by an author or performer (Anderson, 1989). Even if this was at some time true, such an image is now problematic. A typical media audience is not a cohesive membership that behaves according to a shared code. Instead, actors in mass-mediated events use and interpret the "same" text in divergent ways and decide when, where, and how they will engage a medium, subject to the demands and constraints of their social order.

The status of the "text" in mediated communication is also problematic when viewed from the standpoint of the classic audience image. From this conception of audience, media content can be treated either as an artifact of expressive culture or as a representation of social reality. Scholarship that takes the first point of view evaluates texts by aesthetic criteria. Textual meanings are revealed by critics familiar with a long heritage of argumentation and exemplars. From the second point of view, content is understood to be a version of social reality that is shaped by the economic or professional requirements of the media industries. Neither perspective provides much insight into the ways that the meanings of mass media texts are created through the discourse and social practices of specific audiences.

Efforts to reconcile the analysis of mediated texts with notions of an active, interpreting audience extend back at least as far as Hall's (1980) essay on television encoding/decoding. In this chapter, we continue to explore this problem by considering how the idea of "genre" is used to understand media participation. In general, popular genres are thought of as texts that share characteristic content, themes, and reading experiences. The audiences for generic texts—romance readers, mystery readers, or, here, science fiction readers—are understood as "people who read these kinds of books," or better, "people to whom these kinds of books can be sold." Because generic texts reliably deliver certain experiences, people who enjoy those experiences can seek out generically identified texts. Thus, the marketing category, genre, at least nominally identifies an audience, and in most discussions popular genres and the audiences they attract are conflated, and the readers of generic texts are thought to be using and understanding them in similar ways.

Our intention is to make this construction more complex. What we have in mind are questions like the following: To what extent is it true to speak of a single audience for a popular genre? (Audience, here, could be understood as a gloss for "groups of people who use and understand texts in similar ways.") What common properties do readers recognize in a market-defined category—such as science fiction—that allow the texts belonging to that category to be put to particular uses? If, in fact, there are several identifiable audiences for a single genre, each identified by strategies of interpretation and use, what does it mean to speak of text or genre at all?

This chapter looks empirically at interpretation among genre users in terms of consensus and dissensus, that is, in terms of a schism over the purposes and methods of reading. We suspect that this sort of conflict is characteristic of the phenomenon of "audience." Rather than a singular group of readers who share codes of interpretation and textual practice, the notion of audience represents (and hides) divergently correct ways of categorizing texts in which "capital" is gained or lost in the struggle over effective symbolism (Bourdieu, 1984; Fenster, 1991). The marginalization of certain kinds of mediated texts and the cultural and political interests that grow up around them both reflect and engender interpretive conflict. What audiences gain in these struggles, especially in subcultural arenas, is the ability to produce shared imaginative worlds.

INTERPRETIVE COMMUNITIES AND POPULAR GENRES

Social-semiotic approaches to mass communication view media reception and use as social practices that operate in institutions and interpersonal relationships (e.g., Anderson & Meyer, 1988; Fiske, 1987; Jensen, 1991; Lindlof & Meyer, 1987; Morley, 1980, 1988). Rather than simply receive meanings from media content, audience members creatively fashion meanings that are, in part at least, their own. Researchers try to understand the logics people use to construct media-related discourses and the constraints that limit those constructions.

Within social semiotics, the concept of the "interpretive community" has often been used to explain how media audiences produce meanings that are variable, yet socially intelligible. *Interpretive community* is seen as a way to resolve the tensions between the contention that reception is a creative act and the apparently normative qualities of messages. The term is widely associated with literary critic Stanley Fish, whose early arguments are collected in *Is There a Text in this Class?* (1980). At the time, Fish was seeking a way to incorporate the dynamic process of reading texts into the practice of criticism. As Pratt (1986) observed, "Fish embark[ed] on the task of working out in the reader-response arena the theory of the socially constituted subject, the social constitution of reality, the collapsing of subject and object" (p. 46). Fish proposed that legitimate readings are constrained by the interpretive community to which a person belongs. Essentially, an interpretive community is a collectivity of readers who share certain strategies for textual interpretation. The interpretive community establishes conventions, mostly tacit and subject to negotiation, concerning how people recognize, create, experience, and talk about texts. An object comes to life as a "text" only to the extent that readers (including critics themselves; see Griswold, 1987) employ strategies to produce an interpretation. One of Fish's major contributions to criticism, then, was to posit the text as a socially constituted event. Although its physical character is fixed, only a reader can activate the codes and strategies that create meaning from a text. In order to produce a recognizable, approved interpretation within an interpretive community, readers must learn the practices that produce such readings. Through socialization, community members come to view the standards of their community as natural and right and may not credit readings derived from other standards as valid. For Fish, there is no meta-discourse that can decide what is the best or most desirable interpretation. Thus, the theory of interpretive communities is a relativistic view of reading activity, which is seen by some as either apolitical (Carragee, 1990) or as justifying only the readings of the most powerful reader/critics (Pratt, 1986).

Fish's formulation of the interpretive community was so broadly sketched that it left much to be filled in—and criticized (e.g., Pratt, 1986; Scholes, 1985). This lack of specificity, combined with its heuristic appeal, invited others to adapt the concept to their own purposes. For scholars concerned with mass media audiences, the interpretive community represents a bridge between critical/cultural and social-scientific approaches to communication (Gray, 1987; Jensen, 1987), micro- and macrosocial levels of analysis (Jensen, 1991), and concerns of literacy and communication (Liebes, 1989; Long, 1986; Radway. 1984).

Within audience research the study of interpretive communities is an active area of cultural analysis (Jensen & Rosengren, 1990). It is often allied with other forms of reception study, which examine interpretation through such paradigms as psychoanalytic theory (Mailloux, 1982; Walkerdine, 1986) and uses and gratifications (Liebes & Katz, 1986). A distinguishing feature of the interpretive community concept, however, is its emphasis on the social constitution of semiosis. Recently, the notion of interpretive communities has been employed in studies of women's reading practices (Grodin, 1990; Radway, 1984), serial-drama viewers (Feuer, 1989), *Star Trek* fans (Jenkins, 1988), and family video use (Lindlof & Shatzer, 1989).

Much of this work proceeds from an interest in popular genres and the competencies and pleasures that characterize audience engagement with them. Genre is a starting point of investigation for several reasons. First, mass media content is marketed through genre categories which offer prima facie evidence for the existence of shared normative interpretations. Second, genre analysis recognizes the importance of reading in its explications of the generic text (see Rabinowitz, 1987). Finally, genre provides a convenient way to define the field of study (including the setting and human subjects) by limiting the respondents to users of a particular genre.

However, by accepting the genre-community linkage too uncritically, researchers may not recognize when readers disagree or are ambivalent about a genre. Moreover, if the researcher uses a genre definition to "qualify" people as members of an audience community, the social-action component of reading or television viewing may be neglected or distorted (see Lindlof, 1988). The "interpretive community" that is thereby constructed may be empirically unreal. An alternative is to study how readers themselves configure a genre; how they appropriate formal features, narrative conventions, authorial style, themes, and tropes into a generic scheme. Such an approach refocuses attention on those elements that are vital to the audience's sense-making activity.

It is unclear whether audience interpretations develop out of social categories of class, gender, and race, or from communicative practices that span or criss-cross the social structure (Anderson & Meyer, 1988, pp. 184-185). Lindlof (1988), for example, argues that interpretive communities represent "overlays" of information processing that operate within social formations without being confined to them. Certainly the many forms of media technology, software, and literacies make it possible for diversely situated people to share certain interpretive strategies—although this does not hold true for all cultures or for all types of media attendance. Lindlof also suggests that interpretive communities can be nested within such groups as families. Styles of media discourse might last only for as long as people have certain kinds of relationships.

Jensen (1991) argues that an interpretive community may apply multiple strategies to a textual object; strategies may overlap for a given group of recipients; and the strategies themselves may be mutually inconsistent or contradictory. Clearly, this skepticism about consensual unity within interpretive communities attacks Fish's argument at one of its weakest points because he does not account for differential power between agents within communities, or the possibility of change in modes of interpretation through encounters with other communities (cf. Fish, 1987). However, if media-related discourses are more loosely coupled to the structural positions of audience members, then interpretive strategies might exhibit more heterogeneity, conflict, and change.

This study does not investigate the mechanisms by which interpretive communities develop and defend their standards. Rather, we are interested in whether a genre-based readership is in fact made up of a certain degree of disunity, and if true, what that disunity might look like. Evidence for heterogeneity in the strategies of readers—as well as a technique for identifying same—would be a productive step in articulating notions of disunity in audience decoding. Such data may cast light on the extent to which the genre expectations that readers bring to their reading practices are culturally engendered (cf. Bennett, 1987).

The genre we selected is the popular mainstream of science fiction literature (excluding avant-garde or esoteric varieties). Many popular genres would have been good candidates for study, but science fiction was chosen for reasons that are pertinent to our interests. As we discuss more fully in the next section, aside from a few ideas about its mission as fiction, science fiction is characterized by ambiguity of textual definition. Yet its general readership is arguably more socially active than other genre audiences and may even be considered a subcultural phenomenon. Thus, science fiction offers an intriguing case of a mass-marketed literature whose properties are relatively open to a knowledgeable "community" of consumers or fans.

THE SCIENCE FICTION GENRE AND READERSHIP

The definition of science fiction has always been elusive, partly because critics cannot decide whether it is literary genre or substantive topic that constitutes science fiction (Nichols, 1985). For example, Wendland (1985) provides this definition: "Science fiction is fantasy posing as realism because of an apparently scientific frame" (p. 11). He argues that science fiction's ability to *seem* authentic and plausible depends on extrapolations of known scientific fact and theory. In other words, the "science" is what distinguishes the genre, and it is the rhetoric of science that is used to achieve artistic effect. This definition is less useful, though, if one admits texts that show little evidence of scientific or technological frameworks. Science fiction's reliance on the narratives, myths, and metaphors of other genres also inspires doubt about its identity. In fact, nearly every other popular genre is represented in books that are widely accepted as belonging to science fiction: There are mysteries-in-space, westerns-in-space, romances-in-space, and variants that do not occur in space at all.

Science fiction is probably most commonly associated with *speculation*—about life forms, matter and energy, technology, and alternative societies. From its beginning, science fiction has attempted to interrogate the limits of possibility such as depicting intergalactic conflict or the lurid results of accidental mutation. A great deal of science fiction continues to offer loathsome BEMs (bug-eyed monsters), as well as the latest and most optimistic possibilities of genetics, physics, artificial intelligence, and so on. However, a large part of science fiction's readership is drawn to the genre for more than melodramatic fare. Especially since the "new wave" of the 1950s and 1960s, science fiction has addressed salient concerns of the human predicament. For example, one can find in science fiction meditations on ecology (e.g., Brunner's *Stand on Zanzibar*), gender identity and gender relations (the novels of Joanna Russ and Ursula Le Guin), and "critical utopias," in which the possibilities of human emancipation in the face of oppression are explored (Moylan, 1986). In other texts, technology is evaluated in terms of its effect on humanity and the natural world. Biological science is considered as it might influence the mind, and religion is viewed as a means of salvation or domination.

A recent trend of some interest is the merging of some elements of science fiction with what is known as "fantasy" literature. Fantasy embodies a diversity of story types which includes sword-and-sorcery tales; parallel or alternate world themes; saga, myth, and legend; faery stories; and animal fables (Rosenberg, 1986). Rosenberg observes that "a very simple distinction [between science fiction and fantasy] can be made: science fiction deals with the possible (though not necessarily probable) because it is based on scientific (hard or soft) knowledge, however tenuously at times; fantasy deals with the impossible, being based on magic or the supernatural" (p. 227). Thus, authors of fantasies are not constrained by the kind of minimal plausibility that seems to be demanded by science fiction. Recently, however, thematic elements from fantasy have been adapted to science fiction-associated settings and stories.

In spite of its ambiguity, or perhaps because of it, science fiction has inspired a large body of scholarly work (Lerner, 1985; Parrinder, 1980). Scores of books and several journals (e.g., *Extrapolation, Science Fiction Studies*) are devoted to science fiction criticism and research. Many science fiction writers are recognized as highly skilled auteurs, and a few have even ascended in critical estimation to the level of moralist (e.g., Kurt Vonnegut and J. G. Ballard). In addition, and more pertinent to this study, there exists a science fiction subculture that is visible through artwork, artifacts, conventions, fanzines, computer bulletin boards, and other manifestations.

Far from being a private act, reading science fiction is the basis for social participation with others who hold similar values, interests, and practices (Fleming, 1977). Experience in reading a common corpus of science fiction texts (along with familiarity with science, technology, and mythic lore) forms the cultural initiation for dedicated readers. According to Parrinder (1980):

> Science fiction . . . has given rise to a sub-culture because it promotes a shared view of reality towards which the rest of society is felt to be significantly hostile or indifferent. . . . Thus a sub-culture like that of the fans can well span differences in temperament between the radical and the conservative, the zealot and the dilettante. What holds them together, besides a mere habit of reading, is a shared vision of possibilities which only those within the circle of initiates seem to comprehend or take seriously. (pp. 36-37)

In other words, the science fiction subculture's view of its own sociopolitical position as marginal may have been a major factor in its formation.

Like other subcultural phenomena (Fine & Kleinman, 1979), competence in the science fiction culture probably develops out of participation in a variety of social domains in which "science fiction" is a topical resource as well as a set of performed activities. Science fiction texts are even creatively taken far beyond what the author originally inscribed (Jenkins, 1988). Thus, what is canonized in the reader community is not the author's work but rather the significant activities surrounding science fiction as they are manifested in members' discourse. Investigation of reading practices and perceptions provides the opportunity to examine the degree of cohesion that exists in an audience community, and indeed whether and how genres can be characterized at all.

METHOD

This study employs Q methodology, a technique used to develop clusters of persons who view a domain of interest in similar ways (Stephenson, 1953). Q methodology enables researchers "to make more intelligible and rigorous the study of human subjectivity" (McKeown & Thomas, 1988, p. 12). This technique offers an effective way to learn how readers prioritize those elements of science fiction that mean the most to them.

In most studies using Q methodology, subjects perform a sorting task in which they indicate the relative importance of various statements to their understanding of a domain (Brown, 1986). Each statement's position in a Q-sort is interdependent with the placement of all other statements, and each subject's sort is compared with every other subject's sort. By using factor analysis with these data, respondents are grouped together (i.e., "factored") in terms of similarities and dissimilarities in their subjective perceptions of the domain.

Items employed in the Q-sort for this study were generated from three sources: (a) a focus group interview with a group of dedicated science fiction readers; (b) extensive consultation with (community-sanctioned) "expert" science fiction readers who know the principal texts and are acquainted with many of its subcultural constituencies; and (c) a review of literature concerning science fiction. The statements we collected seemed to fall into three categories. (All statements are listed in the tables below.)

The first set of 40 statements concern the *practices* of science fiction reading. These statements describe characteristic ways of engaging texts, the uses to which those texts are put, the social context surrounding their use, and the motivations that readers cite to account for their reading. Participants were instructed to sort these statements into nine categories ranging from "describes me well" to "does not describe me well."

The second set of 50 statements describe the *aesthetic* aspects of science fiction. These items include narrative structures, character types, themes, plots, tropes, and stylistic conventions that could influence a reader's enjoyment of a story. These items incorporated ways that readers normally conceive of and refer to aesthetic elements in their discourse about the literature, at least as revealed in our focus group and other sources. Participants were instructed to sort these statements into nine categories ranging from "prefer the most in the science fiction I read" to "prefer the least in the science fiction I read." Although we expected that the aesthetic evaluations would relate to reading practices, we could not predict the nature of those relationships. The emergent, inductive character of Q-analysis, particularly when applied to an unexplored domain, prevents one from being able to specify dimensions in advance with any exactness.

Finally, a 50-item sort of well-known science fiction and fantasy *authors* was developed. Participants were instructed to sort these statements into nine ranks ranging from "like the most" to "like the least."

The objectives of our investigation and the practical aspects of the sorting task were explained to subjects, along with the understanding that by "science fiction" we also meant what some respondents refer to as "fantasy" literature. (There is disagreement over the proper separation of these literatures.) Decks were sorted in the order, (1) Practices, (2) Aesthetics, (3) Authors. In addition to the sorting task, the participants completed a questionnaire eliciting additional reading-related details and demographic data.

Altogether, 27 readers (16 males and 11 females) assisted us in the study, representing a wide range of ages, occupations, and education and income levels. They held in common a self-identification as a "regular" or "dedicated" science fiction reader, along with our ad-hoc criterion of reading an average of at least one science fiction book a month in the recent past. The readers were mostly assembled through personal referrals. Public announcements generated a small number of additional respondents. There was no material reward for participation.

Statistical analysis was performed using QUANAL (Van Tubergen, 1980), a software package designed for the analysis of Q-sort data. Essentially, a matrix of ranks is entered, transposed, and then a standard factor analysis (in this case, principal components) is performed on the transposed matrix. Factors are based on correlations between subjects, rather than test items, and can be described as structures of persons having like viewpoints present in the population. Factors were rotated to oblique simple structures, based on the notion that natural groups of persons can be correlated with one another. Types of persons are derived from the factor structure on the basis of factor loadings, with factors that have both positive and negative loadings split into two types (this occurred in only one of the sorts). Factor solutions were selected on the basis of interpretability and least number of factors. For all three Q-analyses, expert readers were consulted to insure the emic validity of the typal descriptions.

For interpreting the characteristics of types, the QUANAL program offers a summary of the composite response pattern for all persons included in each type. The response pattern is represented as z-scores (i.e., deviations from the mean of the item distribution, where 1.0 is one standard deviation above the mean). Each table in this chapter displays the z-scores (rounded to nearest tenths) for each of the items for each of the groups generated from the three sorts. Two conventional criteria were used in selecting items for interpreting the meaning of the types: (a) typal z-scores that exceed +1.0 and show a relative difference of at least +1.0 from the other types, and (b) typal z-scores that are greater than the average of the other typal z-scores by a difference of at least + 1.0. In other words, only those items that strongly define the types were used for analyzing and describing typal characteristics. Item numbers from the respective tables are noted in brackets in the text.

PRACTICES

Description of Types

Four groups of people sharing science fiction reading practices emerged, whom we named "involved," "leisure," "serious," and "immersed." The three-factor solution for the Practices data accounted for 53% of the total variance (65% of trace). Correlations between factors are as follows: -.10 between factors one and two; .73 between factors one and three; and -.39 between factors two and three. Despite their relatively high correlation, we view factors one and three as distinct for reasons that we make clear. Factor two had significant positive and negative loadings and was divided into two further types (leisure and immersed), for a total of four types overall. (Table 12.1 displays the Practices items, with average ranking by types expressed as z-scores.)

Involved. These readers are distinguished by the characteristic manner in which they engage texts during and after the act of reading. Involved readers get "lost" when they read [11], spend time pondering books after reading [37], savor books [27], sometimes read more than they intend [40], and, in general, seem to be absorbed in the ideas of the science fiction they read. They describe themselves as careful readers, always finishing a book once they have begun reading [25], rereading books [3],

Table 12.1. Practices.

Statements	Typal Z-Scores*			
	Involved	Leisure	Serious	Immersed
1. I sometimes imagine that I am (favorite SF character).	-0.2	**-1.7**	-0.6	**1.8**
2. I have built a large collection of SF books.	**1.3**	0.6	**1.9**	**1.7**
3. I reread my favorite SF books many times.	**1.1**	0.1	**2.1**	**1.3**
4. I read SF to expand my imagination.	**1.3**	-0.8	-0.7	**1.9**
5. Friends often introduce me to new SF books.	0.7	0.2	0.7	-0.5
6. If a book I like is part of a series, I'll read the entire series	**1.2**	**1.2**	**1.1**	0.6
7. For some SF books, I will read the last parts first.	**-2.0**	**-1.1**	-0.5	-0.9
8. I categorize books and authors into genres.	-0.8	0.1	0.5	**-1.0**
9. I get involved with a SF book in order to change moods.	0.2	0.4	**-1.2**	**-1.2**
10. I get involved with a SF book in order to enhance a mood.	-0.1	-0.5	-0.9	-0.4
11. I get "lost" while reading a SF book; nothing distracts me	**1.7**	0.7	-0.1	0.2
12. I sometimes role-play the characters in SF I read.	-0.0	**-2.2**	-0.6	**1.6**
13. I read most of my SF in short periods of time	-0.6	0.6	**-1.6**	-0.9
14. I read SF books on a regular basis.	**1.1**	**1.8**	**1.7**	**1.2**
15. I will read a SF book after seeing a similar movie or TV program.	-0.8	**-1.3**	-0.8	0.0
16. I reinforce the SF interests of other SF readers I know.	0.2	-0.3	**1.0**	-0.6
17. I recommend my favorite SF books to others.	0.9	0.6	**1.6**	0.8
18. I skim a book the first time through.	**-1.6**	**-0.8**	**-1.1**	**-1.2**
19. I read a book very carefully the first time through.	0.5	0.5	-0.3	-0.1
20. I reread certain parts of a book that were very enjoyable.	0.1	-0.8	0.5	0.3
21. I talk with bookstore workers (or librarians) about SF.	-0.7	-0.6	-0.1	-0.9
22. I sometimes discover people who also share SF interests.	0.2	0.3	0.9	0.3
23. I read SF when getting to sleep is difficult.	-0.7	0.8	-0.3	-0.1

Table 12.1. Practices (con't).

Statements	Typal Z-Scores*			
	Involved	Leisure	Serious	Immersed
24. I always finish a chapter during one reading session.	0.7	0.7	-0.2	**-1.2**
25. I always finish a book I start.	**1.1**	**2.0**	0.1	**-1.4**
26. I will quit a book that starts slowly for me.	**-1.1**	**1.0**	-0.8	-0.8
27. I will take my time reading a good SF book.	0.9	0.8	-0.0	-0.1
28. I try to convince non-SF readers that SF is worthwhile.	-0.5	-0.5	0.3	-0.1
29. I try to understand the views of people who don't like SF.	-0.2	-0.6	-0.3	0.0
30. I save my SF reading until important activities are done.	**-1.2**	**1.0**	**-1.8**	**-1.9**
31. I avoid books by SF writers I have never heard of.	**-1.6**	0.3	**-1.6**	**-1.6**
32. I discuss the books I read with friends who have also read them.	0.8	-0.3	**1.7**	0.3
33. I examine the reviews or endorsements of a SF book by notables.	**-1.1**	**1.1**	-0.7	-0.5
34. I trade books I have already read with others.	**-1.3**	0.8	-0.5	**-1.2**
35. I write SF stories or plays in my spare time.	**-1.5**	**-1.6**	**1.2**	**1.0**
36. I use new words or phrases from SF books.	-0.1	**-1.1**	0.1	**1.1**
37. I ponder a book after I finish reading it.	**1.6**	-0.6	0.3	0.8
38. I examine the cover art of SF books when I am shopping for one.	0.3	0.3	-0.2	**1.1**
39. I create visual art similar to SF	-0.9	**-2.0**	**-1.0**	0.4
40. Sometimes I read more SF than I intend to.	**1.3**	**1.3**	0.8	0.2

* Z-scores used to interpret factors (at least one standard deviation above or below the mean of an item) are shown in bold.

and never reading the last chapter of a book first [7]. More so than the other three types, the involved reader does not "skim a book the first time through" [18]. This type claims the expansion of their imagination [4] as a major purpose for reading.

In terms of social interaction over science fiction, involved readers evidence no particular pattern except for being relatively unconcerned about assessing the reputation of a book [31, 33]. Along with leisure readers, involved readers engage in no writing related to science fiction [35]. In sum, the involved type is more exclusively and methodically engaged with science fiction literature as a textual experience than the other types.

Leisure. For these readers, science fiction seems to function as a diversion, something with which to relax. Compared to the rest of the sample, leisure readers do not reread books [20] or invest much thought into science fiction [37]. They are more likely than the other three types to read to change moods [9], get to sleep [23], in short periods of time [13], and not until more important activities are completed [30]. These readers also "read more science fiction than [they] intend to" [40], perhaps indicating a tension between the time they allocate to reading and the actual amount used for reading. One relationship emerging from this analysis is particularly interesting: Although they tend to quit a book that starts slowly [26], they always finish books that they start [25]. This suggests a reader who has specific criteria for what a good book is and is not shy about invoking them.

They do not claim to have a large science fiction library [2], as the other types do, and are more likely to trade science fiction books [34]. The leisure type rates nearly all of the items relating to personal science fiction-inspired fantasy and artistic endeavor at the "does not describe me well" end of the distribution. In all, these readers have assigned science fiction to a well-defined and limited role in their lives. Their reading does not seem to include social or cognitive practices characteristic of a functioning subculture.

Serious. These readers differ from the first two groups most markedly in their social practices. They discuss books with others [32], recommend books for others to read [17], and "reinforce the science fiction interests of other science fiction readers I know" [16]. In terms of reading itself, they most definitely do not read in short bursts [13], to change moods [9], and are the least likely to become "lost" while reading [11]. Of the four types, they place the greatest emphasis on rereading favorite books [3]. Their orientation to reading seems more focused and less affective than the other types.

Serious readers seem to engage in creative literary activity regarding science fiction [35]. Judging from questionnaire and interview responses, the majority of the respondents in this type were writers (one of whom only wrote critical essays). Most of the serious readers in our sample were somewhat involved in fandom. Serious readers seem to read much like the involved readers (hence the relatively high correlation between the types), but their social and creative activities set them apart.

Immersed. Immersed readers are easily distinguished by the way their identities are tied up in social activities surrounding science fiction. They participate in role-playing games [12], use jargon from science fiction books [36], and are heavily involved in science fiction fandom. Like serious readers, immersed readers are writers [35], and are the only ones to show an interest in both creating science fiction visual art [39] and "the cover art of science fiction books when I am shopping for one" [38]. Interestingly, though, the immersed type is not very concerned with author or genre familiarity [8, 31].

With regard to reading activity, the immersed types, like the involved readers, read science fiction for the expansion of their imagination [4]. But in clear contrast to all of the other types, while reading they fantasize that they are their favorite characters [1]. The immersed readers are distinguished by the high priority they place on reading science fiction in ordering their lives [30]. Also, immersed readers do not seem to be as methodical or as committed in actually executing their book reading [24, 25]. It is conceivable that reading is a more spontaneous occurrence for these respondents.

Comparisons of Types

Leisure readers tended to be the oldest respondents and had the highest incomes and the most formal education. Immersed readers rated the lowest in all of these categories. The other two types fell in the center. There was no pattern in the gender composition of the types.

In addition to the Q sorts, participants provided information concerning the size of their science fiction libraries, the amount of time spent reading, and the number of books they had read over the previous six months. In general, our respondents are voracious readers, spending approximately 20 hours per week reading, and completing 60 books over six months, of which half were science fiction.

All of the Practices types spent about the same amount of time per week reading, but reported completion of different numbers of books over six months. Involved readers reported reading 36 books, 27 of which were science fiction; leisure readers reported 62 books, only 7 of which were science fiction; serious readers reported 87 books, 51 of which were science fiction; and immersed readers reported 31 books, 21 of which were science fiction. Most striking is the leisure readers' low percentage of science fiction as part of their overall reading regimen, and the involved readers' rather "pure" involvement with science fiction. Involved readers had the largest science fiction collection, with a mean of 671 books. Serious readers own 496 books, immersed 173, and leisure 71. Again, leisure readers are shown to be less committed to science fiction than the other types.

AESTHETICS

Description of Types

The Aesthetics sort generated three types, which we named "emotional," "intellectual," and "heroic." The three-factor solution accounted for 40% of the overall variance (61% of trace). Factors one and three show a substantial negative correlation (-.53), with factor two relatively uncorrelated with either of the other two. Items and z-scores are displayed in Table 12.2. There are no striking demographic trends in the Aesthetics types, and Aesthetics are unrelated to Practices.

Emotional. Emotional readers particularly enjoy stories centered on the emotional and personality development aspects of characters [7,11, 12, 18, 44, 50], including an interest in strong, independent female characters [12]. It is clear that these readers' science fiction sensibility is very much focused on exploring the subjectivity of the principal characters. Their rejection of aggressive actions by characters [26] and "beautiful, romantic female characters" [13] underscores this interest in the complexities of character psychology. Their preference for "ideas" in the science fiction they read [5] probably relates to this interest in subjectivity and interpersonal relationships.

Emotional readers show a distinct lack of interest in some of the elements of classic adventure stories [37, 49]. They are also averse to political conflict [6], perhaps because they perceive such themes to hold little promise for character development. Of the three aesthetic types, emotional readers are by far the most uninterested in science and technology [1, 23]. Interestingly, these readers do not care for skillfully rendered or "omniscient" stories [20, 21]. In summary, one could infer that emotional readers are not particularly attracted to science fiction for reasons that have to do with the traditions of science fiction tropes and narrative elements. Rather, these readers are attracted to the ways that richly described characters relate to each other.

Table 12.2. Aesthetics.

Statements	Typal Z-Scores*		
	Emotional	Intellectual	Serious
1. The possibilities of science or technology.	0.0	1.5	1.5
2. Visual description	0.2	-0.6	1.2
3. Lots of time spent introducing characters and settings.	-1.4	-1.2	-0.7
4. Several plots at the same time.	0.3	0.9	-0.6
5. The themes expressed in the stories.	1.3	1.5	0.5
6. Themes about political conflicts.	-2.0	1.2	-0.1
7. Development of the personalities of the characters.	2.5	1.0	0.6
8. The motivations of characters.	1.6	1.1	1.4
9. Themes about exotic cultures or civilizations.	0.4	0.6	0.4
10. High adventure.	0.3	-0.6	1.9
11. Character conflict.	1.1	0.7	0.5
12. Strong, independent female characters.	1.0	0.1	0.8
13. Beautiful, romantic female characters	-2.0	-1.0	-0.1
14. Fast-paced action.	0.1	0.2	1.4
15. Stories written in first person.	0.4	-0.1	-0.0
16. Stories written in third person.	-0.2	-0.5	-0.6
17. Romantic interplay.	-0.0	-1.5	0.2
18. Stories that emphasize characters' emotions.	1.8	0.0	-0.3
19. A great deal of detail about characters' lives.	0.0	-0.2	0.4
20. The sophistication of the writer's style and use of language.	-0.1	1.7	1.4
21. Knowing more than the characters do about their situation.	-1.1	-2.0	-0.7
22. Stories involving time travel.	0.1	0.9	0.0
23. Valid, up-to-date scientific information and theory.	-0.8	1.4	1.3

Table 12.2. Aesthetics (con't).

Statements	Typal Z-Scores*		
	Emotional	Intellectual	Serious
24. The use of magical power by characters.	0.6	-0.5	-1.3
25. Stories that involve earlier periods of human history.	-0.7	-1.4	-0.0
26. Aggressive actions by the characters.	-1.4	-0.3	0.2
27. Stories in which the characters operate in teams.	-0.8	-1.3	-0.8
28. Surprise endings.	0.8	-0.4	-1.4
29. Characters who use deception or intrigue.	-0.6	0.2	0.2
30. Stories in which the characters have clearly defined goals.	0.1	-0.5	-0.1
31. Themes about the fate of the earth and/or human species.	0.2	1.5	-0.4
32. Main characters who are very human or human-like.	0.0	0.3	0.6
33. Main characters as life forms very different from humans.	0.0	-1.0	-0.7
34. Stories that are difficult to figure out.	-0.4	0.6	-2.4
35. Characters using exotic weapons.	-0.9	2.0	-0.5
36. Themes about other dimensions.	1.3	0.8	-0.8
37. Themes of great conquest and empires.	-2.0	0.6	-0.1
38. Courageous heroes/heroines.	0.1	-0.8	1.1
39. Themes with relevance to current issues.	-0.5	1.2	-0.6
40. Stories centered around great myths and legends.	0.5	0.2	-0.7
41. Creatures that are extraordinary in appearance or abilities.	0.5	0.2	-0.8
42. Aliens that threaten human life.	-1.8	-1.2	-1.1
43. The survival of main characters at the end of the story.	0.2	-1.0	0.3
44. Main characters with qualities I can identify with.	1.4	-1.4	2.3
45. Lots of colorful minor characters.	0.4	-0.1	-0.2
46. Themes that satirize current values or morality.	0.4	0.8	-1.5

Table 12.2. Aesthetics (con't).

Statements	Typal Z-Scores*		
	Emotional	Intellectual	Serious
47. Main characters who claim victory at the end of the story.	-0.6	**-1.5**	-0.4
48. Endings that are open to different interpretations.	0.2	0.6	**-2.2**
49. Stories that span great sweeps of history.	**-1.6**	**1.5**	**-0.8**
50. Humorous characters and situations.	**1.3**	-0.3	**1.5**

*Z-scores used to interpret factors (at least one standard deviation above or below the mean of an item) are shown in bold.

Intellectual. Type two, intellectual readers, seem to read primarily for intellectual stimulation. This is the only group that likes satire or cares about the social relevance of science fiction [5, 6, 31, 39, 46]. They are "literary" in the sense that they enjoy stories that are difficult to figure out and attend to the language and style of the author [20, 34, 48]. In sharp contrast to the other two types, the intellectual reader does not prefer "main characters with qualities I can identify with" [44]. Although satire is valued, "humorous characters and situations" [50] are not, again in contrast to the other types.

Taken together, these items suggest that these readers are not threatened, confused, or disappointed by the complexity of some science fiction writing. This conclusion is supported further by this type's negative response to stereotypical and melodramatic elements [17, 33, 35, 38, 47] . In a related vein, elements of the literature associated with vividness of depiction are rejected [2, 10] . This reader type is attracted to abstract concerns, told in a subtle manner. Any style that smacks of the simplistic, lurid, or romantic is devalued. Their preference for historicity [37, 49] and science/technology [1, 23] indicates the contexts in which these readers' concerns about social relevance, moral decision making, and fate are encountered.

Heroic. As is evident from the three highest z-scores [44, 10, 50], respondents of the third type seek science fiction material that intensely involves them with humorous, adventuresome characters. This type is labeled heroic due to the strong interest, contrasting sharply with the other two types, in characters whose descriptions and deeds exemplify positive, unambiguous traits. For example, accompanying the appreciation of humor and heroism in the characters they read about [10, 38], there is also a negative response to the use of magical powers by characters [24], "extraordinary creatures" [41], mythic tropes [40], "themes about other dimensions" [36], satire [46], and nearly all of the items relating to character development and conflict. Thus, especially in contrast to Type 1, heroic readers seem to desire characters whose actions are virtuous and straightforwardly human. There is also a pragmatic cast to the scenes in which their preferred characters appear. In particular, these readers do not regard the fiction they read as particularly "speculative" or as having much relationship to larger frames of reference.

These readers display an interesting pattern in their preferences for writing technique and strategy. Although "sophistication of writer's style and use of language" [20] does matter to them, heroic readers shun ambiguity in story construction and story resolution [28, 34, 48]. They also do not appear to enjoy the interpretive work of following a story with several plots [4]. More than the other two types, they like stories that are vividly described and contain "fast-paced action" [2, 14] . The kind of action they prefer is indicated in their interest in aggressive character action [26] and "characters using exotic weapons" [35]. Their preference for science and technology [1, 23] may relate to their liking for descriptive detail in characters' uses of advanced hardware. In summary, then, heroic readers approach science fiction as a good, undemanding "read," with strong melodramatic elements at its narrative core.

Comparisons of Types

There were no striking demographic trends in the Aesthetic types with the exception of income. Emotional readers tended to report lower incomes, and heroic readers reported higher incomes than the overall sample distribution. Again, cell sizes were too small to infer clear significance from the relationships. The Aesthetics types were unrelated to the Practices types, and reading frequency and library size did not differ substantially among the Aesthetics types.

AUTHORS

For the author sort, two (uninteresting) factors emerged which accounted for 27% of total variance (40% of trace) and are correlated at .17. The two types can be generally described as fantasy and science fiction authors. Within the science fiction type, Asimov, Heinlein, Clarke, Niven, and Bradbury rated highest; within the Fantasy type, McCaffrey, Tolkein, Bradley, Norton, and McKillip rated highest. For the most part, those same authors showed the greatest z-score differences between the two types. Items and z-scores are presented in Table 12.3.

There was a moderate association of emotional type from the Aesthetics sort with the fantasy Author type. Given the interests of the emotional readers in character portrayal and interaction and "themes about other dimensions," the relationship is not surprising. The other Aesthetic types, intellectual and heroic, showed a moderate preference for the Science Fiction author type. (Cell sizes were too low to calculate statistical significance.) No associations between Aesthetics types and Practices types, or between Practices types and Author types, were observed.

Interestingly, the only demographic variable to differentiate the two author types was gender ($X2 = 3.50$; $p < .06$). Nine women were associated with the fantasy type, and three with the science fiction type. Eight men were associated with the science fiction type, and only three with fantasy. These results could support the common assumption that men are more interested in the technological, scientific, and abstractly speculative

Table 12.3. Authors.

	Typal Z-Scores*	
Items	Fantasy	Science Fiction
1. Anderson	-0.6	**1.2**
2. Asimov	0.4	**2.2**
3. Clarke	0.7	**1.8**
4. Heinlein	0.8	**2.3**
5. Herbert	0.7	**1.3**
6. Pohl	-0.5	**1.1**
7. Aldiss	**-1.3**	-0.4
8. Blish	0.3	0.2
9. Bradley	**1.7**	**-1.3**
10. Burroughs	0.0	**1.1**
11. Dickson	0.4	0.5
12. Farmer	-0.9	-0.3
13. Harrison	-0.1	-0.1
14. Dick	**-1.1**	-0.1
15. Ellison	-0.9	0.1
16. Moorcock	-0.3	-0.1
17. Sturgeon	**-1.2**	0.1
18. Zelazny	**1.0**	0.4
19. Bradbury	0.8	**1.5**
20. McCaffrey	**2.2**	0.4
21. Silverberg	0.2	**1.2**
22. Bova	-0.7	0.0
23. Cherryh	0.4	-0.8
24. Le Guin	0.9	0.7
25. Niven	0.5	**1.4**
26. Pournelle	**-1.1**	0.1
27. Saberhagen	-0.1	-0.1
28. Davidson	**-1.8**	-0.9
29. Anthony	**1.5**	-0.1
30. Laumer	-0.9	0.2
31. Leiber	-0.3	0.5
32. Hubbard	**-1.0**	**-1.3**
33. Lee	-0.8	**-1.2**
34. Brackett	-0.6	*-1.3*
35. Howard	**-1.2**	0.2
36. McKillip	0.9	**-1.5**
37. Norton	**1.5**	-0.4
38. Chalker	-0.3	**-1.3**
39. Vance	-0.9	-0.6
40. Stewart	0.9	-0.9
41. Donaldson	0.9	-0.6

Table 12.3. Authors (con't).

	Typal Z-Scores*	
Items	Fantasy	Science Fiction
42. Brooks	0.8	**-1.5**
43. Tolkein	**2.0**	**1.6**
44. Delaney	-0.7	-0.3
45. Asprin	**1.2**	**-1.0**
46. McIntyre	0.9	-0.6
47. Offut	-0.8	-0.9
48. Paxton	-0.3	**-1.5**
49. Amis	**-1.5**	-0.9
50. Kornbluth	**-1.7**	-0.4

*Z-scores used to interpret factors (at least one standard deviation above or below the mean of an item) are shown in bold.

concerns represented in the work of the science fiction authors and that women are attracted to the historical and characterological attributes of the fantasy authors' work.

CONSENSUS

Another resource for assessing the solutions of a Q-factor analysis are those items that rank highly, but similarly, for all the types. By evaluating items for which consensus exists, we can identify commonalities experienced through participation in science fiction by all of its readers. Such items can be seen as representing the broadest level of competence and preference for science fiction readers.

In analyzing the average z-scores for the Practices items that display a high consensus across the four types, three emerge as interpretable at an acceptable level (a z-score greater than +1.0 or less than -1.0). Two of these were rated "describes me well": "I read science fiction books on a regular basis" (1.46), and "If a book I like is part of a series, I will read the entire series" (1.0). The third item was rated on the "does not describe me well" end of the distribution: "I skim through a book the first time through" (-1.16). For these consensus items, this notion is clear enough: One must read regularly, but one must also demonstrate adequate levels of seriousness (by not skimming through books the first time through) and connoisseurship (by reading entire series).

For the Aesthetics sort, three items showed a high consensus, of which only one rated highly on the "prefer the most" end: "The motivations of individual characters" (1.34). Two Aesthetics items rated high on the "prefer the least" end: "Aliens that threaten human life" (-1.36), and "Lots of time spent introducing characters and settings at the beginning of the book" (-1.10).

The consensus Aesthetics items make up a less understandable picture than do the Practices items. It could be that skilled science fiction readers look on a lengthy descriptive phase at a book's beginning as a sign of amateurish authorship. The negative response to the threatening aliens figure may reflect either a low prevalence of this device in the literature read by our sample or a belief that it falsely represents the sophistication of science fiction literature. Comments from the participants lend somewhat more credence to the latter interpretation.

CONCLUSION

These findings clearly indicate the presence of prominent cleavages of reading practice and aesthetic judgment within the science fiction "community." It may not even be accurate to speak of science fiction readers as a community, or of science fiction as a genre. Thus, the consensus items did not reveal the kind of marginalist concept of self proposed by Parrinder (1980) for the whole science fiction readership. There is no ethos or archetypal imagery driving their interests as a subculture. Science fiction readers seem to share an *attitude of seriousness* rather than sets of strategies or substantive ideas about science fiction.

The Practices sort in particular disclosed the heterogeneity of audience life worlds that is concealed by the terms "readership" or "audience." One pole of audience interest is represented by the leisure readers, whose lifestyle relegates science fiction to a durable, but not central, niche. Notably, science fiction represents a low percentage of their substantial reading diet, and ownership of science fiction books is not at all important. The other pole is occupied jointly (but differently) by the involved readers, whose affective involvement in science fiction far exceeds the others, and the immersed readers, whose communicative involvement most closely resembles the recognized cultural forms of"fandom." The practices of serious readers are also more engaged in science fiction than the leisure readers, but without the high level of identification at the psychological and cultural levels as the involved and immersed readers, respectively. Serious readers' science fiction-related ties with others are almost entirely discursive.

In reviewing the Aesthetics sort, the 27 readers conceptualized science fiction in at least three ways that are internally coherent and substantially separate from each other. In a sense, these three modes of evaluating science fiction texts—emotional, intellectual, and heroic—correspond to prominent traditions of science fiction writing as indicated in their associations with the two Author types. However, the lack of positive correlation among the Aesthetics factors, and the presence of only one consensus item preferred by all three, shows conclusively that science fiction readers have very separate and self-contained tastes. Apparently they sample very little science fiction outside their own set of interpretive strategies.

This study indicates that it is not accurate to speak of a unitary interpretive community for a corporate-defined genre of mediated content, particularly one as textually heterogeneous as science fiction. This sort of schism, though, does not mean that interpreters' activity is either indeterminate or free-floating (cf. Evans, 1990). If all readers constructed substantially different messages, criticism would become a pointless activity and scientific study of meaning construction would be impossible. If, on the other hand, the text is part of a broader constellation of competencies, interests, and rule-governed operations in the world, then the text is no longer isolated or indeterminate, but is fundamentally generic. The genres, though, are those of the actions of interpreting audiences.

In the novel and other popular forms, the text is interpreted by readers through intersubjective agreements about genre and intertextuality (how texts cross-reference each other), and the social actions that allow knowledge to be reinvented in everyday life (Bakhtin, 1981, 1986; Lindlof, 1988). Although a few demographic and socioeconomic associations could be discerned, especially for the Practices sort, a case can be made that uses and understandings of science fiction are only weakly affected by position in the social structure. Certainly, there appear to be minimal cost or literacy requirements imposed on readers by most of the science fiction market. It is more likely that science fiction reading is a different socializing practice than other kinds of media use, and one which changes across the life span. This phenomenon of "readers who are socially disparate though united by a secondary collusion" (Dubois & Durand, 1989, p. 153)—the collusion of reading science fiction—is evident in the present study. Among the issues that need to be explored is how readers who vary in social structure location can classify genre elements similarly, yet in a way different from other "groups" of readers who have experienced roughly the same body of literature.

DiMaggio (1987) has examined the structural processes involved in the relationships between genres and the social groups that produce and consume them. Among the several propositions he advances is the claim that the greater the range of social networks in a social system, and thus the greater the range of roles, the greater the level of genre differentiation (p. 447). On the other hand, the more intergroup social contact that occurs in a system, the more likely that genre classifications will be salient to all groups (p. 448). The data analyzed in the present study exhibit both of these phenomena. Although the Practice types indicate little intergroup communication concerning science fiction as a topic, the split of fantasy and science fiction Author preferences points to a widespread recognition of science fiction's basic classification scheme. At some level, then, any serious reader must learn how the whole science fiction-fantasy domain is organized. At the pragmatic level of personal taste, however, science fiction's salience may be limited to a subset of authors, texts, and attendant elements of the science fiction culture.

The heterogeneity of science fiction may have its origins in the diversity of its audience in recent decades. What once may have been a cohesive science fiction subculture during the "golden age" of the 1940s and 1950s—marked by in-group language, canonical texts, and a close author-reader community—began fragmenting by the late 1960s (Parrinder, 1980). Many new readers were "recruited" to the science fiction genre by the successes of *2001: A Space Odyssey, Star Wars, Star Trek,* and other mainstream productions, and the rapid diffusion of fantasy role-playing games contributed to a growing fantasy literature (Fine, 1983). This bigger science fiction audience was acquainted with the older traditions, but its interpretive strategies grew more complex due to the greater range of readers' class and lifestyle positions and the influx of other media forms. Although we did not measure communication networks, the lack of an association between the Aesthetic and Practice types points to a general absence of intergroup contact.

For communication researchers, the interpretive community concept permits us to study reading (and other kinds of media reception) as an accomplishment of social negotiation. But the concept will have to become concerned with relations of power and discourse if it is to be something other than a way to generate readings. Rabinowitz (1987) argues that the act of reading is political; it reflects "the systems of power relations among groups (genders, races, nationalities, social classes, among others) in any social situation—systems that may in part be formalized (for instance, through law), but that are always invisible" (p. 5). Thus, the political structure within which acts of reading are situated privileges certain strategies, while casting others as deviant. If authors anticipate the strategies that their communities of readers will employ (see Mailloux, 1982), then we need to ask questions about how readers with particular histories and interests develop interpretations both before and during the act of reading. How do readers empower or disable the economic, political, and/or aesthetic intent of a book's strategies?

Finally, many texts, from erotica to self-help to science fiction, come endowed with reputations that require their users to develop complicated and delicate means of engagement (Fry, Alexander, & Fry, 1990; Lindlof & Grodin,1990). Here, too, constraining public definitions may elicit such stances by the individual as concealment, self-depreciation, subversion, or opposition. Alternatively, readers may adopt social identities and modes of "face work" that give support to their media use. Although this study addresses the issue of interpretation, the methods by which readers engage and debate generic texts also need to be studied. Q methodology's contribution to this kind of understanding can certainly be greater if it is supplemented with methods that are more sensitive to the processual and historical aspects of media use.

REFERENCES

Anderson, J. A. (1989, August). *Some preliminary thoughts on the elaboration of audiences.* Paper presented at the annual meeting of the Association for Education in Journalism and Mass Communication, Washington, DC.

Anderson, J. A., & Meyer, T. P. (1988). *Mediated communication: A social action perspective.* Newbury Park, CA: Sage.

Bakhtin, M. M. (1981). *The dialogic imagination* (C. Emerson & M. Holquist, Trans.). Austin: University of Texas Press.

Bakhtin, M. M. (1986). The problem of speech genres. In C. Emerson & M. Holquist (Eds.), *Speeeh genres and other late essays* (V. W. McGee, Trans.; pp. 60-102) . Austin: University of Texas Press.

Bennett, T. (1987). Texts in history: The determinations of readings and their texts. In D. Attridge, G. Bennington, & R. Young (Eds.), *Poststructuralism and the question of history* (pp. 63-81). Cambridge: Cambridge University Press.

Bourdieu, P. (1984). *Distinction: A social critique of the judgment of taste.* Cambridge: Harvard University Press.

Brown, S. R. (1986). Q technique and method: Principles and procedures. In W. D. Berry & M. S. Lewis-Beck (Eds.), *New tools for social scientists* (pp. 57-76). Beverly Hills, CA: Sage.

Carragee, K. M. (1990). Interpretive media study and interpretive social science. *Critical Studies in Mass Communication, 7,* 81-96.

DiMaggio, P. (1987). Classification in art. *American Sociological Review, 52*(4), 440-455.

Dubois, J. & Durand, P. (1989). Literary field and classes of texts. In P. Desan, P. P. Ferguson, & W. Griswold (Eds.), *Literature and social practice* (pp. 137-153). Chicago: University of Chicago.

Evans, W. A. (1990). The interpretive turn in media research: Innovation, iteration, or illusion? *Critical Studies in Mass Communication, 7,* 147-168.

Fenster, M. (1991). The problem of taste within the problematic of culture. *Communication Theory, 1,* 87-105.

Feuer, J. (1989). Reading "Dynasty": Television and reception theory. *The South Atlantic Quarterly, 88,* 443-460.

Fine, G. A. (1983). *Shared fantasy: Role-playing games as social worlds.* Chicago: University of Chicago Press.

Fine, G. A., & Kleinman, S. (1979). Rethinking subculture: An interactionist analysis. *American Journal of Sociology, 85,* 1-20.

Fish, S. (1980). *Is there a text in this class?* Cambridge, MA: Harvard University Press.

Fish, S. (1987). Change. *The South Atlantic Quarterly, 86,* 423-444.

Fiske, J. (1987). *Television culture.* New York: Methuen.

Fleming, L. (1977). The American SF subculture. *Science Fiction Studies, 4*(3), 263-271.

Fry, V., Alexander, A., & Fry, D. (1990). Textual status, the stigmatized self, and media consumption. In J.A. Anderson (Ed.), *Communication yearbook 13* (pp. 519-544). Newbury Park, CA: Sage.

Gray, A. (1987). Reading the audience. *Screen, 28*(3), 24-35.

Griswold, W. (1987). The fabrication of meaning: Literary interpretation in the United States, Great Britain, and the West Indies. *American Journal of Sociology, 92,* 1077-1117.

Grodin, D. (1990). T*he interpreting audience: The therapeutics of self-help book reading.* Unpublished doctoral dissertation. University of Kentucky, Lexington.

Hall, S. (1980). Encoding/decoding. In S. Hall, D. Hobson, A. Lowe, & P. Willis (Eds.), *Culture, media, language* (pp. 128-138). London: Hutchinson.

Jenkins, H., III. (1988). *Star Trek* rerun, reread, rewritten: Fan writing as textual poaching. *Critical Studies in Mass Communication, 5,* 85-107.

Jensen, K. B. (1987). Qualitative audience research: Toward an integrative approach to reception. *Critical Studies in Mass Communication, 4,* 21-36.

Jensen, K. B. (1991). When is meaning? Communication theory, pragmatism, and mass media reception. In J.A. Anderson (Ed.), *Communication yearbook 14* (pp. 3-32). Newbury Park, CA: Sage.

Jensen, K. B., & Rosengren, K. (1990). Five traditions in search of the audience. *European Journal of Communication, 5*(2-3), 207-238.

Lerner, F. A. (1985). *Modern science fiction and the American literary community.* Methuen, NJ: The Scarecrow Press.

Liebes, T. (1989). On the convergence of theories of mass communication and literature regarding the role of the "reader." In B. Dervin (Ed.), *Progress in communication sciences, vol. 9* (pp. 123-143). Norwood, NJ: Ablex.

Liebes, T., & Katz, E. (1986). Patterns of involvement in television fiction: A comparative analysis. *European Journal of Communication, 1*, 151-171.

Lindlof, T. R. (1988). Media audiences as interpretive communities. In J. A. Anderson (Ed.) *Communication yearbook 11* (pp. 81-108). Beverly Hills, CA: Sage.

Lindlof, T. R., & Grodin, D. (1990). When media use can't be observed: Problems and tactics of collaborative audience research. *Journal of Communication, 40*(4), 8-28.

Lindlof, T. R., & Meyer, T. P. (1987). Mediated communication as ways of seeing, acting, and constructing culture: The tools and uses of qualitative research. In T. R. Lindlof (Ed.), *Natural audiences: Qualitative research of media uses and effects* (pp. 1-30). Norwood, NJ: Ablex.

Lindlof, T. R., & Shatzer, M. J. (1989). VCR usage in the American family. In J. Bryant (Ed.), *Television and the American family.* Orlando: Academic Press.

Long, E. (1986). Women, reading, and cultural authority: Some implications of the audience perspective in cultural studies. *American Quarterly*, 591-612.

Mailloux, S. (1982). *Interpretive conventions.* Ithaca, NY: Cornell University Press.

McKeown, B., & Thomas, D. (1988). *Q methodology.* Newbury Park, CA: Sage.

Morley, D. (1980). *The Nationwide audience: Structure and decoding.* London: British Film Institute.

Morley, D. (1988). Changing paradigms in audience studies. In E. Seiter, H. Borchers, G. Kreutzner, & E.-M. Warth (Eds.), *Remote control: Television, audiences, and cultural power* (pp. 16-43). New York: Routledge.

Moylan, T. (1986). *Demand the impossible: Science fiction and the utopian imagination.* New York: Methuen.

Nichols, A. (1985). Complementary and critical descriptions of science fiction. *Extrapolation, 26*, 309-315.

Parrinder, P. (1980). *Science fiction: Its criticism and teaching.* New York: Methuen.

Pratt, M. L. (1986). Interpretive strategies/Strategic interpretations: On Anglo-American reader-response criticism. In J. Arac (Ed.), *Postmodernism and politics* (pp. 26-54). Minneapolis: University of Minnesota Press.

Rabinowitz, P. J. (1987). *Before reading: Narrative conventions and the politics of interpretation.* Ithaca, NY: Cornell University Press.

Radway, J. A. (1984). *Reading the romance.* Chapel Hill: University of North Carolina Press.

Rosenberg, B. (1986). *Genreflecting. A guide to reading interests in genre fiction.* Littleton, CO: Libraries Unlimited.

Scholes, R. (1985). *Textual power.* New Haven: Yale University Press.

Stephenson, W. (1953). *The study of behavior.* Chicago: University of Chicago Press.

Van Tubergen, N. G. (1980). *QUANAL user's guide.* Lexington: Department of Communication, University of Kentucky.

Walkerdine, V. (1986). Video replay: Families, films, and fantasy. In V. Burgin, J. Donald, & C. Kaplan (Eds.), *Formations of fantasy.* London: Methuen.

Wendland, A. (1985). *Science, myth, and the fictional creation of alien worlds.* Ann Arbor: UMI Research Press.

Author Index

Subject Index